Liverpool: 1

Football, Popular Music and Extraordinary Success

© Tommy Allen 2016

All rights reserved

Acknowledgements

I would like to thank the staff at the Local Record Office in Liverpool Central Library for all their support in my research for this book.

Other books by Tommy Allen

Liverpool 1840-49: A Decade of Change and Challenge, Triumph and Tragedy

War Poets on the Mersey: Poetry and Protest in First World War Liverpool

Contents

Introduction 3

1. Help! 1950-1959 6
2. From Me to You: January – July 1960 25
3. We Can Work It Out: August – December 1960 41
4. A Hard Day's Night: January - July 1961 60
5. Please Please Me: August – December 1961 80
6. I Feel Fine: January – July 1962 102
7. Ticket to Ride: August – December 1962 118
8. I Like It: January – July 1963 141
9. You'll Never Walk Alone: August - December 1963 166
10. Needles and Pins: January - July 1964 189
11. …and in the end: 1964-2016 218

Introduction

On 1 January 1960, the idea that Liverpool and Everton football clubs would both be First Division champions within four years would have seemed absurd to supporters on Merseyside. The idea that one side could go on to win the league title would have appeared fanciful enough; the idea that the two sides could do so, absurd indeed.

Why would this have been so? Why would an idea that both Merseyside clubs winning the First Division title in January 1960 be viewed as absurd?

To begin with Everton. At the time the team were in 17th place in the First Division and struggling to avoid relegation, an annual occurrence for the past six seasons. The club had failed to finish higher than 15th for the past five seasons. For Everton supporters, staying in the division was a great achievement, never mind winning the title.

As for Liverpool, they were lying ninth in the division; except that it wasn't the First but the Second Division. A fair way off the top of the table, they were not looking likely to achieve promotion. During the past five seasons the team had annually struggled and failed to achieve their aim of a return to the top flight of English football. Liverpool supporters' first thoughts would have been on getting into the First Division, not winning it!

On 1 January 1960, if someone were to suggest that a group of teenagers calling themselves The Quarry Men (forerunner of the Beatles) would, by the summer of 1964, have had a string of number one hit records and achieved world fame, well that would have seemed far more absurd than the idea of the football clubs winning the First Division title.

The Quarry Men, a group of musicians without a drummer, at college or working nine to five, were struggling to convince audiences and booking agents alike that they were a band worth listening to. They were, for the moment, seemingly drifting nowhere.

Remarkably though, four years later, Everton and Liverpool had both won the First Division title and the Beatles had achieved a string of number one hits. Moreover, the Beatles were not the only Merseyside band, nor the first, to do so. That distinction goes to the Gerry and the Pacemakers hit, *How Do You Do It?* Before the summer of 1964, several other Merseyside artists, often classified as Mersey Beat, also reached the top of the charts including The Searchers, Billy J Kramer and the Dakotas and a female solo singer, Cilla Black.

So how did they do it? How did the football clubs and Merseyside musicians achieve success as rapidly as they did?

To appreciate the incredible progression and speed of achievement in the four years from 1960, the opening chapter rewinds the clock ten years to reflect upon the relatively poor state of Everton FC and Liverpool FC and their subsequent disappointing football campaigns through the 1950s. The chapter also provides the background to the efforts of the hundreds of teenagers across Merseyside striving to become successful musicians. The young men and women, influenced by the revived, simple musical style of skiffle and the new exciting, electronic sound of rock 'n' roll, formed groups to perform at local venues such as church halls and social clubs. The ultimate hope was to catch the eye of a record producer or such like.

The book's twice yearly main chapters begin in 1960. They detail how the football clubs and Mersey Beat musicians progressed and ultimately achieved their remarkable levels of success. Such success would never have been accomplished without substantial financial investment and the services of knowledgeable and skilled managers. Short biographical details of those responsible for financing and managing the teams, the bands and artists are included.

It wasn't success for everyone, however. Several individuals, footballers, musicians and managers, did, for a variety of reasons, a few of which were acrimonious, miss out on the success of their contemporaries. Some of their stories are addressed in the text.

Unsurprisingly, the parallel rise and eventual success of the football clubs and musicians, did not go unnoticed by those participating at the time. Those involved, were contributors and witnesses to an extraordinary period in the region's cultural history. For example, Bill Shankly, manager of Liverpool's championship winning team, stated in his 1976 autobiography, *My Story*:

> "The whole of the city came alive in the 1960s. It became world famous because of The Beatles and other pop groups. The whole thing was boiling and bubbling."

Fellow Scotsman, centre forward Alex Young, a member of Everton's title winning side, commented in his 2008 autobiography, *The Golden Vision*:

> "*I arrived during the early days of Mersey Beat. In addition to the Fab Four* (the Beatles) *there were hundreds of boys strumming guitars and banging drums in local clubs such as The Cavern and Blue Angel. I think the music scene mirrored that of the football (scene)."*

Young's observation perfectly summarised events. The mirror image he writes of is the extraordinary, improbable rise and eventual success of football and music on Merseyside in the early sixties.

1. Help! 1950-1959

The great majority of the 48,668 spectators leaving Liverpool's Anfield stadium on 20 January 1951, if told, would not have believed that they had just witnessed the last Liverpool v Everton league match of the 1950s. A 2-0 win for Everton, failed to save the club from First Division relegation at the end of the season. A future without a derby match for a decade or so, would have seemed incredible for Liverpudlians and Evertonians alike to contemplate.

Less than nine months earlier, the football outlook on Merseyside appeared much brighter, as the clubs faced the prospect of a possible first ever all Merseyside FA Cup Final. Both had reached the semi-final stage of the competition, but were eventually drawn to play each other at Maine Road, Manchester. Liverpool went on to win the game 2-0, before losing the 1950 final by the same score to Arsenal.

Everton's demotion began a miserable decade for the club. Liverpool, though, fared little better, their form also declined over the same period. In 1954, the club reached their lowest point when they too were relegated from Division One. By an incredible coincidence, Everton won promotion at the end of the same season to replace their neighbours in the top flight.

The difficulties faced by the Merseysiders resulted in management changes in 1956. At Liverpool, Don Welsh, manager since 1951, was replaced by Phil Taylor; at Everton, Ian Buchan took over from Cliff Britton who had been in charge at Goodison for eight seasons. Buchan was not, however, designated manager, he was given the title of chief coach.

For the remainder of the decade, the new managers endured frustrating campaigns. Liverpool, despite quality players such as crowd favourite Billy Liddell, tried desperately, but ultimately failed to win promotion. Everton, meanwhile, battled annually to retain their place in the First Division.

The teams were nothing if not consistent in an era of perennial failure. The First and Second Divisions consisted of 22 teams; in 1955, at the end of their first season in Division Two, Liverpool finished in eleventh place. The team performed much better for the remainder of the decade, but, with just two teams eligible for promotion, finished every season frustratingly third or fourth.

Everton also achieved a remarkably similar level of consistency, but at the other end of the league table. They too finished in eleventh place in 1955 and ended all other seasons that decade poorly positioned in either fifteenth or sixteenth place.

The FA Cup competition provided little solace either. In the second half of the decade, both clubs managed to reach the quarter final of the competition on one occasion, but other than that it was third, fourth or fifth round defeats for both. Liverpool though did have one consolation, a January 1956 thumping 4-0 fourth round win over Everton at Goodison Park in front of an unbelievable 72,000 spectators.

Always looking to improve their playing squads, in 1958 both clubs turned to the Scottish League to recruit new players. Liverpool signed a promising under-23 international inside forward Jimmy Harrower from Hibernian. Later in the year, Everton also captured an inside forward from Glasgow Celtic. Of small stature, renowned for his leadership skills and combative nature, five feet four inches tall Bobby Collins earned the nickname *"The Little General."*

The two Scotsmen had not been on Merseyside long when they were involved in matches which were to become legendary, for the wrong reasons, in Everton and Liverpool's respective histories. The two games illustrate the relatively depressing condition of both clubs in the 1950s and arguably provide the most embarrassing results ever recorded by the pair.

On 11 October 1958, Everton travelled to White Hart Lane to face Tottenham Hotspur. On the morning of the match the London side appointed Bill Nicholson its new manager, a man who went on to achieve great success with club. Everton on the other hand arrived manager less. The club had, following a run of six straight defeats, dismissed its chief coach Ian Buchan two weeks earlier. A directors' sub-committee oversaw first team affairs on the day of the match.

From the off, the game was a disaster for the Blues. Nicholson's team had romped into 6-1 lead by half time and went on to score a further four goals in the second half. Regardless of a Jimmy Harris hat-trick, and Collins scoring his second goal for the club, Everton were on the end of a 10-4 thrashing. A depressing trip home for Evertonians followed.

The result exposed Everton's desperation for a new manager. A week later, Johnny Carey, a 1948 FA Cup winning captain of Manchester United, who moved into management soon after, was recruited from Blackburn Rovers.

Three months following the Everton catastrophe, on 15 January 1959, Liverpool faced semi-professional, Southern League side Worcester City in an away third round FA Cup tie. Liverpool, in second position in Division Two on the day of the game, were clear favourites to go through. Just nine minutes had elapsed when Worcester took the lead. In the 81st minute, thanks to a Liverpool own goal, the non-league side doubled their advantage. A Geoff Twentyman penalty wasn't enough to prevent Liverpool from a shocking 2-1 defeat and an embarrassing cup exit.

With the new decade approaching, could it get any worse for the Merseyside clubs?

The following season, 1959-60, Liverpool manager Phil Taylor and club supporters were hopeful that a promising 21-year-old, Roger Hunt, recently signed from non-league football, who had impressed in reserve team football, could provide the goals in the push for promotion. Though by no means terrible, it was a mixed start to the season for Liverpool. By the end of September, the team had won five of ten games and were not too far off promotion places. Hunt had scored three goals to date. Results, though, were poor in October, as the team failed to win any of its games and picked up just four points from five played. The pressure on Taylor was now enormous.

Meanwhile, come mid-September, the annual gloom and doom had settled on Goodison Park. Everton, having gathered a mere three points from six games, were bottom of the First Division having failed to win a match. Thankfully, for supporters, three victories and a draw in the following seven fixtures saw the team improve its league position, before a single goal by a prodigious young Chelsea forward named Jimmy Greaves, consigned the Blues to a 1-0 defeat at Chelsea.

To Everton supporters' surprise, centre forward Dave Hickson, the club's main goal scoring threat and fans' favourite, missed the club's next match against Leicester City. Despite a fantastic 6-1 victory, rumours abounded that Hickson had requested a transfer, deeply worrying Evertonians. A few days later, the worries turned to shock and anger when they learned on 6 November that the centre forward's request had been granted and he had indeed left the club.

The anger was compounded by the news that Hickson had been transferred to none other than neighbours and rivals Liverpool! Hickson, alongside Liverpool Chairman TV Williams, was photographed at his new club and quoted saying that he was *"Delighted to sign for Liverpool."* The move led *Liverpool Echo* football journalist Leslie Edwards, to write:

> *"Never in the history of this city has there been such a rumpus about a player from one club joining neighbours and rivals. Everton fans have written that if Hickson goes they go with him and Liverpool fans that if he arrives they will depart. It remains to be seen if they are as good as their word."*

For different reasons, the subsequent two games for both teams were dramatic. The day following Hickson's transfer, Everton journeyed north to face Newcastle United. The result was almost identical to the dreadful one at Spurs a year earlier. Travelling Evertonians saw their team thrashed and humiliated 8-2. Many of them wrote to the *Liverpool Echo,* expressing their total dismay at the result and the current plight of their club.

Leslie Edwards, prior to the Newcastle game, asked if Everton supporters would in effect boycott the next home fixture in protest at Hickson's departure. On 3

October, in one of Hickson's final appearances, more than 40,000 attended a 2-1 home victory over Arsenal. On 14 November, the first home game after his transfer, less than half that total, a measly 19,172, watched an impressive 4-0 win over Birmingham City. Edwards got his answer.

Liverpool's fixtures on the corresponding dates, though different, were equally dramatic. Although some supporters threatened to boycott Hickson's debut match at home to Aston Villa on 7 November, the great majority did not. In fact, a record attendance for the season to date, 49,891, witnessed the ex-Evertonian make a fantastic start to his Liverpool career, scoring both goals in a 2-1 win.

The drama did not end with Hickson's signature and immediate impact. In their next game at 17th placed Lincoln City, and regardless of a Hickson goal, Liverpool suffered a humiliating 4-2 defeat. The game proved to be the breaking point for manager Phil Taylor. After 23 years at the club as a player, coach and team manager, on Tuesday 17 November, he tended his resignation. He told the press "*I am tired. The strain of trying to win promotion has proved too much.*" The *Daily Mail* on the 18th suggested that Taylor lacked authority at the club and it was this lack of command which brought on his resignation. Its reporter wrote:

> "*I hesitate to call him manager – his official title for the last four years – for he never had complete charge of the team. But Taylor's job was always difficult with half of Liverpool screaming for promotion and has been ever more difficult since Reuben Bennett's appointment as chief coach caused a reorganisation of duties last Christmas.*"

Liverpool immediately began their search for a new manager. Taylor, who oversaw a 4-3 win over Leyton Orient, pledged to stay on until a replacement was found. The club's directors turned their attention to Yorkshire and fellow Second Division side Huddersfield Town, a club which had thrashed the Reds 5-0 a year earlier. Results such as this attracted Liverpool to Town's Scottish manager, Bill Shankly. For the moment, the approach was on hold as the club's next fixture on 28 November was against ... Huddersfield Town. Shankly would be approached after this game.

William Shankly, the son of John, a tailor and mother, Barbara, was born in the village of Glenbuck, Scotland on 2 September, 1913. Football was *'in the blood.'* Two uncles on his mother's side, Robert Blyth and William Blyth, were both professional footballers in England. Growing up, he and his four elder brothers were keen to emulate their uncles. At school, all the Shankly boys played football at any given opportunity. In his autobiography, he revealed his schoolboy love of the game:

> *"We played football in the playground, of course, but we never had an organised school team. It was too small a school. If we played another school we managed to get some kind of strip together, but we played in our shoes."*

Glenbuck was a mining village, so when Shankly left school at 14 he went to work at the local colliery. His first job was to empty trucks coming up from the coal face and then to sort the coal from the stones. Six months later he went to work underground.

While at the colliery, Shankly played junior football for a local team, Cronberry Eglinton. In 1932 a Carlisle United scout was sent to run the rule over him. The scout was impressed enough to recommend the club offer young Shankly a contract. He had achieved his ambition of playing professional football, as had his brothers earlier. He wrote

> *"All the boys became professional footballers and once, when we were all at our peaks, we could have beaten any five brothers in the world."*

Shankly's time at Carlisle was short-lived; he was transferred to Second Division Preston North End in 1933. Considered a powerful wing half (a midfield player in today's terminology), in the 1933-34 season, he helped the club win promotion to the First Division. Rarely missing a game, he subsequently played an important part in helping the side reach the 1937 FA Cup Final at Wembley, where Preston were defeated 3-1 by Sunderland.

Preston progressed well in the pre-war years. finishing third in Division One in 1937-38. The team also reached another FA Cup Final, this time successfully defeating Huddersfield Town 1-0. Victory came via a last minute extra time penalty. By all accounts, Shankly had an exceptional season, topping it on 9 April 1938, with his first Scottish international cap against England at Wembley. The scorer of the winning Cup Final goal, George Mutch, did likewise on Shankly's debut as Scotland defeated the *"auld enemy"* 1-0.

A further four caps followed, but, like all professional footballers, his playing career was interrupted when Britain declared war with Germany in 1939, the day after his 26th birthday. War led to the suspension of national professional football leagues and the FA Cup, although some competitive matches were played during the conflict.

Shankly joined the RAF and, depending on where he was stationed, managed to play in wartime league, cup and exhibition matches for Norwich City, Arsenal, Luton Town and Partick Thistle. He played one game for Liverpool in 1942, oddly enough, a 4-1 win over Everton. He met his future wife Nessie while in the RAF and they were married in 1944.

Peace time professional football resumed in 1946 and Shankly returned to Preston. With age now moving against him and retirement beckoning, he needed to consider other options in the game. Though still playing, he was appointed coach for Preston North End reserve team.

Aware of his reported coaching talents, in 1949 Shankly's first professional club, Third Division North side, Carlisle United, offered him the post of manager. He accepted, and upon joining the club, immediately retired from playing. He departed Preston on a sour note, however. The club, angered by his actions, refused him a benefit match. Shankly called Preston's spiteful act, *"the biggest let down of my life in football."*

Carlisle immediately improved under Shankly's stewardship, achieving a third-place finish in 1950-51. He believed the club, with a couple of acquisitions, were strongly positioned for promotion the following year. In finishing third, moreover, he was of the understanding that the team performed well enough to have earned the players a bonus payment. Carlisle's Board of Directors, however, informed him that the club lacked the required funds and therefore bonuses could not be paid. The board's decision led to his resignation; the first, but not the last of his managerial career.

Shankly wasn't out of the game for long. In 1951, he was appointed manager of Grimsby Town, a club that had been relegated twice in recent seasons, dropping from the First to the Third Division North. He, however, believed he had *"good players to work with."* Settling in, he immediately encouraged his players to take training seriously, for instance telling them to play five-a-side matches *"as if your lives are at stake."*

Grimsby made a strong challenge for the title in 1951–52, but just failed to gain promotion finishing second (only one team was promoted to the Second Division at the time). The following season proved a disappointment, as the team slipped to a fifth-place finish. Again, believing the club should show ambition, Shankly sought investment from a Board of Directors; again, he was refused and again he resigned, departing Grimsby before the season was out.

Cumbrian club, Workington Town quickly snapped up his services next. Workington, a club beset with problems, shared its ground with the town's rugby league club, a situation with which Shankly disapproved. That, however, was not his only concern. Apart from managing the team and overseeing training, he was also responsible for most of the club's administrative duties, including dealing with the mail and picking up the players' wages at the local bank.

He achieved relative success at Workington, improving both their league position and attendances, but in November 1955, he shocked the club by tending his resignation. The reason, a better offer had arrived from Yorkshire club, Second Division, Huddersfield Town. His new club required a reserve team coach and Shankly was only too willing to take up the offer. He had been in post for just a year when Huddersfield's first team manager surprisingly resigned. He was offered and accepted the promotion to the top job.

On Huddersfield playing staff at the time was a young Scottish prodigy, 16-year-old Denis Law. On Christmas Eve 1956 Shankly handed the teenager his first team debut. Many top clubs were aware of the young man's talents and his manager spent a lot of time fending off suitors.

On Huddersfield's playing staff was a young Scottish prodigy, 16-year-old Denis Law. On Christmas Eve 1956 Shankly handed the teenager his first team debut. Many top clubs were aware of the young man's talents and his manager spent a lot of time fending off suitors.

Huddersfield's primary aim was to win promotion to the First Division, but Shankly only managed to achieve mid-table finishes in his three full seasons in charge. In late November 1959, lying seventh in the league table on 19 points, Huddersfield were approached by fellow Second Division club Liverpool, requesting a meeting with their current manager. Shankly was surprised but willing to talk to the Merseyside club. However, he had first to prepare his Huddersfield team for their next home match against ... Liverpool.

On Saturday 28 November, Huddersfield defeated Liverpool 1-0. Following the game Shankly accepted the offer of an interview for the vacant manager's position at *Anfield*. He arrived in the city on 1 December; impressed Liverpool's Board and was appointed team manager. Meeting the press, Shankly announced:

> "I am very pleased and proud to have been chosen as manager of Liverpool Football Club, a club of such great potential. I make no promises, except that from the moment I take over I shall put everything I have into the job I so willingly undertake."

Shankly didn't start work immediately. Liverpool agreed that he could stay in charge at Huddersfield until the club appointed his successor. Liverpool's backroom staff of Rueben Bennett, ex-player Bob Paisley and coach Joe Fagan took over first team duties until the new manager was in place.

Liverpool won their next two games, 3-1 at Anfield over Ipswich and 2-0 at Bristol City. Meanwhile, Huddersfield were struggling to replace Shankly. The directors, however, decided that it didn't help either club if he remained in charge any longer. Replacing him with the reserve team coach, on 15 December Shankly departed Yorkshire for Liverpool. The Anfield coaching staff may well have feared for their futures with the arrival of a new manager who would have been within his right to bring in his own people. Shankly, however, placed great faith in the current backroom team and all three were kept in post.

On the pitch, it was a distinctly inauspicious start for Liverpool's new boss. Two poor performances resulted in two poor results; the first, albeit against promotion chasing Cardiff City, was a disconcerting 4-0 home defeat. A 2-0 Boxing Day loss in London to Charlton Athletic followed. At least the year ended on a happier note for supporters when Shankly managed to produce his first ever Liverpool victory, defeating Charlton 2-0 in the return match two days later at Anfield.

Meanwhile, over at Goodison Park, in the concluding fixtures of 1959, Everton produced a familiar set of results. The odd victory was followed by the odd draw, which in turn was followed by the odd defeat, until a fine 2-0 Boxing Day win over Manchester City at Goodison. It was not to be a Happy New Year for Evertonians though, as the return match with City on the 28 December, resulted in a 4-0 hammering.

Could the 1960s bring about an upturn in fortunes for the Merseyside clubs? Could Shankly inspire a Liverpool team lying in ninth place to mount an unlikely promotion challenge? Could Carey ease the fears of the doom-laden Evertonians by pulling clear of the relegation places? Perhaps the FA Cup, coming up in January, could offer an alternative path to success. Everton had been handed a decent looking draw against Third Division mid-table opponents Bradford City; Liverpool meanwhile were set to face fellow Second Division side Leyton Orient at Anfield.

* * * * *

Three teenage boys living in south Liverpool in the mid-fifties were not much interested in football. Their first love was music. John Lennon, Paul McCartney and George Harrison had been captivated by the new, exciting sound of rock 'n' roll and the re-emerging sound of skiffle, a mixture of jazz, blues and folk.

Skiffle's main attraction to young musicians was its simplicity and low cost of creation. The acoustic guitar was lead instrument, but all other sounds were usually produced using homemade or improvised instruments, such as a washboard and a tea chest bass. The latter instrument was made from a pole, traditionally a broomstick, placed into a tea chest, with one or more strings stretched along the pole and plucked.

In the UK, skiffle's main exponent was a Scotsman, Lonnie Donegan, a popular singer and performer who produced several hit records. His first, *Rock Island Line*, entered the Record Retail Chart (although there were other charts later, this will be the chart referenced in this book) in January 1956. He quickly followed that success with two more hits, including an EP entitled *Skiffle Session*. More hits followed in 1956 before he finally achieved his first UK number one, *Cumberland Gap*, in January 1957.

Lonnie Donegan played the *Liverpool Empire* on Sunday 11 November 1956 and in the audience, the day after his mother's death, was 14-year-old Liverpool Institute schoolboy, Paul McCartney. Donegan's Liverpool appearance, sparked his desire to play the guitar; costing £15, the instrument was bought for him a short while later by his father, Jim.

Donegan also had a great influence on another *Institute* schoolboy, 14-year-old George Harrison. Speaking to the Beatles' official biographer, Hunter Davies in 1968, Harrison said:

> "I'd been aware of pop singers before him, like Frankie Laine and Johnny Ray, but never really taken much interest in them. I don't think I thought I was old enough for them. But Lonnie Donegan and skiffle just seemed made for me."

Alongside skiffle, a relatively new style of music, rock 'n' roll, became something of a sensation in the UK. In 1954 the sound of Bill Haley and His Comets landed on British shores with the revolutionary sound of their hit single, *Shake, Rattle and Roll*. Haley followed up in January 1955 with a moderately successful second number, *Rock Around the Clock*. The song remained in the UK charts for just two weeks.

However, released in the UK later in the year, a Hollywood movie bearing the same title proved extremely popular with young cinema goers. The movie's success led to a re-issue of *Rock Around The Clock*. Second time around, it became a smash hit, reaching number one in the UK in December 1955, where it stayed for a total of five weeks. The record continued to sell well into the new year and went on to spend a total of 36 weeks in the charts.

1956 was a boom year for rock 'n' roll in the UK. The new US sensation, Elvis Presley, produced seven top twenty hits that year including his first *Heartbreak Hotel* and others such as *Blue Suede Shoes, Hound Dog* and *Love Me Tender*. Other vibrant, energetic musicians, such as Little Richard, Eddie Cochran and Gene Vincent were extremely popular in the UK too.

Their successes were followed the next year by US stars Chuck Berry and Buddy Holly and the Crickets. On a tour of England in 1958, Holly appeared before a sell-out audience at Liverpool's *Philharmonic Hall* performing such massive hits as *Peggy Sue* and *That'll Be the Day*.

With respect to the UK charts in the 1950's, Merseyside produced a few successful artists. US singer and actor Al Martino with *Here in My Heart* was the first to produce a number one UK hit single. Five months later, 23 April 1953, 37-year-old Lita Roza hit the top spot with her novelty song *(How Much Is) That Doggy in the Window*. Lita, the second of seven children of a Spanish father and English mother, was born in Toxteth, Liverpool. She holds the distinction of being the first Liverpool recording artist to reach number one in the UK.

Following closely on the heels of Roza's success were two male singers both born in 1928. In February 1954, Frankie Vaughan produced a top twenty hit, *Istanbul (not Constantinople)*. A half dozen top twenty hits followed, before he eventually made number one in January 1957 singing *Garden of Eden*. Vaughan, a traditional singer known for performing in top hat, white tie and tails, had several more chart hits before the end of the decade.

Vaughan was raised in the city centre while Michael Holliday, labelled the *"British Bing Crosby"* owing to his crooning style, was born and raised in Kirkdale, north Liverpool. Holliday made the top twenty for the first time in April 1956 with *Nothing To Do*. Following two further top ten entries, *The Story of My Life* became Holliday's first number one hit. The song remained at the top for two weeks. Before the end of the decade, two further Holliday singles reached the top thirty.

It wasn't the sound of Vaughan or Holliday in which the young Merseyside musicians were interested though, but that of a younger Liverpool singer who emerged on the music scene towards the end of the fifties. Born in 1940, Ronnie Wycherley, left school at 15 and as a teenager was employed in a variety of jobs. Wycherley had a strong desire to become a musician and singer. After several auditions, he managed to earn a few bookings. His act consisted entirely of covers, but he was keen to perform his own material composed at home.

In May, 1958, Wycherley cut six tracks at *Phillip's Recording Studio*, Kensington, Liverpool. They were mainly covers of Elvis songs, though one, *Yodelling Song*, was a composition of his own. He sent the tracks to London and Larry Parnes, an impresario and manager of a crop of young singers, such as Tommy Steele and Marty Wilde, who had recently burst on to the UK music scene. Wycherley received no reply. His incensed mother wrote to Parnes imploring him to listen to the recordings and give her son a chance.

The letter had its desired effect. The impresario invited Wycherley to *The Larry Parnes Extravaganza* taking place at the *Birkenhead Essoldo Cinema* on 1 October

1958. Wycherley expected to play Parnes his own songs in private. Parnes wanted to see and hear more. He cajoled the teenager on to the stage. Although nervous, Wycherley made a great impression on the audience and Parnes immediately incorporated him on his national tour. The following night in Stretford, Greater Manchester, Wycherley made his full debut.

To add excitement and exhilaration, as well as to make his artists more memorable, Parnes changed their names. Hence, Tommy Steele (from Tommy Hicks) and Marty Wilde (from Reg Patterson). He therefore reasoned that Ronald Wycherley was an unlikely name for a rock star; his new artist needed a more exciting appellation; Parnes renamed Wycherley...Billy Fury.

In virtually no time at all, Billy had signed a seven-year recording contract with *Decca* and his first song *Maybe Tomorrow*, made the top twenty in May 1959; this was followed two months later by a top thirty hit, *Margo*. By the end of the decade, Fury was indeed an inspiration to young Merseyside musicians.

On 6 July 1957, seven months after Lonnie Donegan's *Empire* appearance, Paul McCartney met up with 15-year-old art college student John Lennon. Lennon was lead singer in a local band called The Quarry Men, and they were performing at the Woolton Festival, south Liverpool.

Advertised as a skiffle group and performing the songs of Lonnie Donegan, The Quarry Men impressed the watching McCartney. After the show, he was introduced to Lennon. Within weeks, impressed with what he saw and heard, Lennon made McCartney a member of the band. On 18 October 1957, at the *New Clubmoor Hall*, Back Broadway, Norris Green, Paul McCartney made his debut with The Quarry Men.

In February, the following year McCartney introduced his younger school friend George Harrison to Lennon. Harrison's guitar skills also impressed Lennon and, despite the reservations of a couple of the Quarry Men, invited him to join the group.

Skiffle and rock 'n' roll had not only inspired The Quarry Men, but hundreds more young, budding musicians on Merseyside. As the fifties were closing, new bands were being formed on an almost weekly basis in the region. Gerry and the Pacemakers, Cass and the Casanovas, Rory Storm and the Hurricanes, Faron and His Flamingos, The Undertakers, The Coasters, Earl Preston and The TTs, and The Remo Four, just a few of those performing live in an ever-increasing number of venues.

Stretching from central Liverpool to the suburbs and outer Merseyside towns, the bands performed in a variety of locations including dance halls (sometimes called jive halls), town halls, church halls, social clubs, youth clubs and cinemas. Popular venues in the city centre included *The Blue Angel* on Seel Street, *The Jacaranda Coffee Bar* on Slater Street and *The Iron Door* on Temple Street. Thousands of music fans watched and listened to bands in the city suburbs and in towns such as Birkenhead, Widnes and St Helens.

Audiences were not always polite and respectful. It was not unusual for trouble to break out at some shows. Local gangs often clashed in the Hambleton Hall, Huyton, for example. To prevent them being used as missiles, chairs at the *Aintree Institute* were bolted down. A few venues had to employ doormen/bouncers. Thankfully, the disorder, though sometimes disturbing, was rare.

In the late fifties, two of Liverpool's most famous music venues opened. On Wednesday 16 January 1957, the cellar of a former fruit warehouse at 10 Mathew Street in Liverpool city centre was converted into a music nightclub and given the name the *Cavern*. Owner, Alan Sytner, named the club after a Paris jazz club, *Le Caveau De La Huchette* and held ambitious plans for it to become the top jazz venue outside London. The popular local combination, the Merseysippi Jazz Band, topped the bill on opening night in front of a sell-out audience.

Jazz, with famous performers such as Humphrey Littleton, Ronnie Scott, Kenny Ball and local group The Bluegenes making regular appearances, dominated the early *Cavern* years; the club also played host to skiffle. 7 August 1957 is commonly regarded as the date The Quarry Men first played the club. A member of the group at the time, banjo player Rod Davis, however told BBC *Radio Merseyside* in August

2011 that the Quarry Men played the club a few weeks earlier but, as the sessions were not pre-advertised, they had been overlooked by music historians.

Despite the club's popularity, in 1959, Sytner sold the *Cavern* to 32-year-old Ray McFall. Quick to recognise the growing influence of rock 'n' roll, McFall consciously decided to increase the number of performances by such bands, handing a weekly booking to Rory Storm and the Hurricanes, for instance.

The Hurricanes, Merseyside's leading rock 'n' roll band at the time, were formed in 1958 by Broadgreen born Alan Caldwell. Caldwell's love of Hollywood Westerns led him to originally name his group Al Caldwell's Texans. The band's lead guitarist was Caldwell's good friend, Johnny Byrne and, sticking with the Western movie theme, he called himself Johnny Guitar in homage to the eponymous character played on screen by Sterling Hayden.

In early 1959, Caldwell changed the group's name to The Raving Texans and brought in drummer Ritchie Starkey. A change of name for Starkey also, he called himself Ringo Starr. The group quickly morphed to Al and the Hurricanes before settling on the more dynamic and memorable Rory Storm and the Hurricanes.

When speaking, Caldwell had a noticeable stammer, but as Rory Storm his singing stage performances were unaffected and his renown grew. He became known for flamboyant stage wear and eccentric, sometimes dangerous stunts. The group wore red suits while Rory donned a garish pink outfit and, if the opportunity arose, he would climb around the stage to daringly leap about, a sight unseen before by Merseyside audiences. His sometimes-perilous stunts would occasionally lead him into trouble and endanger his personal safety. John Lennon was more than impressed, later admitting that he was in *"awe"* of Rory Storm.

The Hurricanes went on to perform many gigs at the *Cavern* before the end of the 1950s. The club soon developed a reputation, not just for its eclectic music, but also for its unique atmosphere owing to its narrow stage, viewing area and cocktail of smells, few of them pleasant. Access to the club was down a single 18 step, steep stone staircase with a 90 degree turn at the bottom where the pay desk was situated. There the audience found themselves in a claustrophobic, three-arched, red brick auditorium.

Below ground the smell of the toilet and drains, mixed with body sweat, was at times overpowering. Club goers talked of the odour remaining with them sometime after their visit ended. Others spoke of being able to *"smell the Cavern"* on people sitting near them on the bus. If they found the smell in any way offensive, it didn't appear to put off visitors. The *Cavern's* distinctiveness played a great part in the club's success. No other venue could claim to have what the *Cavern* had.

Emulating the *Cavern*, a coffee bar and club in the cellar of a large Victorian house at 8 Hayman's Green, West Derby, about three miles from the city centre, opened as a music venue, specifically targeting the youth of Liverpool. Its owner, local woman Mona Best who named the venue *The Casbah*, persuaded her son, aspiring drummer Pete, and local band members to renovate the newly purchased building with the promise of paid performances as reward for their efforts.

The club opened its doors on 29 August 1959 with The Quarry Men and its reduced line-up of Lennon, McCartney, Harrison and drummer Ken Browne, the first act to perform. All popular Merseyside bands, including Rory Storm and Cass and the Casanovas, played *The Casbah*.

The Casanovas, formed in the spring of 1959 by Brian Casser, an ex-Merchant Navy seaman, quickly earned a positive reputation. Casser, a singer and rhythm guitarist, initially formed a trio, with singer and guitarist Adrian Barber and drummer Brian J. Hudson. Hudson left soon after to be replaced by Johnny Hutchinson. In need of a bass player, the trio brought in Johnny Gustafson in December. Playing a wide range of music, from Latin American to rock 'n' roll, the group's popularity increased on Merseyside.

The Quarry Men meanwhile were going through a quiet period, playing the odd college and Casbah gig, but little else. In November John Lennon took time out to visit the *John Moores Art Exhibition* at Liverpool's *Walker Art Gallery*. The exhibition was the brainchild of *Littlewoods Football Pools and Mail Order* owner, John Moores.

In 1923 Moores established the football pools; after a slow start it grew into a successful business. Moores, though Blackpool born, moved the company's operation into a purpose-built building on Walton Hall Avenue, Liverpool 4, just a mile from Goodison Park and not much further from Anfield. He expanded his business empire in the early 1930s, creating *Littlewoods Mail Order* store. In 1937 he established his *Littlewoods* department store in Blackpool. At the outbreak of war in 1939, there were 25 *Littlewoods* stores across the UK. By 1952, Moores owned more than 50 stores and his pools business was stronger than ever.

By now a multi-millionaire, Moores was looking to expand his interests beyond business. In 1957 he inaugurated the *John Moores Painting Prize* which culminated in an exhibition held at Liverpool's *Walker Art Gallery*. In 1959, Lennon's friend and fellow art college student, Stuart Sutcliffe entered the competition with a piece entitled *Summer Painting*. Sutcliffe's artwork failed to win the competition, but Moores admired its quality so much, he purchased the canvas for £65.

What then was Sutcliffe to do with his remuneration? Paul McCartney, during an interview on a 1995 ITV programme, later a book, *The Beatles Anthology,* said that he and Lennon convinced the artist of how best to spend his £65:

> *"We all reminded him over a coffee: 'Funny you should have got that amount, Stuart - it is very near the cost of a Hofner bass.' He said, 'No, I can't just spend all that.' It was a fortune in those days, like an inheritance. He said he had to buy canvases or paint. We said, 'Stu, see reason, love. A Hofner."*

Suitably cajoled, Sutcliffe bought a Hofner bass; he was now part of the band, although there remained a problem, he had never in his life played the instrument. He would need to learn quickly.

As the decade ended, Merseyside's leading bands continued to be in great demand. The Hurricanes performed regularly at the *Cavern*. The ever-busy Cass and the Casanovas and Gerry and the Pacemakers were performing at various venues on a regular basis. On 16 December, both were booked to play an arts' ball in the *Mardi Gras* club, Bold Street. The show's promoter, Allan Williams, owner of the *Jacaranda Coffee Bar*, was a budding local impresario in the mould of Larry Parnes. Williams had quickly made a name for himself managing bands and organising shows, such as the one in Bold Street.

One group not considered for inclusion by Williams were The Quarry Men. They were a struggling band, now minus a member. Drummer Ken Browne had had enough and quit to form his own group. The Quarry Men may well have acquired an expensive Hofner bass, but without a full complement of musicians would not be able to compete with the likes of The Hurricanes, Casanovas and Pacemakers. The acquisition of a drummer in the New Year was essential.

*

Would a change of decade bring a change of fortune for The Quarry Men? Could any of Merseyside's most popular bands attract the attention of record companies and earn a recording contract?

On the football front, could Liverpool's new manager finally inspire the club to win promotion? Could Everton avoid relegation once again and instead of constant struggle, show signs of progress?

2. From Me to You: January – July 1960

For Everton, the new decade began where the previous ended, a 1-0 home defeat to Bolton Wanderers. Bill Shankly's Liverpool, though playing catch-up in the league, picked up their second consecutive victory beating Hull City 1-0 at Anfield. A break from league football, the FA Cup was up next the following Saturday, 9 January. Bookmakers didn't hold out much hope for the Merseyside clubs' chances of lifting the trophy, offering odds of 66/1 for both.

Liverpool, at home to Leyton Orient, got off to a flying start with a first minute Hunt goal. Orient equalised midway through the second half. In a hard-fought last quarter, a replay appeared inevitable, but Hunt struck again with virtually the last kick of the game to send his side through to the fourth round.

3,000 Evertonians travelled nervously but hopeful to Yorkshire in support of their team playing Third Division Bradford City. Supporters were once again badly let down by the side. Everton produced a *"woeful performance"* to lose the tie 3-0. The *Liverpool Echo* headlined the defeat, *"An Inglorious Exit."* In its report, the paper claimed that the *"Bradford goalkeeper Stewart can hardly have had an easier match as so ineffective was Everton's attacking play."*

Mr Rigby of Litherland, one of the travelling supporters, wrote to the *Echo* on the 12th to express his disappointment and anger at the Everton performance.

> *"Never in my life have I been more humiliated watching Everton. It was the worst exhibition from a First Division team that I've ever had the misfortune to witness."*

He and other correspondents were firmly convinced that Everton were destined for relegation. Manager, Johnny Carey had a massive job on his hands to prevent such an outcome.

Following the loss at Bradford, Everton were desperate to improve their playing squad. They made substantial offers for two players, Maurice Setters of West Bromwich Albion and Roy Vernon of Blackburn Rovers. The club chauffeured Vernon and his wife to the city to show them around the ground and to look at prospective homes. On his return to Blackburn, Vernon informed Everton that he would be remaining at his current club. Setters meanwhile chose Manchester United over Everton.

The embarrassing cup defeat and the rebuff of two players led the *Echo* to label the period, *"One of the blackest weeks in Everton's history."* The outlook was indeed bleak.

In the meantime, Shankly was in the process of changing several aspects of his new club. The team were performing in a run-down stadium and training in outdated facilities. Melwood, the training ground was in a pitiable state, overgrown, lacking care and attention, with only one mains water tap in the changing rooms. Finding the situation unacceptable, he arranged for the players to arrive for training at Anfield from where they would travel by coach the couple of miles to Melwood. After training, the team would return to Anfield to shower, change and eat a communal meal

He further believed the players were not fit enough for competitive action and he observed the efforts of every one of them during training. *"I would train amongst them,"* he wrote in *My Story*. *"I would know who wanted to train and who didn't. Each player was being watched."* He would demand some players work harder than others, constantly pushing them give more.

He changed the footwear too, getting rid of the heavy boots and importing *"continental"* ones, which he reasoned were better for balance and control. The players wore them for first time in their next home game with Sheffield United, a match they won comfortably by three goals to nil.

The contest however had a *"nasty edge to it"* reported the *Echo*. Dave Hickson had a running battle throughout with the United centre half. The Liverpool man was eventually dismissed for an apparent bad tackle, a decision which angered many Liverpool supporters.

One fan ran from the Kop to the centre circle to jostle the referee. It took the efforts of a half dozen policemen to remove him from the pitch. The *Echo* reported that after the game, hundreds of Liverpudlians gathered outside the ground to *"howl for the referee."* The scenes were *"unprecedented and ugly."* It took police reinforcements to clear supporters and allow the referee, Mr J.S. Pickles of Stockport, to safely leave the stadium.

Inquiring into the sending off and the protests a few weeks later, the FA concluded that Hickson's dismissal was an error and the club bore no responsibility for the after-match events.

Following Everton's third straight league defeat, 2-0 in their next game at Fulham, the club found itself just one place from relegation. It seemed the doom-laden feelings of supporters were coming true. At least the club had finally managed to sign a new player, Tommy Ring, an experienced 29-year-old outside left, from Scottish Second Division side, Clyde, for a fee of £12,000.

On 23 January, his debut at Goodison Park against Nottingham Forest, Ring made an immediate impact as he inspired the Blues to a fantastic 6-1 victory. He left the pitch to a standing ovation. His surname proved a newspaper sub-editor's dream. *"Everton buy a 22-carat Ring"* was the Daily Post headline, while the Echo declared: *"Ring signing was right on the button."*

The same afternoon Liverpool played out a 3-3 draw at Middlesbrough with two of their opponent's goals coming from a future successful English club manager named Brian Clough. Liverpool supporters though were more focussed on their upcoming fourth round FA Cup tie at Anfield the following Saturday. Liverpool had been drawn to play against Lancashire rivals, First Division Manchester United, in a game the *Echo* described as the Reds' *"biggest game since the 1956 Everton cup match.*" United contained several star players, such as England international forward Bobby Charlton.

The match, an all ticket affair, attracted a sell-out crowd of 56,738 and generated a great deal of national newspaper interest before and after the game. Following the game The *Sunday People* wrote:

> "Bobby Charlton became a V.I.P. footballer once again at rainy, muddy Anfield. Two expertly-taken Charlton goals in the first half knocked hotly-fancied Liverpool cold. Back-in-form Charlton was the hero all right. Liverpool did equalise United's first goal with a Wheeler right-foot cross-drive. Then in the second half came United's best attacking spell and Bradley scored the third goal with a rising left-foot shot."

United won the tie 3-1 and the *Liverpool Daily Post* was equally praiseworthy of Charlton's performance as too was Billy Liddell, who in the *Echo* said the United man *"flittered as the rest struggled."*

Liverpool soon got over the defeat and a decent run of results followed in February as they picked up five points from a possible six, though they failed to make headway on leaders Cardiff City and Aston Villa. With eleven games remaining league positions had not changed. Liverpool were ten points in arrears of second place Aston Villa and, with just two points for a win, promotion was looking a tall order.

The excellent Nottingham Forest result gave Everton supporters renewed optimism, but they were to be disappointed and fearful in February. From three games, only a single point was accrued and the club found itself third from bottom of the league and staring relegation full in the face. The club's supporters insisted that only urgent efforts in the transfer market could save the team from the dreaded drop.

Manager Carey and the Board of Directors were fully aware that the acquisition of new players was crucial. In response, Everton made a renewed offer for one of their earlier targets, the Blackburn forward, Roy Vernon. Much to the delight of

Evertonians, Vernon was persuaded the second time to make the short journey to Goodison Park for a fee of £27,000. Carey held the player he once managed in very high regard, describing him as *"the best forward in the country."*

Vernon was quickly snapped up as a weekly columnist for the *Liverpool Daily Post*. In his first column on 4 March, entitled *The Whole Truth* he explained why he first turned down the opportunity to join Everton, but eventually changed his mind. At the beginning of the year, he said he had fallen out with the Blackburn manager. Shortly afterwards, to his surprise, he awoke to read in a newspaper that he was *"up for sale."* Everton manager, Carey, immediately contacted Rovers. The next day Vernon and his wife were in Liverpool *"looking at houses."*

This *"was too much too soon"* Vernon said. He needed time to think over Everton's offer, so returned to play for Blackburn. As the weeks went by he realised that the move to Goodison was too much of an opportunity to miss and hoped Everton would return with an offer. The club did and this time, *"I did not hesitate to sign,"* he said.

Another addition to the squad was made a few days later when right winger Mick Lill joined Everton from Wolverhampton Wanderers for a fee of £20,000

The Blues continued to seek reinforcements and Carey travelled next to Scotland to persuade Dundee wing half Jimmy Gabriel to move south of the border. Gabriel's manager, Bob Shankly, brother of Liverpool's Bill, when asked, told the press that, *"no amount of money would persuade the club to sell the player."* Carey wasn't listening and his bid of £27,000 was too much for the Dundee board to reject. Gabriel, the costliest transfer from Scottish to English football at the time, was on his way to Goodison to join the other new signings.

Could the recent recruits help Everton stave off relegation? Club supporters certainly hoped so.

Evertonians were immediately delighted as their new signings made an instant impact. Vernon and Lill scored three goals between them in a 4-0 win over Preston North End. Vernon went on to score another two in Gabriel's debut game, a 2-2 draw at West Ham. The new signings were having the desired effect as Vernon and Lill were on target yet again, scoring a goal each in an excellent 6-1 home win over Chelsea.

Full of praise for the new look Everton, *Echo* reporter Michael Charters wrote on 16 March:

> *"For a team of such talent, relegation is unthinkable. I am thrilled as the next man with the possibilities of next season. What a difference Roy Vernon, man of this match, makes. He is destined to play a leading role in the good things which promise to come Everton's way."*

Evertonians were feeling better about themselves as the club climbed to the relatively safe position of 15th, their highest league position of the season. But, complacency can be a dangerous thing. Football does have the nasty habit of turning against you and the reality of relegation soon again raised its head.

Before March was out, Everton were on the end of a 6-2 hammering at West Bromwich Albion and a week later they suffered a 2-1 defeat at home to Newcastle, which pushed the club once again down to 19th place, closer to the relegation zone. There was still a great deal of hard work to be done.

As Everton were suffering reversals, news emerged from Goodison Park which was sure to please many Evertonians. On 23 March, John Moores, the millionaire businessman who purchased Stuart Sutcliffe's painting a few months earlier, filled a vacancy on Everton's Board of Directors. Ignoring the threat of relegation, he instantly outlined his ambitions for the club. *"We want to win the European Cup with the best team, the best coaches, the best club and the best directors."*

Many people had questioned how Everton could afford the recent new signings. Moores' appointment answered the question. Interesting times lay ahead for Everton.

March would define if there was any possibility of Liverpool winning an unlikely promotion. An excellent 5-1 defeat of Stoke at the start to the month kept slim hopes alive. The remainder of the month was however to prove a disappointment. The *Echo* reported that there *"was an air of inevitability"* about the result of the away Portsmouth fixture as Liverpool, leading 1-0 at half time, lost the game 2-1. *"Most players appeared to be going through the motions,"* the paper added. The Portsmouth game was followed by a 2-2 draw at home to Huddersfield and yet another draw, a thrilling 4-4 at Aston Villa.

With the outlook of eight scheduled games for all teams, April was a *"heavy month"* for football clubs. The pressure of trying to stay in touch at the top of the table finally told on Liverpool and hopes of promotion were finally extinguished with two defeats in the first three games of the month. With pressure off, the team appeared more relaxed on the season's run-in. Four of the final five games were won, the other drawn. The team scored thirteen and conceded just two in the process.

The final league table made frustrating reading for Liverpudlians. Their side again finished in third place behind Aston Villa and Cardiff City. Shankly had undoubtedly improved his side in the second half of the season, but his task now was to improve the team by at least one place to fulfil fans' ambition of returning the club to the First Division.

Across Stanley Park, in the meantime, Everton supporters remained in a state of nervous tension as the fight against relegation resumed in April. A decent 2-2 draw away to Birmingham was followed by arguably the best result of the season. 66,000 spectators at Goodison roared the team on and the players responded with an unlikely but magnificent 2-1 defeat of league leaders Tottenham Hotspur.

The result and the new signings led to a surge in confidence and another great home win followed, a thumping 4-0 defeat of Blackpool. With fears of relegation easing, the team only required a couple of more points from their remaining four games. They did more than enough, claiming away draws at Leicester and Blackpool before a final 1-0 home victory over Leeds United. Although the season ended in a disappointing 5-0 defeat at Manchester United, the end target of playing First Division football next season had been achieved. Everton ended the season in 15th place.

Like Shankly, Everton manager Johnny Carey could now start planning for a campaign aimed towards the top of the table rather than a struggle at the other end.

The football season may have ended for both clubs, but the summer brought news of events that were to immediately and spectacularly transform the fortunes of Everton. Liverpool too would be beneficiaries of events.

Evertonians woke on the morning of 24 June to news that at Everton's Annual General Meeting, held at Goodison Park the evening prior, major changes had taken place on the Board of Directors.

Before the board changes were announced, Johnny Carey first addressed the meeting. He told those present that the team was in good shape for the future, adding:

> *"I am quietly confident that the task of rebuilding a great Everton is in progress. There is much work to be done, but we are going ahead in the belief that in the future there will be a team worthy of such wonderful support."*

The news that followed had the greatest impact on supporters. Everton announced the appointment of a new Chairman, John Moores. In just three months, the Pools millionaire had been promoted from director to club chairman. It also became clear why the club had elevated Moores to the position. He had granted the club a £50,000 interest free loan, which substantially helped to bankroll the recent signings and therefore crucially helped in the avoidance of relegation.

Moores spoke to the press after the meeting revealing that he had tried to attract the *"best British players,"* including Shankly prodigy Denis Law from Huddersfield. Unfortunately, and despite the riches possessed by Moores, Manchester City had outbid the Blues, paying a record British fee of £55,000 for the 20-year-old.

Moores made a further surprising revelation. He declared that he wished not only success for Everton, but for Liverpool too. The Football Association's rules barred an individual from having simultaneous involvement in more than one club. Moores said if rules allowed he would have also joined the Board at Liverpool to help bring success to Anfield as well as Goodison. He wasn't allowed to personally join the Board but this would not prevent Moores having great influence at Anfield.

One week after Everton's AGM, on 1 July, Liverpool's AGM took place at Anfield. Shankly spoke first, announcing that it was:

> *"Time to forget about the past, a new chapter has begun at Anfield and by joint efforts of the Board, myself and the playing staff I am sure that success will come much sooner than some people anticipate."*

Again, as at Everton, it was the composition of Liverpool's Board of Directors which made the more interesting reading. In February, Liverpool director, Robson Roberts, had tragically died of a heart attack during the away fixture at Plymouth Argyle, leaving a vacancy on the Board. The club received six nominations for the position, but, after the meeting, Chairman Williams announced that Eric Sawyer had been unanimously voted in to fill the vacancy.

Crucially for the Reds, Sawyer was employed as an accountant at John Moores' *Littlewoods Mail Order Company*. The public later learned that the Everton Chairman had recommended Sawyer's appointment to the Liverpool Board. It appeared that the new director was the proxy of Moores at Liverpool. Liverpool, like Everton, now had relatively substantial funds available to improve their playing squad.

Shankly later declared in his autobiography that Sawyer was the most important man at the club at the time. He said that he *"often held official and unofficial meetings"* with the director, particularly when it came to discussing potential signings. Thus, with Sawyer's appointment, Moores had in one way or another, secured positions on the boards of both Merseyside clubs.

Moores had bankrolled the recent spate of Everton transfers, but didn't plan to ease the spending. Buying expensive footballers may be a costly business, but it did not necessarily mean no return on expenditure. Moores concluded that the policy of buying players was an investment which would ultimately lead to a return on outlay. He reasoned that as the clubs played in large stadiums, success on the field would inevitably lead to an increase in attendances.

Liverpool had recently shown against Manchester United that it could fill its ground to capacity while Goodison Park could accommodate crowds of 75,000. Gone would be the days of 40-50,000 fans attending one week followed by less than half that the next. Regular full houses would certainly recoup much of Moores' money, but only success would guarantee it.

Prior to Liverpool's AGM, the Board handed Shankly the funds required for one of his transfer targets. In mid-June, Liverpool paid Sheffield United £14,000 for winger Kevin Lewis. Interviewed by the *Echo* on 21 June, Shankly confidently told the paper that *"there will be more new men at Anfield before very long."* Shankly's statement was good news for Liverpool supporters.

With the new season weeks away and investment in players promised, both Merseyside clubs and their fans could look forward to August with renewed optimism.

* * *

For British lovers of rock 'n' roll, 1960 started with a bang. Organised by impresario Larry Parnes and beginning the first week of January, two of America's biggest rock 'n' roll stars were lined up for a nationwide tour. Joint star Eddie Cochran was a handsome, hugely talented 21-year-old guitarist and singer. Cochran, also a proficient bass guitarist and drummer, composed his own songs, two of which, *Summertime Blues* and *C'mon Everybody*, were hits on both sides of the Atlantic.

20-year-old Gene Vincent was the tour's other star. Vincent had been badly injured in a motorcycle accident in 1955 and was close to having a leg amputated. He was subsequently left with a permanent limp and considerable chronic pain.

The injury however did not prevent him becoming one of the original rock 'n' rollers. An energetic stage performer, in 1956, he produced a massive hit single, *Be-Bop-A-Lula*.

The tour began on 6 January with Billy Fury and other Parnes' managed stars such as Joe Brown and Georgie Fame on the bill. The tour rolled into the *Liverpool Empire* on 14 March and over six nights played to packed audiences. Among those gripped by the performances of Cochran and Vincent were the likes of Rory Storm, John Lennon, George Harrison, Paul McCartney and Gerry Marsden.

Also in attendance was Allan Williams, the budding impresario and owner of the *Jacaranda*. Williams was determined to persuade Parnes to add an extra date to the tour with a return to Liverpool. Williams planned to include on the bill some of the local talent under his control.

Having experienced the enthusiasm for rock 'n' roll in Liverpool, Parnes agreed to a joint enterprise with Williams. One of Merseyside largest venues, the 6,000 seater *Liverpool Stadium* was hired and Merseyside acts were booked, including Rory Storm and the Hurricanes and Cass and the Casanovas. Posters were published and distributed; ticket sales were going extremely well when tragedy struck threatening the show.

On Saturday 16 April in the county of Wiltshire, southern England, a taxi carrying Vincent, Cochran and two other passengers was travelling along a road near the village of Chippenham. The driver was speeding and his vehicle blew a tyre; he lost control and smashed into a lamppost. Cochran received severe head injuries and tragically died in hospital in Bath the following day, Easter Sunday. Rock 'n' roll had sadly lost one of its biggest, rising stars.

Receiving non-life threatening injuries, Vincent and the other passengers were luckier. When fit enough to do so, Vincent returned to America to recover.

Despite the tragedy, Parnes and Williams were determined not to cancel the show and contacted Vincent to persuade him to return to the UK. They suggested that the event be dedicated to the memory of Eddie. Vincent agreed to return for the show re-arranged for 3 May. Once again posters were published for the *Stadium* announcing it as *"The greatest beat show ever to be staged in Britain"* featuring *"America's Great Gene Vincent."* One of the groups added to the bill to replace Cochran were Gerry and the Pacemakers.

Formed by Gerry Marsden in 1959, Gerry and the Pacemakers began life as Gerry and the Mars Bars. Marsden, a guitarist, also sang vocals. His brother Fred was drummer, with Les Chadwick on bass and Arthur Mack on piano making up the quartet. Marsden said he was watching athletics on TV when the commentator mentioned a *"pacemaker"* and from there changed the group's name to Gerry and the Pacemakers. The band swiftly established itself on the Merseyside beat circuit, and their performances were impressive enough for Williams to use them as a substitute for Eddie Cochran.

The *Stadium* show was a roaring success with the Pacemakers one of the most commended bands performing. The biggest gig in which Merseyside beat groups had performed and they demonstrated they could well and truly hold their own.

After the Vincent tour, Parnes began organising a new nationwide summer tour for many of his acts, including Billy Fury. Parnes required either backing groups or performers to support his star turns and, having witnessed some of the talent on Merseyside, believed Liverpool the best place to find the necessary support. He contacted Williams to organise an audition of the city's best available bands.

On Tuesday 10 May, at the *Wyvern Social Club* (soon after *The Blue Angel*) on Seel Street, with Billy Fury watching on, Williams gathered together several hopeful bands including Derry and the Seniors, Bob Evans and his Five Shillings, Gerry and the Pacemakers, Cass and the Casanovas and the band formerly known as The Quarry Men now calling themselves The Silver Beetles. Rory Storm and the Hurricanes did not attend the audition, their performances having earned the band a forthcoming summer season at *Butlin's Holiday Camp*, Pwllheli, North Wales

At the suggestion of Williams, The Silver Beetles had acquired a new drummer, Tommy Moore, a 28-year-old fork lift truck driver working at a Garston bottle factory. Moore did not show up on time, so for their first couple of songs, Cass and the Casanovas' drummer, Johnny Hutchinson, substituted. Moore arrived during The Silver Beetles audition to complete the band's set.

The audition concluded, the performers waited for the results. While doing so they continued to perform across Merseyside. On Sunday 15 May, for example, The Silver Beetles and Cass and the Casanovas played the first lunchtime session at the recently opened *Iron Door* club on Temple Street in the city centre.

Three days later Parnes contacted Williams with news of the audition. He revealed that he hadn't selected any bands to support Fury. The news apparently did not come as a surprise to many of the Merseyside musicians. They believed the 'Billy Fury Audition' was a Parnes pretext for him to choose acts to support his other stars. The Silver Beetles were chosen to back one of Parnes' new discoveries, Johnny Gentle, on a tour of Scotland. The band were delighted to take up the offer and hastily prepared.

On 20 May, and never having met Gentle, the excited five-piece Silver Beetles travelled north to the Scottish town of Alloa, situated about 35 miles west of Edinburgh. Also, performing that first evening was Tommy Steele and a Scottish group, The Alex Harvey Beat Band.

The Silver Beetles were not identified on posters which simply read, "*Johnny Gentle and his group.*" To the packed Alloa hall, and then other locations, Gentle and The Silver Beetles, covered the music of Buddy Holly, Elvis Presley, Eddie Cochran ad other US stars.

While travelling between shows, the ensemble was involved in a minor traffic accident when the band's van, driven by Gentle, crashed. Drummer Moore was the only one injured, losing his front teeth in the accident. He was taken to hospital, but was persuaded by Parnes' tour organiser to re-join the band and tour. He did so, but had seemingly decided to quit The Silver Beetles after the band's return to Liverpool.

The accident apart, the tour was a reasonable success for the group. Performing regularly certainly helped to hone the talents of individuals, including bassist Stuart Sutcliffe, as well as improving the group's cohesiveness. When they returned to Liverpool they were a group more in demand than previously.

Through June and July, The Silver Beetles began to pick up regular weekend bookings as well as playing the occasional midweek show. Having informed his co-band members in advance, drummer Moore quit the group on 13 June, following a performance at the *Jacaranda*. He felt that regular work at the Garston bottle factory offered the financial security that irregular performances with the band could not. The Silver Beetles were yet again on the lookout for a drummer.

During the Scottish tour, a musical *"experiment"* took place at *The Cavern*. Starring Rory Storm and the Hurricanes, together with Cass and the Casanovas, on 25 May owner Ray McFall arranged the club's first full *"Beat Night."* Although jazz fans boycotted the show, the evening was considered a huge success, with many young music fans attending the club for the first time.

From there on, Wednesday evenings became Beat Nights at the club and the process of the *Cavern* becoming a full-time Beat venue was set in motion. Because of McFall's publicity posters, it's probable that the term *'Mersey Beat'* entered popular parlance.

A band performing at the Fury audition, Derry and the Seniors, formed at the beginning of the year by Derry Wilkie, one of the few black performers on the Merseyside circuit, received news from Williams that they had impressed Parnes who had arranged a residency in London, for the group. Guitarist, Howie Casey, told *Mersey Beat* music magazine the following year what happened next:

> *"We were initially told we would be backing one of Parnes' artists in Blackpool. We were all chuffed and gladly gave up our day jobs. Then, some little time later, we found out that it was all cancelled."*

Having committed themselves, they were furious and went to see Allan Williams.

"We went down there, irate and upset but Allan sort of wriggled out of it by saying he'd take the band down to London, to the 2i's club in Compton Street, Soho. Days later, we all piled into two cars and went off. There were no sound checks, nothing like that, you just got up and played and did our rock and roll 'Good Golly Miss Molly', 'Ain't That a Shame', that sort of thing."

Performing one evening, a German nightclub owner, Bruno Koscchmider was in the audience watching the Seniors. Koscchmider, owner of a Hamburg nightclub, the *Kaiserkeller*, was a lover of live British and American music, who had recently lost his regular band, The Jets, to another Hamburg establishment. He was on the lookout for a replacement and was impressed enough by the Seniors to invite the band to take up residency at the *Kaiserkeller*. The group did not hesitate to accept the invitation.

The seven-piece group arrived in Germany, quickly settled and proved very popular. Such was the Seniors' success, Koscchmider was keen to book another Liverpool band for another of his Hamburg clubs, the *Indra*. He'd met Allan Williams at the 2i's in the past and asked him to send over one of his bands.

Williams' first choice was Rory Storm and the Hurricanes, but they were committed to the summer season at *Butlin's*. The money the band negotiated to perform at the holiday camp was so good it convinced drummer Ringo Starr to give up his day job. Second choice for Williams were Gerry and the Pacemakers, but Marsden didn't feel the group ready enough to commit to such an undertaking. So, Williams next turned to The Beetles (the group had recently dropped Silver from their name).

Lennon and McCartney saw this as an opportunity to good to miss and didn't hesitate to accept. Philip Norman in *Shout,* his comprehensive biography of The Beatles, stated that upon hearing the news Derry Wilkie wrote in protest to Williams. In an angry letter, Wilkie complained that *"it would spoil it for everyone if he sent over a bum group like The Beetles."*

Williams chose to ignore Wilkie's protests and arranged for the band to travel to Hamburg in mid-August. First, they desperately required a drummer.

For a brief period following Moores' departure, The Beetles thought they had solved their missing drummer problem. Norman Chapman, spotted by Allan Williams, was initially recruited, but only managed to appear with the group on three Saturday nights towards the end of June and the first Saturday in July at the *Grosvenor Ballroom*, Birkenhead. Unfortunately for The Beetles, the following week, Chapman went into National Service.

In the meantime, the drummer less Beetles had been hired to perform for a full week at the *New Cabaret Artistes Club*, on Upper Parliament Street, Toxteth. Though illegal at the time, the *Cabaret* was in fact a strip club run by Harold Adolphus Philips, known as Lord Woodbine, a 31-year-old Trinidadian born musician, and club co-owner with Allan Williams. In September 1962 Paul McCartney, in the *Mersey Beat* newspaper, recalled the group's sessions at the venue.

> "John, George, Stu and I used to play at a Strip Club in Upper Parliament Street, backing Janice the Stripper. At the time, we wore little lilac jackets...or purple jackets, or something. Well, we played behind Janice and naturally we looked at her...the audience looked at her, everybody looked at her, just sort of normal. At the end of the act, she would turn around and... well, we were all young lads, we'd never seen anything like it before, and all blushed...four blushing red-faced lads."

*

The group may well be able to perform without a drummer in a strip club, but performing in a raucous Hamburg night club in the early hours of the morning was a totally different scenario. With the trip to Germany getting closer and time running short, it was back to the drawing board in the search for a drummer.

Football wise, the Merseyside clubs appeared better equipped for the forthcoming season commencing in August? Were they well enough equipped to challenge for their respective titles?

3. We Can Work It Out: August – December 1960

On the eve of the new season, Merseyside football fans were in a much more optimistic mood than they had been for several years. Having ended the previous campaign strongly, Liverpool supporters believed their new manager obtained the skills, knowledge and judgement to finally achieve the much-desired target of promotion. On 19 August, looking forward to the opening game of the 1960-61 season the following day, Shankly told the *Daily Post*:

> "Everybody has worked hard at Anfield to ensure 100% fitness and I must say that I am impressed by the keenness around me. We have left no stone unturned both in training and tactical talks and if we don't show some results for it I shall be a very disappointed man."

Trepidation was the usual sensation for Evertonians at the start of a new season, but it was missing this year. The investment in new players and their optimism gave supporters a more hopeful outlook. Recent signing, Roy Vernon in his weekly *Daily Post* column wrote:

> "These are exciting days. I have never known finer spirit or more impressive confidence. I can hardly believe it is the same club I joined. Gone are the doubts and worries that prevent players from giving their best. In their place comes composure and a burning desire to plunge into our season's new fixtures."

Following the close season signing of Kevin Lewis, Shankly wanted to further strengthen his squad. On the eve of the new campaign, Liverpool tabled a £15,000 bid for Leeds United centre half, Jack Charlton. The player had declared his unhappiness at the club and requested a transfer. Contacting Leeds, the *Liverpool Echo* was informed that the club were willing to sell Charlton, but *"only for a fee of*

£30,000." Liverpool felt the price prohibitive, but remained hopeful of signing the player and would table another bid after their first home game against... Leeds.

The Liverpool team: *Slater, Byrne, Moran, Wheeler, White, Leishman, Lewis, Hunt, Hickson, Melia, A'Court*

In front of more than 43,000, Charlton, the *Post* reported, played well, but he needed to as Liverpool were much the dominant side. Goals from Lewis and Hickson gave Liverpool victory, though the team *"should have scored many more."* Post-match the club returned to its pursuit of the Leeds man, but again were rebuffed.

Everton could not have asked for a tougher opening game, away to title favourites and FA Cup holders, Tottenham Hotspur. The Everton team:

Dunlop, Parker, Jones, Gabriel, Labone Meagan, Collins, Lill, J Harris, Vernon, Ring.

Tottenham controlled much of the game and Everton were holding on for a point until two very late Spurs goals gave the home side a much-deserved victory. Without goalkeeper Dunlop, the *Echo* wrote, *"the score would have been considerably higher."*

For Evertonians, the much anticipated first home game of the season against Manchester United was next up on Wednesday the 28th. More than 50,000 were in attendance to see *"Brilliant Everton Tear United Apart"* as the *Post* headlined the following morning. Two goals each for Lill and Collins, who was *"the star of the show,"* gave the Blues a very convincing 4-0 win. The paper declared that Everton had proved *"they were a force to be reckoned with."*

On the same evening, Liverpool received a huge early season jolt to their confidence with a heavy 4-1 loss at Southampton. Liverpool's defence was reported as being *"completely at sea"* by the *Post*. Liverpool had taken an 11th minute lead through Tommy Leishman, but Southampton went on take total control and the home side *"were not flattered by the margin of victory."*

Next up for Liverpool was an away fixture at Middlesbrough, the game ending in a disappointing 1-1 draw. New signing Kevin Lewis had a goal, which may well have proved to be the winner, controversially disallowed for offside.

Before the final game of the month Liverpool re-entered the transfer market, though not to capture the signature of Jack Charlton, that deal having finally fallen through as the clubs failed to agree a fee. Shankly instead looked to bring in a Preston North End wing half, Gordon Milne. Former Everton boss Cliff Briton, Milne's manager, described him as a player of *"boundless energy, a genuine trier and a good footballer."*

During his time at Preston in the 1930s, Bill Shankly played alongside Milne's father, Jimmy; the 1937 FA Cup final one of the games. While together, the Shankly and Milne families lived as neighbours on the same Preston street. Growing up, Shankly knew all about Milne junior's talents, following his career with interest after he signed professional terms with Preston. On 30 August, Shankly got his man. Milne made the switch to Anfield for a fee of £16,000. He went straight into the first team to play Southampton at Anfield the following evening.

Also selected to make his first start of the season was 38-year-old Billy Liddell, giving him the distinction of being the oldest footballer to play for the club in a post-war senior match.

Milne, who had only been introduced to his team mates one hour before kick-off, had an undistinguished debut, as Southampton went on to complete a quick double over Liverpool with a 1-0 victory. The game was the only time Milne and Liddell played together. The veteran's first team playing career ended that evening.

It was a mixed end to August for Everton. The penultimate game of the month produced an excellent 3-1 home defeat of Leicester, but this was followed by a poor performance. At Old Trafford on 31 August, Everton didn't start badly in the return game with Manchester United but, the *Echo* reported, went in at half time three goals in arrears. They went on to lose the match 4-0. Bobby Charlton, scorer of the opening goal with an unstoppable 25-yard effort, *"was the best player on the pitch,"* the *Echo* concluded.

The previous season, Everton failed to win a single game away from home and started this campaign looking likely to do similar as they lost again 3-2 at Aston Villa. Like Liverpool, Everton's pre-season optimism had been quickly punctured; the team were 14th in the table having picked up only four points from a possible ten.

Evertonians had little time to dwell on the dismal position as just two days later their team faced yet another away game, this time at Blackpool, but they were in for a shock, albeit a pleasant one. A 4-1 win, meant their team had finally ended a run of 25 away games without victory. Leslie Edwards in the *Echo* the following day wrote:

> *"It was a triumph for manager Carey's insistence on trying to play good football all the time. The team has the ability and the talent to play superb football,"*

The *Echo* was equally fulsome in its praise following Everton's next home game, a 3-1 home win over second placed Wolves. *"If this is the new order, let's have more of it."* Two more home games out of the scheduled next three also yielded wins over Blackpool (again) and West Ham United. In the latter game, Vernon scored his sixth and seventh goals of the season. In between the Goodison wins, Everton picked up another two points away at Bolton Wanderers. The excellent five-match winning streak catapulted the team from 14th to third place in the league table. A title challenge was on.

Chelsea at Stamford Bridge were up next for Everton on the first Saturday in October and leading 3-2, the Blues were on track to record their third consecutive away victory. With the game entering its closing stages, recent signing Tommy Ring, chased down a poor Chelsea back pass. Stretching for the ball he collided with Chelsea keeper Reg Mathews; Ring did not return to his feet and lay on the ground clutching his leg. The trainer could do little to assist the stricken player; an ambulance was called and Ring was transferred to hospital accompanied by manager Carey.

There a broken leg was diagnosed and Carey remained at Ring's bedside for most of the evening. The manager later returned to Merseyside to speak to the player's family and to personally pass on the extent of the player's injury. Back at Stamford Bridge, in the days when substitutes were not allowed, ten man Everton could not hold on to their lead and the game finished 3-3.

Sadly, for Tommy Ring, the Chelsea game was to be the last of his Everton career. He never fully recovered and left the club a year later for Barnsley, having played 27 times, scoring six, in a relatively short but successful spell at the club.

The severity of Ring's injury forced Carey to move quickly to find his replacement. The manager brought in an experienced Northern Ireland international, 29-year-old Billy Bingham, (a future Everton manager) from Second Division Luton Town for £15,000. Bingham had scored against Liverpool at Anfield earlier in the season.

October may have started in distressing fashion for one of Everton's players, but on the pitch the team's outstanding form continued. Following an insipid rare goal less draw at Preston, three victories in succession were accumulated beginning with a 3-2 win at Fulham. Everton were rampant in the first half of their next game against Manchester City scoring four without reply. They went on to win the game 4-2. Everton were producing *"sparkling Champagne football when in the recent past they served up warm beer,"* commented the *Echo*.

Another victory on the road at Nottingham Forest 2-1, with Bingham scoring the first goal of his spell at the club, kept Everton in the title chase. Roy Vernon however was sent off late in the match following a dangerous tackle. The player faced the possibility of suspension at a crucial time for his club.

Meanwhile over at Liverpool, the team's start to the season *"was an anti-climax no one expected"* wrote Michael Charters in the *Echo*. They are *"defending reasonably well, but Shankly needs to resolve the situation of his misfiring forwards,"* he added. Shankly was concerned: *"Our backs are against the wall"* he told the paper. *"We will get it right,"* he said, before the team's next game at home to Brighton.

Attempting to resolve the goal scoring problem, Shankly dropped recent recruit Kevin Lewis and recalled winger Ian Callaghan for his first start of the season. The team went on to record a 2-0 win, but the home fans, in an attendance of just 24,390, were unhappy with the entertainment, expressing their disapproval. The *Echo* called the display *"lifeless, uninspiring and singularly untidy,"* before describing the crowd's reaction: *"The fare on offer led the faithful of the Kop to produce a burst of slow handclapping."*

Performances failed to improve; A disappointing 2-2 home draw against Luton Town was followed by away defeats to Ipswich and the return match with Luton,1-0 and 2-1 respectively. Liverpudlians, who expected their team to be challenging at the top of the table were, to be kind, extremely disappointed to find Liverpool languishing in 13th. *"To mention the word promotion would be utterly ludicrous,"* wrote the *Echo*. Shankly clearly had a job on his hands to convince observers otherwise.

Shankly handed Johnny Morrissey his first start of the season for the next game against Scunthorpe United. There were signs of improvement as Liverpool won the home game 3-2. Morrissey performed with enough distinction to be selected for the next fixture.

"Morrissey Crowns Grand Display with Brilliant Goal" read the *Echo* headline following Liverpool's first away win of the season by three goals to one at Leyton Orient. The two successive wins failed to entice supporters to Anfield against Derby County; less than 24,000 attended the 1-0 victory. The Kop were disappointed with the team's performance, again resorting to the slow handicap.

Despite the Kop's response, the victory over Derby was the third in what was proving to be a great run of results. Through October and early November, Liverpool recorded victories at Lincoln City, Shankly's old club Huddersfield Town, Plymouth Argyle and Charlton Athletic. Perhaps playing with some trepidation, results were not as good at Anfield, but the Reds never tasted defeat, battling out draws with Portsmouth and Sunderland before defeating Norwich 2-1 on 12 November.

The storming set of results elevated the club to third place. On 21 points, Liverpool were a point in arrears of Ipswich Town, though seven off commanding leaders Sheffield United.

The victories kept on coming. A 3-1 away victory at Charlton Athletic moved the club up to second in the table, seven points behind their next opponents Sheffield United. The most important match of the season to date. A victory would send a message to United other promotion teams.

After the recent great run of results, Everton's November began in disappointing fashion with two unsatisfactory draws against lowly placed teams, West Bromwich Albion and Cardiff City, slightly denting title hopes. Against Newcastle United next at Goodison, Everton produced a display as good as any to date. They were a single goal ahead at half time, but three goals in eight second half minutes blew away their opponents. The game ended 5-0 with Bobby Collins scoring a hat-trick.

Prior to the Newcastle game. Everton again entered the transfer market to sign two more players. For a joint British record transfer fee of £55,000, Alex Young and George Thomson, joined from Scottish club, Heart of Midlothian. Young's portion of the fee was £44,000. The player attended the Newcastle match and called the Goodison Park atmosphere *"impressive."*

Evertonians would have to wait to see Young in action, though; the Scotsman, who hadn't played for three weeks, was indisposed with a knee injury and was expected to remain side-lined for a similar period at least. Thomson was pencilled in for his debut in Everton's upcoming fixture.

The enjoyment of the Newcastle victory and the signatures of Young and Thomson was however short-lived. In London for their next game, Thomson's debut, the Blues suffered a 3-2 defeat at Arsenal. The loss kept Everton in third place behind Spurs and Sheffield Wednesday. The team were about enter a possible season defining set of fixtures in December, including two home games against the league leaders and nearest rivals.

Liverpool's fine run results and the top of the table position of their opponents brought the crowds to Anfield. 40,000 were in attendance as the game against league leaders Sheffield United kicked off.

In a closely contested first half a Jimmy Harrower opening goal was cancelled out by a Sheffield United equaliser. In the second half, Harrower produced *"his best performance yet in a Liverpool shirt"* reported the *Daily Post*, as the centre forward went on to score a hat trick in an eventual 4-2 victory. Dave Hickson netted the other. The result not only put the team right in the promotion race it put them firmly in contention for the title too.

At 0-0, torrential rain forced the half time abandonment of Liverpool's next game at Stoke City. Swansea City were next at Anfield on 12 December. *"This was never a match, it was an exhibition and the only exhibitors were Liverpool,"* pronounced the *Echo* as the team, *"who played superbly on a hard, treacherous pitch,"* ran out 4-0 winners.

Another away point was picked up with a draw at Leeds United before the final three fixtures of the year. These very crucial games were scheduled to be played over a hectic six day Christmas holiday period.

On 3 December, ex-Everton centre forward, now Sheffield Wednesday manager, Harry Catterick, brought his second-placed team to Goodison Park. Catterick oversaw the league's meanest defence. After 19 games, they had conceded just 16 goals, five fewer than leaders Spurs.

In front of 50,702 spectators, Everton got off to the best possible start with a Vernon goal in the first minute. Wednesday, the *Echo* reported,

> *"... were much the better team in the first half and deservedly went in to the break leading 2-1. Then, as so often happens, Everton slipped into top gear."*

Everton *"tore into"* their opponents scoring three second half goals, including another from Vernon, before running out 4-2 winners, leapfrogging Wednesday in the process, to move into second in the table. Post-match Catterick was very complimentary about the Goodison crowd saying they *"generated a very special atmosphere."*

Prior to Everton's next fixture at Birmingham City, the club received news Evertonians feared; Roy Vernon received a 14-day suspension for his dismissal against Forest in October, therefore becoming unavailable for the game with Birmingham, but, more crucially, the all-important visit of Tottenham Hotspur.

Vernon's replacement at Birmingham, Derek Temple, was making his first start of the season. The result of the match, played on a muddy St. Andrews pitch, was a virtual replica of the Sheffield Wednesday contest. The Blues were 2-1 down after 48 minutes, but once again finished strongly to go on to record a 4-2 win. Although the team were going into the Spurs game minus Vernon and six points in arrears of the league leaders, they were doing so in full confidence.

The build up to the Spurs match generated exceptional interest in the local and national press, being billed as *"Everton's biggest game since the 1950 FA Cup semi-final against Liverpool,"* by the *Liverpool Echo*. One journalist, perhaps overstating affairs, classified the contest as English football's *"Match of the Century."* In a special preview, the early Saturday *Echo* dedicated eleven pages to the match. Many column inches were written about Everton's new acquisition, Alex Young, who was set to make his debut in place of the suspended Vernon. Was the debutant fit enough to make his presence felt?

More than 60,000 spectators arrived at a misty Goodison Park. Supporters behind both goals struggled to see the action at the opposite end of the pitch. Those centrally positioned, including reporters, were better placed to view events. An evenly fought first half concluded with Spurs eventually showing their class, scoring two goals in quick succession.

Everton came out fighting in the second half and within two minutes, centre forward Frank Wignall reduced the deficit. However, as the game wore on the mist turned to fog and visibility worsened, so much so that reporters were no longer able to record the action. Darkness also now fully enveloped the ground and many inside the stadium, expecting the referee to abandon proceedings, departed proceedings. The game however continued and Spurs scored again to run out 3-1 winners to stretch their top of the table lead over Everton to eight points.

In his assessment, based on what he observed, the *Echo's* Leslie Edwards wrote:

> *"Tottenham are the best club side ever. Their understanding is almost perfect. They move the ball from one end of the pitch to the other like lightning."*

As for Everton, Edwards claimed Young, still carrying an injury, was clearly not fit enough for such a daunting task. He concluded *"Everton gave Spurs a decent run, but were beaten by the better team on the day."*

When drawing up the season's fixture list, the football authorities arranged for the Christmas games to be played on Saturday the 24th and Boxing Day the following Monday. The two holiday games at the time were reverse fixtures and if competing teams agreed, the Christmas Eve match could be re-arranged to be played on the extra Bank Holiday, Tuesday 27th. Not many clubs did switch, but two teams, Everton and Liverpool, and their respective opponents Burnley and Rotherham United, did.

The Merseyside teams performed exceptionally well on Boxing Day, both recording victories. Almost 40,000 fans at Anfield saw Hunt and Lewis put Liverpool two up before a late Rotherham consolation. The win moved the Reds up to third in the table. Everton in the meantime recorded an excellent 3-1 win over last season's league champions and current fourth placed team Burnley at Turf Moor. Like Liverpool, Everton also stood in third place in the First Division at the end of the game.

Liverpool's reverse fixture with Rotherham ended in a disappointing 1-0 defeat. The team played reasonably well, the *Echo* reported but *"squandered numerous chances."*

Meanwhile at Goodison chaos reigned. Everton had re-arranged the fixture to allow their supporters time to complete shopping and other Christmas related activities, freeing many of them to attend the Burnley game on the 27th. Attend they certainly did. Thousands began queuing early, long before the scheduled start. It appeared that thousands would be turned away as kick off approached, but the club decided to keep the turnstiles open.

When the numbers were counted, the attendance was calculated at just under 75,000, the second highest league gate in the club's history, only surpassed by the 78,000 who watched the 1948 Liverpool derby match. Worried about dangers to spectators, the police instructed the club to allow younger supporters to sit on the running track to ease the pressure in standing areas.

Following the previous day's excellent victory, thousands of Evertonians arrived in the hope of a repeat performance, but they were to leave extremely disappointed. Everton *"failed to show"* and Burnley comfortably won the game 3-0.

Unsurprisingly many people wrote to the *Echo* complaining about their experience at the game. Most of those in the standing areas said the overcrowding was so bad they could not see the pitch, while others said they feared for their safety and left. Although football during the period was undoubtedly at times a very popular spectator sport, luckily no one at Goodison was badly hurt that day, but Everton Football Club had learned a valuable lesson.

The concluding games of 1960 took place on New Year's Eve, but neither of the Merseyside clubs delivered a celebratory message to their fans. Everton travelled to Leicester City and were trounced 4-1. The *Echo* report read: *"Everton got bogged down dilly-dallying on a muddy pitch. Leicester got the ball forward more quickly and were rewarded for their efforts."*

Liverpool at Anfield led Middlesbrough 3-2 with 15 minutes remaining. They were eventually undone by two late goals from Boro centre forward and later Nottingham Forest manager, Brian Clough. The *"architects of their own downfall,"* late defensive mistakes cost Liverpool the game.

What began as a period of Christmas celebration, concluded in a very *"Unhappy New Year"* for Merseyside football fans. Everton remained third, but a distant ten points behind leaders Spurs. Liverpool too had slipped to third, but their nearest rivals did not have the greatest December either. Liverpool were four points off leaders Sheffield United and one off second placed Ipswich Town. Promotion was by no means out of the question.

Without matches on Saturday 24 December, on its front page the Saturday *Football Echo* ran a wide-ranging interview with Everton Chairman John Moores, who addressed subjects such as footballers' pay, televised games, the future of the First Division and of course, Everton.

He said he was delighted with the team's progress so far: the third-place position had exceeded his expectations. At the start of the season, he hoped to finish in the top six. His ambition was to see the team challenging for the First Division title *"within two to three years"* he said. In addition, he had an *"harmonious relationship"* with Everton's manager, though he believed that if he was in charge he would *"be a little tougher in training"* than Mr Carey. Finally, he stated,

> *"When I joined the Everton Board I knew I must make a go of it. That we have done so well so quickly, surprises and delights me."*

Come the New Year the Merseyside clubs would need to put the recent defeats behind them and get back to winning ways if they were to maintain their respective league challenges.

Next up was the FA Cup third round. For all those concerned at Liverpool and Everton, a busy weekend lay ahead on the first Saturday in January, both teams had been drawn at home. The post war cup competition had been a constant source of disappointment for Merseyside fans; could this season's competition offer something different?

* * * * *

In early August 1960, the nervous, drummer less Beatles, unable to personally find a replacement, placed an advert in the *Liverpool Echo* for the position and awaited a response. Their trip to Hamburg hung by a thread. If a drummer could not be found, the trip may have to be abandoned.

Fortunately, one young, competent drummer came forward; moreover, he was available to travel abroad. 20-year-old Pete Best, the son of the *Casbah Coffee Bar* owner, Mona Best, met the band, auditioned, impressed and was accepted. Fully complemented, the Beatles (having again changed their name) could now make the trip to Germany.

The band, Allan Williams, his wife Beryl, her brother Barry Chang, and co-owner of the *Cabaret* strip club, Lord Woodbine, piled into a minivan to make the uncomfortable road journey to Hamburg. Van driver and trip organiser, Williams, had not obtained work permits for entry into West Germany and all were detained at the port of Harwich. Williams somehow convinced the authorities that the young people travelling with him were holidaying students and they were permitted to continue their journey. Upon arrival in Hamburg, Williams finally obtained official permits.

Permits were not the only problem. Williams hadn't arranged accommodation, so the Beatles found themselves housed in the storeroom of a cinema, the *Bambi Kino*. Paul McCartney, in *Anthology*, described the conditions:

> "We lived backstage in the Bambi Kino, next to the toilets, and you could always smell them. There were just concrete walls and nothing else. No heat, no wallpaper, not a lick of paint; and two sets of bunk beds, with not very much covers, we were frozen".

The Beatles performed immediately at Bruno Koschmider's *Indra* nightclub. They were required to play from 7pm until 2am every day, and until 3am on weekends, with a 15-minute break, each hour. On 17 August, The Beatles played the first of 48 nights at the club.

Their shows mostly comprised covers of their favourite songs. By the early hours of the morning, drunken audiences would urge the band to play songs they preferred, forcing the Beatles to extend their repertoire. It took time, but the group grew accustomed to the long performance hours and the additions to their set. They were forced to regularly adapt, especially as Koscchmider repeatedly insisted they *"Mach shau - make a show."*

In late September, their residency having ended at Butlin's, Rory Storm and the Hurricanes arrived in Hamburg. They too were booked for a residency at a Koscchmider club, the *Kaiserkeller*.

In early October, the Hamburg authorities received complaints of noise from neighbours of the *Indra*, and responded by closing the club. Koscchmider, impressed by the Beatles performances to date, wanted to retain the band, so booked them for a shared residency with the Hurricanes at the *Kaiserkeller*, where they split performance times.

Allan Williams, always on the lookout to further the careers of his performers, arranged a recording session for the Hurricanes at a Hamburg studio. Williams asked Lennon, McCartney and Harrison to play and sing harmonies with the band. By the end of the session, with Ringo Starr on drums, the musicians recorded three songs, *Fever*, *September Song* and *Summertime*.

During one Beatles set at the *Kaiserkeller*, a young German artist, Klaus Voormann, walked into the club and was immediately taken by the band. At his next visit, he was accompanied by his girlfriend, photographer Astrid Kirchherr. The couple quickly became club regulars and befriended the Beatles.

Kirchherr got on well with all members of the band, but particularly with bassist Stuart Sutcliffe. The two shared a passion for art. Sutcliffe arranged for Kirchherr to photograph the band at various Hamburg locations. Her collective images have since provided a definitive portrayal of the Beatles Hamburg era. Kirchherr and Sutcliffe drew close to each other, which led to a split between the photographer and her boyfriend, Voormann.

With a growing reputation, the Beatles were attracting the attention of other Hamburg club owners. One, Peter Erickson, owner of the *Top Ten* club, offered the band more money and better living conditions. Liking the deal, the band jumped at the opportunity. Lennon informed Koscchmider that they were to soon take up residency at the *Top Ten*. The *Kaiserkeller* owner did not take the news at all well. In an act of revenge, he notified the German authorities that 17-year-old George Harrison was underage and therefore ineligible to work in the country. His action had the desired effect. Harrison was deported a few weeks later.

Playing out their contract, the four-piece Beatles continued to perform at the *Kaiserkeller*. However, having found a replacement band, an angry Koscchmider ended the Beatles stay at his club. Preparing for their next residency, on 29 November, the band began to move their belongings from the *Bambi* cinema to the attic above the *Top Ten*. In the dark, McCartney and Best gathered their belongings and, unable to clearly see what they were doing, lit objects. Different accounts have since emerged describing the objects as rags, a wall tapestry and even a condom attached to a nail.

There was a small fire but little damage. Nevertheless, the incident further enraged Koscchmider and he reported it to the police. McCartney and Best were arrested, and spent the night in jail before being released. Deportation was the ultimate punishment for their exploits and the two were expelled from Germany the following day.

Having no band to perform with, John Lennon reasonably concluded that remaining in Hamburg was pointless. On 1 December, he returned to Liverpool. However, such was the relationship between the other Beatle and his girlfriend, Stuart Sutcliffe chose to stay in the city. The couple became engaged and Sutcliffe returned to his first love, enrolling as a student at the city's art college.

While the Beatles and the Hurricanes were performing in Hamburg, in October, Gerry and the Pacemakers played the *Cavern* for the first time. Band member Freddie Marsden later told *Mersey Beat* that the club: *"...was brilliant for sound as there was no echo, so you could hear exactly what you were playing."*

Also in October, owner McFall introduced the first lunchtime sessions at the *Cavern*. He made a further addition, employing a full-time DJ. A passionate lover of the Merseyside music scene and occasional booking agent, Bob Wooler was hired for the role. One for a clever turn of phrase, Wooler opened his set with the announcement: *"Remember all you cave dwellers, the Cavern is the best of cellars!"* From there on club goers were known as *"cave dwellers"* and the club advertised itself as *"The Best of Cellars."*

In December, Merseyside lost one of its most popular groups when Cass and the Casanovas disbanded in acrimonious fashion. One of its members, Johnny Gustafson, told *Mersey Beat* newspaper that the group's founder, Brian Casser was responsible for the split. Referring to Casser as Cass, Gustafson stated:

> *"Cass was both the founder and leader, and the rest of us were getting increasingly fed up with him, so we hatched this plot to disband and reform without him."*

Before the year was out, Casser quit Liverpool for London and he was to miss out on the success of Mersey Beat, unlike his former bandmates who reformed in January 1961.

Following their return from Germany The Beatles managed to perform only twice before Christmas, at the *Casbah* and the *Grosvenor Ballroom* in Wallasey. With Sutcliffe in Germany, they now required a bass player. Pete Best approached a member of one of his earlier bands, friend and college student Chas Newby. Newby to temporary sit in and play the few remaining gigs of 1960.

Worryingly short of bookings, in desperation the Beatles turned to the knowledgeable and influential Bob Wooler at the *Cavern*. Wooler contacted local promoter Brian Kelly, for whom he had occasionally worked. Kelly was reluctant to book the band as they had let him down without warning to support Johnny Gentle earlier in the year. The persuasive Wooler got his way and Kelly booked the group for a show on 27 December in Litherland. They were to perform on a bill with The Del Renas, The Searchers and The Deltones.

A couple of hours after the final whistle of the Everton game against Burnley at an overcrowded, dangerous Goodison Park, The Beatles were preparing to go stage at a venue two miles north of the stadium. Their performance that evening at *Litherland Town Hall* was one that convinced many in the audience that the greatly improved group were now among the best, if not the best, on the Merseyside music scene.

A 17-year-old Bootle apprentice railway engineer, William Ashton, was among those in the audience and he later vividly recalled the opening moments of the Beatles' performance:

> *The curtain opens. There are five guys on stage. The closest one turns and screams: 'I'm gonna tell Aunt Sally, 'bout Uncle John...' His name... Paul McCartney. Everyone runs to the front of the stage. I've never heard a white person singing like that. They are unkempt. They seem unrehearsed, yet they are very together. They are magic."*

The Beatles performance convinced Ashton that his future lay not at British Rail, but in rock 'n' roll. He eventually quit his job to become a singer. Ashton joined a band called the Coasters and together they began to make an impression performing in clubs and halls across Merseyside. He would later change his name to Billy J Kramer and with his backing group The Dakotas, become a very successful Mersey Beat band. The quote above is taken from Kramer's 2016 autobiography, *Do You Want to Know a Secret*.

Promoter Brian Kelly published posters for the Litherland show reading: *'Direct from Hamburg – The Beatles'*. John Lennon in *Anthology* recalled that some in the hall were confused by the band's billing.

> "Suddenly we were a wow. Mind you, 70% of the audience thought we were a German wow, but we didn't care about that. Even in Liverpool, people didn't know we were from Liverpool. They thought we were from Hamburg. They said, 'Christ, they speak good English!' which we did, of course, being English."

Many others at Litherland were equally gripped and awestruck by the Beatles' performance, not least Bob Wooler. Less than a year later Wooler was prepared to make a bold statement and prediction in print. In an August 1961 edition of *Mersey Beat* newspaper, he wrote:

> "The Beatles are the biggest thing to have hit the Liverpool rock 'n' roll set-up in years. They were, and still are, the hottest local property any Rock promoter is likely to encounter. In the Beatles, was the stuff that screams are made of. Here was the excitement - both physical and aural - that symbolized the rebellion of youth in the ennuied (sic) mid-1950's.
>
> This was the real thing. Here they were, first five and then four human dynamos generating a beat which was irresistible. Truly a phenomenon – and also a predicament to promoters! Such as the fantastic Beatles. I don't think anything like them will happen again."

Praise and very prescient praise indeed.

Preventing other promoters from "*stealing*" the Beatles, the initially reluctant, but now equally impressed agent Brian Kelly, immediately booked the group for a series of shows commencing in the new year. Where last December they went into 1960 with very few engagements, now the Beatles were going into 1961 without a free night for the foreseeable future.

On 31 December, the band saw out the old year and let in the new at the *Casbah*. Replacement bass player Newby was due back at college in January, so, with a full set of bookings, the band now required a bass player.

*

At the end of 1960, Merseyside music fans could not get enough of the Hurricanes, Pacemakers and others. The Beatles were now in a much better position to challenge the dominance of those bands. They travelled to Hamburg raw, but their experience in the city produced a more exciting, dynamic, tighter outfit

Despite end of the year setbacks, the Merseyside football clubs were too in a much better condition than a year earlier. Everton were at the right end of the First Division holding an outside chance of winning the league. Liverpool were in a similar position in the Second Division table, standing on the cusp of a return to the First Division.

Could the football clubs and the musicians maintain their progress in the new year?

4. A Hard Day's Night: January - July 1961

On Reflection, Bill Shankly believed the poor results at the end of 1960 were not merely a consequence of a loss of form, but also a result of unfair treatment by match officials. Goals were disallowed and penalty appeals dismissed in the end of year defeats. Shankly concluded that a bit of gamesmanship would not go amiss. He later wrote in his autobiography:

> *"Before the season was over I changed my philosophy for a while. Turning the other cheek did not get us anywhere, so I told my players: 'If you think a decision is wrong, storm up to the referee and surround him, every one of you. Make his life rough.'"*

In his *Daily Post* column Roy Vernon offered an alternative interpretation for Everton's poor end to 1960. He claimed the team's style of play had come *"unstuck on the poor winter pitches."* The Everton manager, Johnny Carey, wanted the team to pass the ball rather than *"lump it forward"* in the hope of bringing reward; winter playing surfaces, however, did not always favour the passing team's approach. Vernon hinted that the manager and players may need to reconsider their tactics in forthcoming games, the first of which was an FA Cup third round tie against Division Two leaders, Sheffield United at Goodison.

Vernon and Everton's other main threat, Bobby Collins, *"were singled out by the opposition,"* the *Echo* reported. *"Some of United's tackling was questionable,"* but effective as United went on to win the match 1-0. *"Everton did not look threatening in front of goal,"* the report added. If the manager and players discussed alternative tactics beforehand, they had clearly not succeeded.

It was also a tough tackling affair over at Anfield in Liverpool's cup tie with Coventry City. A contest so aggressive, the referee on more than one occasion, took time out to speak to team captains, ordering them to control their players.

Liverpool appeared to be in command, taking a two-goal lead, but were shocked by Coventry's response as the Midland club drew level. Liverpool though eventually progressed with centre forward Harrower scoring a late winner.

Merseyside representation in the cup was, however, to follow a familiar pattern, as Liverpool departed the cup in the next round, suffering a 2-0 defeat at home to Second Division rivals Sunderland. Another season, another pair of January exits. Both sides needed now to fully concentrate on their league campaigns.

Liverpool struggled for form in league games between cup ties. Away at Brighton, the Reds were described as *"colourless in attack and uneasy in defence"* by the *Echo,* as their opponents ran out 3-1 winners. Liverpool's forwards were further criticised in the same paper for their performance in a 1-1 home draw with Ipswich, being labelled *"as weak as water."*

One positive from the Ipswich draw; the result prevented a run of four straight league defeats and could be viewed as a point gained rather than lost. Their opponents were a rapidly improving team lying second in the league table and in serious contention for promotion. Ipswich were led by a highly-regarded manager, Alf Ramsey, who would later lead England to World Cup glory in 1966.

On the first Saturday in February, Liverpool finally recorded their first victory of the calendar year winning 3-2 at Scunthorpe, thanks to a late Leishman winner. The result triggered an impressive run of results through the remainder of the month. Leyton Orient were hammered 5-0 at Anfield with Hickson scoring a hat trick in *"his best performance"* since joining the club; two first half Jimmy Melia goals helped Liverpool take a 3-0 lead inside 35 minutes at Derby County, before a Lewis goal ensured a 4-0 win. The same player, and Morrissey, scored the goals which defeated Lincoln City 2-0 at home.

As February concluded, supporters were in a much more optimistic mood than a month earlier. The impressive run of victories kept the club in touch with the top two Sheffield United and Ipswich, and promotion remained a distinct possibility. With twelve fixtures remaining Liverpool were third, two points behind Ipswich and four behind Sheffield United. Liverpool and Ipswich though held two games in hand over United.

If February was a very good month for Liverpool, the opposite applied to Everton. Following their exit from the cup, Everton suffered a bad defeat losing 4-1 to Wolves at the end of January. Just a single point, coming in a 1-1 home draw with Chelsea, was accrued in February. Losses at home to Bolton and away to West Ham and Preston piled the pressure on manager Carey.

The team's poor form prompted an unusual reaction from Chairman Moores. He took it upon himself to meet and address the squad at training. Lecturing the assembled personnel, Moores openly criticised Carey for perceived tactical deficiencies. He then turned on the players, accusing them of a lack of application and effort. Moores singled out Bobby Collins in particular for criticism.

The player was furious with his treatment and went public about the meeting. He told the press that he was not beyond criticism, but believed he could never be accused of lacking effort. Evertonians writing to the *Echo* were supportive of Collins and Carey and fairly damning of Moores with one writer asking, "*How would he know how to play football?*"

Heading to mid-March, Everton at last managed to record victories, winning consecutive home games against Fulham and Nottingham Forest 1-0. Sandwiched between the victories was a 2-1 loss to Manchester City. Approaching the busy weekend Easter period at the end of the month, Everton conspired to lose two games in three days at home to Aston Villa and away to West Brom.

Many Evertonians responded to the dramatic downturn in form by staying away from Goodison; the incredible 75,000 attendance at the 1960 Christmas fixture with Burnley appeared a fading memory as fewer than 30,000 attended the recent home games.

Liverpool began March with a disappointing 2-2 draw at relegation threatened Portsmouth, but Shankly faced the problem of a disappearing attack for upcoming fixtures. The manager lost faith in Jimmy Harrower, preparing to transfer the player to Newcastle; Dave Hickson meanwhile, was on the treatment table and Roger Hunt was out of favour, having failed to score a goal in 1961. Shankly turned to the reserve team and a local teenager, Alan Banks, to solve his goal scoring problem; the player did not disappoint, scoring twice in a 3-1 win over Huddersfield.

The game was notable for the team's response to a non-decision by the referee. At the beginning of the year, Shankly instructed his players to protest if they believed the officials at fault. In the first half, a goal bound effort was diverted wide by a Huddersfield defender. The referee signalled a corner. The *Daily Post* reported:

> "*Virtually the whole team surrounded him. It required one of the most referee-baiting scenes of the season for Liverpool to win a penalty from which Lewis scored.*"

Shankly's ploy had paid off.

Transfer deadline day, 16 March, was fast approaching and, regardless of Banks' efforts, Shankly deduced that promotion would not be won without the addition of a new centre forward. The press reported that Liverpool made a last-minute bid for *"one of the best-known players in the game,"* but the selling club rebuffed Liverpool's approach. A couple of days later, Shankly revealed that the intended target was Middlesbrough's Brian Clough and that the club had tabled a £40,000 bid which Boro rejected.

Without a new centre forward, Shankly, would have to try to win promotion with his current crop of attacking players, in the hope they would find form.

Liverpool could not afford to slip up, but slip up they did. The struggles in attack continued; they picked up just a single point and scored a single goal in games against Swansea and Plymouth. However, all was not lost as Ipswich and Sheffield United also dropped points. With three games in five days to come over the Easter period the league table read:

Ipswich: played 34, points 48

Sheffield United: played 35, points 47
Liverpool: played 34, points 44

With Hickson and a recalled Hunt back in the side, on Good Friday 31 March, Liverpool won their game in hand over United defeating Bristol Rovers 3-0. The following day, Easter Saturday was possibly the most important of the season, away to Sheffield United, no less. Following a goal less first half, United took the lead early in the second period, but a Johnny Morrissey strike rescued a point for the Reds. The two games in two days left Liverpool a single point off United, both teams having played the same number of games.

Three days later, disaster struck in the return match with Bristol Rovers. Liverpool's defence *"fell apart,"* the *Post* reported, conceding four goals inside an hour. Despite Kevin Lewis grabbing a hat trick, scoring his third in the final minute, the result was a massive setback as Sheffield United won at home to open a three-point gap on the Reds.

On Saturday 8 April, all three promotion candidates recorded victories. Ipswich were now in a strong position as league leaders. Liverpool were three points behind Sheffield United with only four matches remaining for the two clubs. Nothing but victory would suffice next at Norwich City on Saturday 15 April.

Thousands of hopeful Liverpudlians made the long, arduous journey to East Anglia, but left the ground in despair. A 2-1 defeat and news of Sheffield United victory meant Second Division football was all but inevitable next season.

Before the next fixture at home to Stoke City, the manager and directors were already planning for next season. They spent most of the week arranging trips across the UK to identify potential close season signings.

In early April, Everton made an announcement that was to shock their fans and, for that matter, many football followers across the country. Rumours of a change of manager began on Monday 10 April with the news that former club centre forward Harry Catterick had resigned as manager of second placed Sheffield Wednesday. The media interpreted his resignation as a manoeuvre to take charge at Everton. The club did not issue a statement to the contrary, so the rumours merely intensified. Current manager Johnny Carey was, unsurprisingly, eager for the club to deny the truth of the rumours.

On the evening of Friday 14 April, he found the opportunity to broach the delicate situation with Chairman Moores. The two men were attending a Football League meeting in London. After the meeting, Carey asked Moores to clarify the position, thereby putting an end to the rumours. Moores suggested they discuss the situation further at their hotel.

As they travelled in a Hackney Cab to the *Grosvenor Hotel*, Carey continued to badger Moores for an answer. Moores responded, coming straight to the point. He informed Carey that he was disappointed by recent performances and he was indeed to be replaced as manager. Carey had famously been sacked in the back of a taxi. When news broke of Carey's dismissal, and its unusual manner, it was no difficult task for the press to assume that Catterick was in line to become his successor.

Despite his dismissal, Carey was courteous enough to volunteer to take charge of team affairs in the game against Cardiff City at Goodison on the following day. As the two men at the centre of the controversy took their places in the stadium, it was difficult for the press to gauge the attitude of most Everton supporters to Moores' decision. *"There were some cheers for Carey and some jeers for Moores"* reported the *Echo* later, though it appeared that most supporters preferred to keep their counsel.

Although too late to save Carey, a great performance ensued; Everton went on to thrash their opponents 5-1. The *Echo's* Leslie Edwards called the display *"the finest I have ever seen from an Everton team."* Following the game, with the team looking on, Carey was photographed in the dressing room cheerily shaking hands with captain Bobby Collins, his last gesture before officially leaving the club.

Evertonians clamoured for more information. Many were incredulous at the news that their manager could be *"sacked in the back of a taxi."* John Moores was forced to issue a statement to explain his and the club's version of events.

> "The question of managerial change had been discussed by the directors for some time and it was agreed at our last meeting that Mr Carey be given the opportunity to resign. This opportunity was turned down and the action of last Friday was taken."

Carey refuted this interpretation of events. He said he was never offered the opportunity to resign, stating:

> "The first I knew of the decision to finish as Everton manager was after the meeting in London on Friday when Mr Moores told me in a taxi."

Irrespective of the truth, Everton needed a replacement for the outgoing Carey. On 17 April, with Harry Catterick present, John Moores chaired an Everton board meeting. At 4.45pm, Catterick was confirmed as the new club manager; Moores announced that Catterick was *"to have total control of all team affairs including training, tactics and signings."*

The following day Catterick met the press and told the assembled journalists:

> "I am terribly proud to have this job offered to me. It is a club of wonderful traditions and I only hope I am able to fulfil expectations."

To coincide with the beginning of the new season in August, Catterick was immediately contracted by the *Daily Post* to write a regular column for the paper.

The only child of parents Henry and Lillian, Harry Catterick was born on 26 November 1919, in Darlington, County Durham. His father began his working life as a steelworker, but was later employed as a miner. Henry, a keen amateur footballer, was spotted by Stockport County who offered him a contract with the club. He accepted, quit the mines and in 1926, moved the family to the north west of England.

Raised on football, young Harry was keen to follow in his father's footsteps, but was advised by his parents not to become too dependent on his ambition. Leaving school at 14 he therefore began employment as an apprentice engineer. Like his father, Harry played amateur football, a prolific goal scoring centre forward, he too was scouted by north west teams. Both Manchester clubs were interested in his signature, but, to his father's surprise, 17-year-old Harry chose to sign for Everton in 1937.

On Everton's books at the time, were two top class centre forwards; one, a renowned record-breaking England international in the twilight of his career, Dixie Dean; the other, a young up and coming goal scorer, signed the previous year from Burnley, by the name of Tommy Lawton. With such distinguished competition for places, young Catterick knew he would have to bide his time. He had though signed for one of the country's top clubs, which was exemplified in 1939 when Everton won the First Division title. Tommy Lawton scored 34 goals en route.

Like Shankly, however, Catterick's professional career coincided with the outbreak of the Second World War in September 1939. He joined the RAF, but was soon demobbed and went back into engineering at the Stockport factory of his apprenticeship. He did play wartime football for Everton scoring an impressive 55 goals in 71 games. During the war, he also played for Manchester United and Stockport.

In 1945, upon the war's conclusion, he returned to Everton as a professional footballer. In November, Everton sold Lawton to Chelsea, so the opportunity arrived for Catterick to make the centre forward position his own. The only competitive professional football at the time was the FA Cup. Everton had been handed a tough third round draw in January 1946; they were to play Bill Shankly's Preston North End.

Without competitive league football, cup ties that season were two-legged affairs. On 5 January, Everton travelled to Deepdale, Preston to play the first leg. Catterick immediately imposed himself on the game scoring in the sixth minute. Preston however fought back with two second half goals and eventually ran out 2-1 winners. The *Evening Express* of 7 January was fulsome in its praise of the Everton centre forward's efforts stating: *"In Catterick Everton have a great leader in his ability and enthusiasm"*

The return leg four days later at Goodison was also a close contest. Everton led 1-0 after 90 minutes and so the game entered 20 minutes' extra-time. Everton took an aggregate lead in the 92nd minute, but Preston quickly equalised. With tie at 3-3 at the end of extra-time, FA Cup rules stated that the match had to be played on until a deciding goal was scored. As it happened, the winning goal came from a Preston penalty scored by Shankly.

First Division football returned to England on 31 August 1946 and Catterick finally made his league debut for Everton, nine years after signing for the club. An inauspicious start for the debutant, though, Everton lost the game to Brentford 2-0. Catterick didn't impress in subsequent games and failed to establish himself in the Everton line-up that season, playing only a handful of games. He had to wait more than a year before he scored his first league goal against Chelsea in September 1947. Repeatedly falling victim to injuries, Catterick played only sporadically over the succeeding two seasons.

Appearances were more regular during 1949-50. Throughout that campaign Catterick played a total of 25 games, scoring twelve goals. Everton had a decent FA Cup run too, but Catterick and his team mates were agonisingly defeated 2-0 by city rivals Liverpool in the semi-final.

Although it began well, the following season was very difficult for Everton. Catterick scored regularly in the first few games, including a hat-trick in a 5-1 win over Fulham. The *Daily Post,* recognising his past struggles with injury, reported on the 9 October.

> *"Catterick's change of fortune came deservedly. His goals were all excellently taken. He will derive much confidence from this performance."*

On the day of the above report, Everton travelled to Aldershot to play its annual game against the British Army. The following day the *Post's* match report was headlined *"Catterick Blow for Everton"*. Having scored an early goal, he pulled a thigh muscle and the immediate diagnosis suggested he would miss a *"few weeks' football."* The injury was though much worse. Over the next five months Catterick did not kick a ball for the first team.

When he returned to action in March 1951, Everton were on a poor run of form and lying in the bottom half of the table. There was talk of relegation but, if the club could eke out a couple more victories, the unthinkable could safely be avoided. Everton, however, embarked on a further disastrous run of results picking up a measly five points from ten games, scoring a paltry three goals in the process.

The final game of the season was away from home against fellow relegation threatened rivals, Sheffield Wednesday. To ensure First Division safety, Everton only required a point. It wasn't to be. In a dreadful performance, with Catterick centre forward, the Blues were thrashed 6-0 and the club were relegated to the Second Division.

The realisation that his playing career was coming to an end, Catterick enrolled on a FA coaching course with ambitions to enter team management. Third Division North club Crewe Alexandra were aware of his aspirations and offered him the post of player-manager. He played his final game for Everton on 27 August 1951 and moved to Crewe shortly afterwards.

There he spent almost two full seasons. In his first season in charge as player-manager, the team finished 16th and he scored eight times in 17 appearances. Finding the dual role difficult, Catterick finally made the decision to retire from playing to concentrate on full-time management. In his first full season in the role, 1952-53, Crewe finished in 10th position.

Catterick, believing he had taken the club as far as he could, sought a fresh challenge. A challenge he certainly gave himself, as he moved on to manage a team in a worse state than Crewe. Of the 24 teams in the Third Division North in 1953, his new club Rochdale, a team that regularly flirted with demotion from the league, ended the year in 22nd position.

Showing few signs of discernible improvement, Rochdale finished 19th at the end of his first season in charge. Determined to improve training methods and tactics, in 1956 Catterick acquired a specialist coach as his assistant, Liverpool born Joe Fagan. The techniques the two employed were relatively successful and Rochdale comfortably avoided the threat of demotion. Fagan however spent just two years at the club, leaving for Liverpool in 1958. Not long after Fagan's departure, a surprise opportunity materialised for the Rochdale manager.

Four times First Division champions, three times FA Cup winners and newly relegated to the Second Division, Sheffield Wednesday called on Catterick's services. An opening too good to dismiss, he was in Sheffield in an instant to prepare for the new season.

Rob Sawyer (*Harry Catterick: The Untold Story of a Footballing Great: 2014*) says Catterick's appointment was controversial with both Wednesday's supporters and some of their directors. Such was the furore; he was not officially appointed until 1 September 1958. Sawyer recounts the new manager's initial impressions upon meeting the players for the first time.

> "*The air of doom and despondency amazed me; never in my 17 years of soccer had I met such a dejected, dispirited set of players.*"

Playing tactics equally amazed him. Defenders had been instructed to "*boot the ball*" up the pitch as quickly and as far as possible. Moreover, Wednesday forwards were financially rewarded for shots on goal, meaning that they usually shot from anywhere. Catterick had therefore to lift spirits and change tactics. He quickly gained a reputation for being a task master in training, working players extremely hard to improve fitness. Believing team discipline was vital, he imposed a system of fines and punishments for misdemeanours or indiscretions.

He further believed in developing and promoting young players to the first team. One such was a tough, skilful wing half and local Sheffield lad, named Tony Kay, who quickly established himself in Catterick's starting eleven. Another promoted youngster, centre half Peter Swan, was, within a couple of years, playing for England.

Catterick's changes and influence brought immediate success. Wednesday, with two points to spare, won the Second Division in his first season in charge, scoring 106 goals in the process. Catterick had proved the doubters wrong with an immediate return to the First Division; promotion though would offer a much sterner test of his management skills.

The 1959-60 season started well for Wednesday with a 1-0 victory at Arsenal, but only five points were gleaned from the following eight games and the team found itself close to the bottom of the league. Despite the pressure, he turned the situation around. From the beginning of 1960 Wednesday lost just three of 21 games and steadily climbed the table, finishing the season in a very respectable fifth position. Catterick also oversaw a great cup run, which ended in a disappointing semi-final defeat to Blackburn Rovers.

His impressive two years in charge at Wednesday made Catterick a manager in demand. In September 1960, Nottingham Forest attempted to lure him away. Forest offered him more money than he earned, or could probably hope to earn, at Wednesday, but the club refused to sanction the move, insisting he see out his contract. Catterick did not dwell on the situation, guiding Wednesday to just one defeat in 16. The team were top of the First Division by mid-November.

Following a run of three defeats towards the end of the year, Wednesday lost top spot to Tottenham Hotspur. The team recovered in the New Year and though not quite good enough to challenge a dominant Spurs side, comfortably remained in second place with the season ending. On 10 April, however, and seemingly out of the blue, Catterick shocked the club and its supporters by submitting his resignation.

In a *Daily Post* column, later in the year, he explained why he took the decision to quit:

> "I had my disagreements with the policy of the club. There was no long-term planning for player development and they were going to great pains to develop a wonderful stadium. There was nothing wrong with that but I

felt their priority was wrong. I would rather have built a top-class side. As there was no point in pursuing my own policy, I resigned."

One week later, he joined Everton.

With Catterick in charge, Everton's final two games of the season both ended in victory. The first of those was ironically a 2-1 defeat of Sheffield Wednesday at Hillsborough. Roy Vernon ended the season on a high, scoring a hat trick in a 4-1 win over Arsenal.

Everton finished the season in fifth place in the First Division.

John Moores in his 1960 Christmas Eve *Echo* interview criticised the previous manager's training methods and his relaxed attitude to the players. Moores knew very well of Catterick's reputation as disciplinarian, a man who insisted on selecting hard working, fit players. Catterick did not dispute this label, as he told biographer John Roberts (*Everton: The Official Centenary History: 1978*).

> *"I think Carey was a bit easy on discipline and one or two players, who were outstanding in terms of ability, had run a little wild. It was one of my jobs to straighten them up, which didn't make me very popular. Any player playing badly but working hard would never be in trouble with me."*

Over at Liverpool yet another third-place finish was guaranteed before the season's end. Like the great majority of supporters, Shankly and many of the club's directors felt that the remaining fixtures were meaningless. While 13,309 spectators, some of whom watched the game seated on the sparsely attended Kop steps, were watching their team defeat Stoke City 3-0, Shankly and all but two directors were attending games across the British Isles scouting potential recruits. That weekend, Shankly identified the player he desperately wanted.

The player would cost a considerable sum of money. At the time, the manager still doubted that funds for a substantial bid were available. In his autobiography, Shankly disclosed the conversation he had with the club's newest director and John Moores' employee, Eric Sawyer. When he asked Sawyer if the club could afford to buy his identified target, the director, Shankly said, simply announced, *"If you can get the players, I'll get the money."*

John Moores' money was undoubtedly available and the Littlewoods owner clearly wanted both Merseyside clubs competing in the top division; he was therefore fully prepared to fund Liverpool's transfers to enable them to join neighbours Everton in Division One.

Two days before Liverpool's season ended in a 3-1 defeat at Stoke City, on 1 May, and before the press were made aware, Shankly received news that the player he long admired was available for transfer. Scottish club Motherwell informed Liverpool that they were prepared to release their star international forward, Ian St. John. Shankly had watched St John and did not hesitate to make his move. He hastily journeyed north to persuade the player that his best interests would best be served at Liverpool.

Immediately captivated by Liverpool's manager, and admitting to not knowing how to find Liverpool on a map, St John was, within 24 hours, in the city looking at houses. Impressed enough by the city and the club, on 2 May, St John committed his future to Liverpool, signing for a fee in the region of £37,000, more than double that of Milne less than a year earlier. St John told the press he was *"shocked"* at the size of the sum.

One week later, on 9 May, St John made his debut in the concluding game of a competition played between teams in the Merseyside area, the Liverpool Senior Cup Final. The match was played at of all places, Goodison Park. Over 51,000 spectators were in attendance to witness his first game, an exciting end to end contest.

Goals from Fell and Vernon gave Everton a 2-0 lead, but Liverpool scored two in quick succession to draw level. An own goal and a Collins penalty re-established

Everton's two goal advantage. The newspaper headlines, however, were grabbed by the scorer of his and Liverpool's third goal of the game, Ian St John. The local press was fulsome in praise of his performance. Though victory went to Everton by four goals to two, it was St John's three goal debut haul which became the story of the evening.

Towards the end of May, and much to Harry Catterick's annoyance, Everton left the UK to participate in an International Soccer League taking place in the USA and Canada. There was little Catterick could do to prevent the club participating, having been agreed before he took over team affairs at the club.

The club faced a heavy schedule of games in the warm north American summer. Much to Catterick's exasperation, the tournament was organised into two groups of eight teams, with the winners of each playing a two-legged final. Beginning on 23 May and concluding on 17 June, Everton had to compete in at least seven games in the space of 21 days. They duly fulfilled their obligations, winning six of their games, beating the likes of Kilmarnock of Scotland, Turkish side Besiktas and the Romanians of Dinamo Bucharest.

Everton topped the group and were set to play the winners of the other group, Czechoslovakian team, Dukla Prague in the final, but not until the first week of August.

While Everton were away in North America, Liverpool were once again busy in the transfer market. To add to his new centre forward, Shankly now required a new centre half. As with St John, the player he identified was in Scotland. At the beginning of July, he and his Vice-Chairman travelled north to meet representatives of Dundee to complete a deal for defender Ron Yeats. Also like St John, Yeats was captivated by Shankly. He later said in an *Echo* column:

> "It was just meeting him for the first five minutes that persuaded me that he was a good man and Liverpool would be a good club to be with. When we were coming down the M6, I didn't know what to say. Bill just turned around and said: 'Ron, I want you to captain the side. You will be my eyes,

my ears and my voice on that pitch.' I thought to myself, 'bloody hell.' It's a big thing at 22."

Yeats arrived on 2 July to put pen to paper for a fee of £30,000. Addressing the assembled football journalists, Shankly famously said to them, *"The man is a mountain, go into the dressing room and walk around him"*

The *Liverpool Echo,* contracted Yeats to produce a weekly column for its Saturday football edition. Yeats, like other recent arrivals on Merseyside including his team-mate Ian St John, Everton's Harry Catterick, Alex Young and Roy Vernon, now had the privilege of reporting on all manner of football related issues.

In the summer of 1961, with the signing of the two Scotsmen complete, Shankly was convinced that the final pieces of his jigsaw were in place to win promotion. Catterick meanwhile believed he had a squad capable of challenging for major trophies, including the league title, but would the North America football competition impact upon his players?

* * * * *

Stuart Sutcliffe, having chosen to remain in Hamburg, and with his temporary replacement Chas Newby back at college, the Beatles needed to find a replacement bass player. The group decided not to bother looking for one and opted instead to stay a four-piece with Paul McCartney volunteering for duty.

Having a virtual monopoly on venues in north Liverpool, agent Brian Kelly was as good as his word. Following the Beatles' *Litherland Town Hall* success, Kelly booked the band for dozens of shows in the coming months. Such was the demand, that on occasion they were required to perform twice nightly at separate venues including the *Aintree Institute, Lathom Hall,* Seaforth and *Blair Hall,* Walton.

Performing twice nightly brought transport difficulties, so with rising incomes, the Beatles employed a roadie, Neil Aspinall, who they originally paid £15 per week.

On 5 January, the band returned to Litherland to play their first show of 1961. It was also the first occasion in which McCartney played bass before a live audience.

Stuart Sutcliffe, accompanied by his fiancé Astrid Kirchherr, returned to Liverpool at the end of January. The Beatles welcomed him back to the band and he resumed duties as bass guitarist.

Also in January, following the departure of Brian Casser, the remaining members of the Casanovas, Johnny Gustafson, Johnny Hutchinson and Adrian Barber reformed as a trio, calling their new group The Big Three.

At the *Cavern*, Ray McFall booked The Bluegenes for a regular Tuesday lunchtime residency. One of the first bands to perform at the club, The Bluegenes were formed in 1957 by Bruce McCaskill as a jazz influenced sextet. There were several changes of personnel during the fifties and by 1961 they were practically a new unit. Come the new decade, McCaskill had quit. The band, now a foursome, were led by guitarists Ralph Ellis and Ray Ennis. Having transformed from a jazz to a beat band, performing rock 'n' roll and rhythm and blues, they adopted a name under which they would later gain fame, the Swinging Blue Jeans.

A consequence of their regular performances, McFall had full confidence in The Bluegenes and so handed the group control over choice of supporting bands. Gerry and the Pacemakers were often booked to play, but on 9 February the group invited the Beatles to make their debut at the club. The session, also the *Cavern* debut of George Harrison, was to be the first of hundreds for the band at the club.

McFall invited the Beatles to headline some lunchtime sessions, which proved extremely popular with audiences. In mid-March, the owner upped the ante and the band were handed a week-long set of shows. There was little stopping the Beatles now and on 21 March they played an evening session for the first time.

The *Iron Door*, the club on nearby Temple Street, was a developing competitor to the *Cavern*. On the weekend of 11-12 March the club held its first *Rock Around the Clock* concert. Beginning at 8.00 pm on the 11th, more than a dozen bands, including The Beatles, Gerry and the Pacemakers and Rory Storm and the Hurricanes, performed non-stop until 8.00 am the following morning.

One band, The Searchers, though not part of the bill that weekend, and a group which struggled to make appearances at the *Cavern*, were to make the *Iron Door* 'home' before the end of the year.

Formed in 1959 by John McNally and Mike Pender, the Searchers, like dozens of others on Merseyside, were originally a skiffle group. The band's name, though disputed by members as to who first came up with the idea, derived from a John Wayne movie of the same title. Their original drummer quit early. Replacement, Chris Crummy, later changed his name to Chris Curtis. Bass guitarist, Tony Jackson, completed the foursome. From 1960 until February 1962, they backed a local singer and were billed as 'Johnny Sandon and the Searchers'.

Three days after the *Iron Door* all-nighter, Stuart Sutcliffe and Astrid Kirchherr returned to Hamburg. The Beatles asked the pair to complete one duty on their behalf, to obtain a summer residency for the band at a club in the city.

The couple attended to some administrative paperwork shortly after arrival, which cleared the way for a trouble-free trip to Germany. Sutcliffe then met Peter Eckhorn, owner of the *Top Ten*. The two agreed on a contract, with band members each to be paid 35 Deutschmarks, about £3, per day. Almost identical to their stint in the city in 1960, the Beatles were required to play from 7pm until 2am each weekday, and until 3am on weekends, with a 15-minute break in each hour.

On 27 March, the Beatles left Liverpool to travel by ferry and train to Hamburg. They began their residency at the *Top Ten* on 4 April. Sutcliffe, though fully supportive, gradually withdrew from performing with the band to concentrate on his art, only playing the occasional show.

In residency and sharing the top of the bill with the Beatles was Norfolk born guitarist and singer, Tony Sheridan. Watching one of the shows at which the Beatles and Sheridan shared the stage, was an agent for the *Polydor* record label. Impressed enough, the agent contacted *Polydor* who booked a recording session for Thursday 21 June. The ensemble arrived for the recording at a school, *Friedrich-Ebert-Halle*. Although set up on a stage, acoustically the performance space was specifically designed for recordings and often used by *Polydor*.

The Beatles, with Sheridan on vocals, recorded four songs over two consecutive days: *My Bonnie*, a beat version of the old standard *My Bonnie Lies Over The Ocean*, The Saints, another beat version of *When The Saints Go Marching In*, *Cry For A Shadow* and *Why?*

The Beatles were paid 300 marks for the sessions. When released in Germany in October, *My Bonnie* was credited to Tony Sheridan and The Beat Brothers. The single reached number five in the German charts.

The Beatles returned to Liverpool on 3 July where Lennon met up with an old friend, Bill Harry. Harry loved the Merseyside music scene and knew most of the performers personally. He believed the local press, the *Liverpool Echo* and the *Daily Post*, did not dedicate enough space to local music. The *Echo*, on a page written by a correspondent using the pseudonym Disker, allowed space in its early Saturday edition to review the latest UK single and album releases, but barely mentioned the talented, emerging bands or the thriving club scene

Harry was exasperated by the lack of coverage. He wanted to take matters into his own hands. Writing later in the paper he established, he said: *"I decided to do something about it myself. I'd write about the local rock 'n' roll scene."*

Working together with his then girlfriend Virginia Sowry, they borrowed £50 to launch a project which would lead to a fortnightly newspaper, called *Mersey Beat*. The paper would be completely devoted to the music of Merseyside, featuring interviews with members of local bands and providing a *'what's on'* section containing information about every musical event taking place in the region over the forthcoming fortnight.

On 6 July, Harry and Sowry published the first edition of *Mersey Beat*. The reaction astounded the couple. All 5,000 copies sold out at the main wholesalers, W.H. Smith, Blackburn's and Conlan's, as well as the two dozen or so other Merseyside newsagents, musical instruments and record stores.

At *North End Music Stores (NEMS)* in Whitechapel, Harry asked to see the manager, Brian Epstein who agreed to take a dozen copies of *Mersey Beat*. All copies sold out almost immediately, so Epstein phoned Harry to ask for more, but none were available. For the second issue, Epstein placed an advanced order for twelve dozen copies.

The Beatles back in Liverpool, joined the other Mersey Beat bands on the club circuit. On 27 July, in one of their final shows of the month at *St John's Hall* in Tuebrook, the group shared the bill with The Big Three. The trio on this occasion were the backing band for an 18-year-old office secretary and aspiring singer named Priscilla White.

5. Please Please Me: August – December 1961

In the first week of August, Everton returned to the United States to play the two-legged final of the International Soccer League in New York. Manager Harry Catterick had had little time to work with his players and was frustrated that the club's pre-season preparations were interrupted by the USA final. An unfit and disinterested Everton were thrashed 7-2 in the first leg and went on to lose the second leg 2-0. Catterick believed the tournament would do his team no favours come the start of the new season.

Disregarding Catterick's concerns and commenting on Bill Shankly's team too, on 18 August, the eve of the new season, the Liverpool *Daily Post* optimistically wrote, *"Everton and Liverpool face promising seasons."* The newspaper was positive in its assessment that come the end of the football year in May 1962, both Merseyside clubs would be in with a chance *"of winning their respective titles."*

Shankly looked forward to an exciting season for supporters not just of his club, but also for neighbours Everton. *"Nowhere is there a greater enthusiasm for the game than on Merseyside"* he declared. Reminded that the atmosphere at football grounds had slipped in recent years he replied, *"I think there is a real possibility it will be re-born on Merseyside."*

On Saturday 19 August both clubs got off to an excellent start, each recording 2-0 victories; Bingham and Young scored for Everton at home to Aston Villa, while for Liverpool, away at Bristol Rovers, Lewis and an own goal were enough for victory. 52,293 watched the game at Goodison, the best attended in the country and 10,000 more than the next highest recorded at Arsenal's game at Highbury, London. There may have been something in Shankly's statement regarding atmospheres at Merseyside grounds.

"*It was pleasing to see Everton get off to a flying start,*" commented the *Daily Post*. In its report of the match on Monday 21st, though, the crowd, the paper added, were a little disappointed with the spectacle on offer. "*Supporters were satisfied with the performance, but the game itself left many spectators dissatisfied... Tackling was unremitting and relentless.*" The reporter hoped Everton's future results would be similar, but the entertainment on offer different.

The *Post* reporter at Liverpool's game concentrated more on the team's performance, writing: "*Liverpool have started well. The first impression is reassuring...The half-back line is reassured, competent and capable.*" Liverpool's next two games yielded convincing home victories at Anfield over Sunderland and Don Revie's Leeds United, scoring eight without conceding. The star of both games, Roger Hunt, scored five of the eight. Liverpool topped the table on Saturday 26 August.

Following the victory over Sunderland, Shankly later recalled how delighted he was with his new attack and how quickly the players gelled. He stated in his autobiography:

> "*Hunt's understanding with St John and Melia was enough to satisfy one even as critical as myself and it augured well for the future.*"

One of the biggest early season talking points concerned the crowd at the Sunderland game played on the 23rd. The official attendance that evening was 48,963; the ground capacity at Anfield at the time was 57,000.

The following day the *Liverpool Echo* reported that lengthy queues were in evidence long before kick-off. Almost all spectators at football matches at the time paid cash at the turnstile, so queues for well attended games were the norm. Turnstiles closed gradually and a few minutes before kick-off, they were all eventually shut; consequently, thousands of supporters were turned away.

Some disgruntled, locked-out supporters making their way home spoke to the *Echo* and expressed their dissatisfaction and disappointment at their experience. The paper went on to question the police and club officials; both blamed each other for the debacle and both pledged to get it right next time. The attendance for the Leeds game was down 6,000 on the Sunderland fixture. On the pitch, Liverpool's August ended with the reverse fixture against Sunderland and another victory, making if four wins from four played.

Everton's next two fixtures after the opening day victory over Villa ended in defeat, quickly puncturing pre-season optimism. They suffered their two losses away to West Bromwich Albion 2-0 in the first and a 2-1 loss at Fulham in the second. The *Echo* believed extenuating circumstances were responsible for the defeats, particularly the first setback at West Brom. Everton had to effectively play most of the match with nine men as two of their star players, Young and Collins, suffered early injuries. Substitutes had yet to be introduced, so the injured players remained on the field as ineffective wingers. The *Echo* claimed that the aim there on *"was to keep down the score."* Everton were consequently forced to play a weakened team in the defeat at Fulham.

The opportunity for revenge over West Brom for Everton came on the 30th. Although still without the injured Collins, they went on to comfortably win the contest 3-1, in front of a disappointingly low attendance of 35,000. The *Echo* praised the performance of Everton's 20-year-old centre half, Brian Labone.

> *"Here is a man who is rising fast in the football firmament. He has established himself as an Everton (and maybe England) pivot for years to come."*

Labone and his team mates were though given something of a footballing lesson in their next fixture, a humiliating 4-0 defeat away to Harry Catterick's former club Sheffield Wednesday. *"It wasn't effort that Everton lacked it was skill and brains,"* commented the *Echo*.

After the Wednesday loss, Catterick took the opportunity to bemoan the effects of the US summer tour, claiming it was an enormous contributory factor in team's relatively poor start to the season. He conjectured before the tour that it would impact on performances and now believed he had been proven right. Whether to appease supporters' concerns and take the pressure off, the club released a statement in support of Catterick's judgement. It read:

> "It does appear that it was a mistake to go to America...The players appear to be jaded after playing in the intense heat over there."

The rest of September continued much in the same vein; three defeats at the hands of Manchester City, Leicester and Burnley were counter-balanced with victories over Ipswich Town, the reverse contest against Manchester City and, the best result and performance to date, a 4-1 home defeat of Arsenal on 30 September. Appraising Everton's start to the season, Leslie Edwards writing in the *Echo* on 2 October stated:

> "Mr Catterick I think has improved Everton. He has asked of the team greater physical effort. Arsenal were astonished by the intensity of Everton's play."

The league table however made frustrating reading for Evertonians as the club found itself 11th of the 22 teams. Catterick faced a stern test if he was to turn his promising team into potential title challengers. Excellent home wins such as those against Arsenal needed to be replicated away from home. The team had managed to accumulate a mere two points on the road.

Liverpool's September began as August left off with another victory, on this occasion a 2-1 win at Norwich City. Ron Yeats writing the following Saturday in the *Echo* felt the team deserved more credit than usual for the result as their train had broken down on the way to the game. The players arrived at the ground only 20 minutes before kick-off. Liverpool were a goal down at half time, but Yeats said that it was in the second half, "...*when team spirit, fighting spirit and fitness really told.*

After a 2-1 home defeat of Scunthorpe the club dropped its first point of the campaign drawing 0-0 at Brighton and Hove Albion. The month concluded with a victory at Newcastle and thumping 4-0 and 5-0 defeats at home to Bury and away to Charlton respectively. Hunt had scored an incredible twelve goals in the opening ten games.

The non-use of substitutions was rarely out of the news. Alex Young was an advocate of substitutes, as was Yeats who, in his *Echo* column, addressed the issue after the Bury match. Liverpool's opponents had lost a player after only 30 seconds due to serious knee ligament damage and Yeats believed that it was grossly unfair for Bury to have to play virtually the entire game with ten men. He wrote: *"Why those in authority do not see the logic of having a pool of at least twelve players, I cannot understand."*

By the end of September, the club were a comfortable four points clear at the top of the Second Division and had the clear look of champions. Liverpool had made a remarkable start to the season. On closer examination, the results appear even more remarkable.

First up, Shankly played an unchanged side in the first ten games. Second, to complete their away fixtures, the team travelled to all points of the compass; to the north, Sunderland and Newcastle; to the south, Charlton and Brighton; to the east, Norwich and to the west, Bristol, round trips totalling almost 2,500 miles by road or rail. Referring to the road journeys, Yeats stated, *"If you happen to be over six foot and travel by coach, it's murder."* Third, to make the record more impressive, Liverpool conceded just four goals in ten games, mainly due, said Shankly, to his *"colossus"* of a centre half, Ron Yeats.

In October, an emphatic 6-1 home win over Walsall was sandwiched between Liverpool's first setbacks. Yet another trip north resulted in a 2-0 midweek loss to Middlesbrough, the two goals bizarrely coming from a Liverpool defender, Dick White. A similar defeat occurred at Derby a week later, but it was not the result that made the headlines, it was trouble on the pitch.

Trailing 2-0, Yeats tackled Derby forward Curry near the touchline and left the player *"in a crumpled heap on the running track."* Curry was carried off, but Derby supporters were incensed at the Liverpool centre half and booed him for the remainder of the match. At the final whistle hundreds of Derby fans invaded the pitch with one or two aiming kicks at Yeats. The situation further deteriorated as fights broke out on the pitch between opposing fans and the police were forced to clear the playing area.

In his *Echo* column, Yeats was rather restrained with regards to the attempted assaults upon him, merely referring to the incident as *"a most degrading melee."* He was more concerned about the potential repercussions of such incidents. The match at Derby was just one of several recently in which trouble had spilt onto the pitch. Yeats wrote:

> *"Some people have spoken of fences being erected to prevent such problems, as happens in some South American countries. I would not like to see that happen in Britain."*

Liverpool's month concluded with a 3-3 home draw to one of their nearest challengers, fourth placed Leyton Orient, now led by ex-Everton manager Johnny Carey. As the team had worryingly doubled the total number of goals conceded in their last four games, reports later suggested that Shankly was concerned about the form of his goalkeeper, Bert Slater.

Despite the draw and the form of the goalkeeper, there was little doubt which team the *Daily Post* believed would finish as Second Division champions. With Liverpool holding a five-point lead over nearest challengers Southampton going into November, the *Post* claimed that it was:

> *"...not a question of whether Liverpool will win the league, but merely a question of by how many points they will win it."*

Following a 3-1 win at Preston North End at the beginning of the month, Liverpool were *"cool and efficient"* the *Post* claimed, handing its Man of the Match award to Ian Callaghan, playing his first game of the season and a scorer of one of the goals. Despite the death of a son earlier that week, Ian St John also played and scored in against Preston. His child sadly passed away within a couple of days of his wife giving birth. In his column on 8 November he thanked those who sent his family messages of support following their loss, saying they had been of *"enormous help"* to him and his wife.

Moving on, he wrote of the *"great support"* the team received both at Anfield and away from home. The Preston game almost *"...felt like a home match with the magnificent following."* He went on, *"I openly admit that I feel happier when the crowd is roaring for us, it makes such a difference, especially at home."* The following evening St John went on to represent his country and scored both goals in Scotland's 2-0 Home International win over Wales at Hampden Park, Glasgow.

The fantastic form continued through November with two more victories; the first a 2-1 away win at Huddersfield Town; the second a resounding 5-0 home win over Swansea City with Roger Hunt scoring three second half goals. The hat-trick was Hunt's third of the season and the goals made it a terrific total of 19 from 20 appearances to date. At the end of the month, Liverpool had extended their lead at the top to eight points. London side Leyton Orient, were now nearest challengers, but surely if the club could maintain its form, the title would soon be won.

With Liverpool in fine form, Roger Hunt, Jimmy Melia, Gerry Byrne and Gordon Milne were performing with enough distinction to be thought worthy of a call up to the England squad. The World Cup in Chile was just seven months off and all players were looking to impress the England manager, Walter Winterbottom.

Winterbottom was in the stands for Liverpool's next fixture away to third place Southampton on 2 December. As can happen on such occasions, it wasn't a good day for Liverpool or the players trying to impress the England manager. Liverpool lost the match 2-0, just their second defeat of the season. Few Liverpool players performed with distinction, but the setback did not prevent Winterbottom giving Roger Hunt a chance. He invited the forward to join an England squad training session later that month. His team mates would have to wait a while longer for their opportunity.

Without dwelling on the defeat at Southampton, Liverpool won their next two home fixtures against Plymouth and Bristol Rovers, 2-1 and 2-0 respectively, St

John scored in each of the games. The *Post* was not overly enthusiastic with the display in the first of those games, reporting that Liverpool barely deserved the win over Plymouth. The performance was such, it claimed, that supporters' *"...nerves were stretched to breaking point until St John scored the late second goal."*

In a very commanding league position, Liverpool supporters looked forward positively to the final two fixtures of the year. The games were away to Yorkshire opposition. The team however performed very poorly in both, particularly in front of goal. They were first beaten at Rotherham United 1-0 and then on Boxing Day lost by the same score line at Leeds United. Nearest league rivals, Leyton Orient, who were on a fine run of form, recorded two victories on the days of Liverpool's setbacks. Consequently, the Reds' once comfortable lead at the top of the table had been cut to four points. To add further pressure, Orient also held a game in hand.

The defeat at Rotherham, St John later revealed, caused Shankly great consternation. He was even more concerned with the quality and stature of his goalkeeper Bert Slater. Writing in his autobiography, the Liverpool forward said:

> *"I overheard Shankly saying to Bob Paisley, 'the boy's not big enough.' I knew that was the end of Slater's time at Anfield."*

Slater, at five feet nine inches tall, it must be said, was on the short size for a goalkeeper.

Over at Goodison Park, Everton finally began to show the form supporters eagerly awaited. October proved a very productive month and a gradual climb up the First Division table ensued. The period started in the best possible fashion with a 6-0 thrashing of Nottingham Forest. As much was expected of him, Evertonians had waited for one of their favourites, Roy Vernon, to hit form. He'd missed a handful of games through injury, but did score his first two goals of the season in the Arsenal game at the end of September. He doubled his tally against Forest.

His playing partner, Alex Young, was also playing well. The *Echo* wrote of his performance against Forest:

> "It was the finest exhibition of centre forward play since the days of Dixie Dean and Tommy Lawton – that is how I rate the performance of Young."

Everton supporters hoped that early season expectations were finally being met.

To add to supporters' delight, the Blues had at long last managed to win another away match, a convincing 3-0 win at Wolverhampton Wanderers. The victory was followed by a 1-0 win over Sheffield United at Goodison. Hopes were high for a 100% October return as Everton travelled to bottom club Chelsea. It wasn't to be. Everton had to be content with a disappointing 1-1 draw. The league table at the end of the month did though read much better. Considering the club were in 21st place at the end of August, they were now in 5th following an exceptional turnaround in form.

On 18 October, the Merseyside teams took time off league duties to contest their annual *'friendly'* derby match at Goodison Park. Alex Young writing for the *Echo* on the day of the game asked *"What are the odds against a league double by the city clubs?"* He believed it a distinct possibility. Supporters of both clubs yearned for derby matches as evidenced by the attendance of more than 60,000.

The following day the *Echo* was effulgent in its praise of the entertainment on offer. It said the match was:

> "…one of the finest the clubs have ever produced. It stormed and raged for 90 minutes. It produced some of the hardest, fastest, finest football seen for seasons… the sooner the fixture is off the friendly list the better. Both teams have enough to grace the First Division"

For the record, the game ended 2-2.

Into November and at Goodison, Everton began with an outstanding performance on the 4th against the league's best team, last season's double winners, Tottenham

Hotspur. The *Post* described Everton as not *"...just at their best, but at their bravest and most spirited,"* in their 3-0 victory. Vernon was portrayed as *"a near genius"* and Young as all *"poise and perfection."* Echoing Young, the report ended with a question; *"Can Everton depose Spurs as champions?"*

Everton drew their next game 1-1 at Blackpool, but most local and national newspaper football talk the following week centred on the likely transfer of a goal scoring sensation currently playing in Italy. The player wasn't Italian, but English; his name, Jimmy Greaves.

Greaves made his debut for Chelsea in 1957 and went on to score an incredible 124 goals in 157 appearances before his world record transfer of £90,000 to AC Milan in the summer of 1961. Despite making an excellent start at Milan – scoring nine goals in twelve appearances in the notoriously difficult Italian Serie A – he was clamouring for a return to England. Several clubs including Manchester United and his old team Chelsea were linked with his signature, as too were Everton.

Regardless of the recent upturn in form, some Evertonians wrote to the *Echo* urging the club to sign Greaves. Harry Catterick, in his *Daily Post* column on 15 November, sought to put a dampener on supporters' hopes. Spurs had placed a bid of £100,000 for the forward, the six-figure sum Catterick regarded as *"unacceptable."* Such a fee, he added, *"will have a knock-on effect for all other buying clubs as sellers would demand larger fees,"* he argued. Greaves would certainly not be arriving at Everton. As it was, the player did go on to sign for highest bidders Spurs in December, not for the much expected a six-figure sum, however, but for the five-figure sum of £99,999.

Everton's penultimate game of November was a 1-0 home defeat of Blackburn Rovers with Vernon again providing the winner against his former club. However, the month ended in defeat as the team suffered a 3-1 loss at West Ham United, their first setback since 23 September. After the West Ham loss, Everton, stood third in the table, six points off leaders Burnley, still healthily positioned for a title challenge.

Everton began December in great form with a resounding 5-1 win over Lancashire rivals Manchester United. The victory was made extra special by *"a blistering first half display"* in which all five goals were scored without reply. United, the *Echo* reported:

> "...were left bewildered by the speed and skill of Everton's attack. They simply were not able to cope with the intensity of Everton's game... Everton declared at half time."

If this was indeed a true reflection of events, the *Echo* report irritated some supporters as well as the scorer of two Everton goals, the paper's own columnist, Roy Vernon. He refuted the allegation the following week. *"Nothing could be further from the truth,"* he wrote. He believed that United manager, Matt Busby, was determined to avoid total humiliation and ordered his players *"to win the second half."* The United players, Vernon said, responded with a much improved second half performance.

The win moved Everton into second place. Nevertheless, and fairly typical of season to date, the team's away form was their downfall. What appeared on paper to be winnable opportunities against mid-table opposition, Cardiff City and Aston Villa, resulted in two disappointing draws, with just a single goal scored in the process. Vernon called their away form, *"a real mystery."*

Although the prolific Jimmy Greaves had signed for Spurs, more than a few supporters continued to lament what they believed was a missed opportunity for the club. In letters to the *Echo*, supporters complained about Everton's inability to score sufficiently away from home; the team had managed just twelve goals in eleven away games. The correspondents pointed out that to date Everton had the third worst away goal scoring record in the league. The two bottom placed teams, Chelsea and Manchester City, had both scored more away than Everton. It would be impossible to win the league, they deduced, with such a record.

Predictably Everton, back at Goodison, picked up maximum points in their next two games. Victories over Fulham, 3-0, Bobby Collins scoring twice, and a 1-0 defeat of Bolton Wanderers, made it at least a Happy Christmas for Evertonians; to make the holiday even happier, league leaders Burnley suffered a 2-1 home defeat to Arsenal. The result left Everton at the turn of the year a mere two points in arrears of the north Lancashire team.

Despite the impressive end to the year, all was not well at Goodison Park. Catterick was not entirely satisfied with the performances of some his players. One was Booby Collins who, despite scoring twice against Fulham, was on the end of what he called a *"rollicking."* In his autobiography, penned by David Saffer, (*Bobby Collins: The Wee Barra:* 2004) he wrote:

> "After scoring two against Fulham, Catterick told me I was not the player I used to be. I was not happy and told him so. I'd been the best Everton player that day and I'd got a rollicking. I knew my days were numbered."

So, with Liverpool's Second Division lead at the top of the table being pressurised by Leyton Orient and Everton, despite showing signs of disharmony, gaining ground on First Division leaders Burnley, what would the New Year bring for the Merseysiders.

First up however in January, cup ties, with Liverpool at home to first Division strugglers Chelsea and Everton, to play on the face of it a much easier game, also at home to non-league side, King's Lynn.

* * * * *

An unusual music venue was added to the increasing list of locations used for showcasing the talents of Merseyside musicians. In August 1961, *Cavern* owner Ray McFall hired the iconic Mersey ferry, the *Royal Iris,* for an event he titled the *Riverboat Shuffle*. It wasn't a show for Mersey Beat bands alone, but a mixture of musical styles. Acker Bilk, and his Paramount Jazz Band headlined the show, while the Beatles, reflecting their developing progression, were second on the bill.

Bilk enjoyed his experience aboard about the *Iris*. Interviewed by author Spencer Leigh for his book *The Cavern*, the jazz man stated:

"The boat used to go down the Mersey a bit and out in the channel and the Beatles did our interval spots. They wore black leathers and I liked the tunes they played. I was quite impressed to be steering the boat as the captain gave me the wheel whilst The Beatles were playing."

Beginning and ending at the Pier Head, the shuffle lasted for over three hours. Pete Best, in a co-authored book also written by Spencer Leigh, *The Best Years of The Beatles*, said that when the show was over, *"... we had a great drinking session with Acker and his band who brought their own crates of beer and told us to get stuck in."*

To celebrate his upcoming 21st birthday on 8 October, John Lennon, accompanied by Paul McCartney, began hitchhiking from Liverpool to Paris. Lennon received a £100 early birthday present, and decided that he would like to spend most of the money in the French capital. Lennon told his aunt Mimi that he was travelling abroad to sell his paintings.

Back home and on stage, on 15 October, Lennon, McCartney and the other Beatles were just one of a dozen or more acts on the bill of a variety show at the *Albany Cinema* Maghull. The headline act was a star of the Merseyside comedy circuit, Ken Dodd. The Beatles, tenth on the list of performers, went on and played a couple of rock 'n' roll numbers. Thoroughly disliking what he heard, an angry Dodd complained to the show's promoter Jim Gretty. Dodd urged him to eject the band from the stage before the end of their set, which the promoter duly did.

A couple of years later, prior to an early TV appearance, the Beatles met Dodd and Paul McCartney asked the comedian whether he recalled having them thrown off stage. Dodd said he remembered the incident taking place, but never realised it was the Beatles he'd asked to be removed.

The eighth issue of the now very popular music paper *Mersey Beat* was published in late October. A long Bob Wooler article listed 273 bands performing in Liverpool alone. A writer with a penchant for a witty pronouncement, Wooler claimed that most groups were merely *"makeweights,"* their longevity *"measured more by the clock than by the calendar."* There was, however, a much more determined bunch who believed they'd soon come good, and that fame and acclaim were just around the corner. Wooler reeled off the top ten names on that list with the Beatles coming out at number one.

On the day of publication of the Wooler article, the Beatles, Gerry and the Pacemakers and Karl Terry and the Cruisers were all in performance at *Litherland Town Hall*. One of the musicians, it's not known who, suggested that for the night group members *'mix and match,'* have a bit of fun and collectively call themselves 'The Beatmakers'. The musicians swapped guitars, Paul McCartney did a turn on drums and all performers made general mischief. Despite the anarchic nature of the evening, the show still went down well with the audience.

*

> *"At about three o'clock on Saturday, October 28, 1961, an 18-year-old boy called Raymond Jones, wearing jeans and a black-leather jacket, walked into a record store in Whitechapel, Liverpool, and said: 'There's a request I want. It's My Bonnie and it was made in Germany. Have you got it?'*
>
> *Behind the counter was Brian Epstein, 27, director of the store. He shook his head. 'Who is the record by?' he asked. 'You won't have heard of them,' said Jones. 'It's by a group called the Beatles…"*

So runs the prologue to *A Cellarful of Noise*, the 1964 autobiography of Brian Epstein. Many Beatles historians claim Epstein conceived the story to add a touch of mystery and romanticism to the soon to be established relationship between himself and the promising pop group.

In 1958, on Great Charlotte Street, next door to Yates's Wine Lodge a popular public house in Liverpool, *North End Music Stores (NEMS)* opened its first city centre outlet. Selling musical instruments, radios and record players, *NEMS* was also a record retailer and in charge of the department was 24-year-old Brian Epstein, son of store owner, Harry.

The business was healthy enough for Harry Epstein to branch out and open a second city centre store on nearby Whitechapel, with Epstein junior transferring to manage the new store's record department. Brian Epstein proved to be an excellent manager so much so that by the turn of the decade *NEMS*, Whitechapel was Liverpool's leading record retailer. Moreover, it became a very fashionable place to be seen, as customers mixed with members of local bands.

Brian Epstein, son to mother Queenie and father Harry, was born at number 4 Rodney Street in Liverpool city centre on 19 September 1934. The Epstein family had been in the furniture trade since 1901, owning a shop in the Walton district of the city. The store, situated on the corner of Walton Road and Royal Street, was less than a ten-minute walk to each of the city's football grounds, Anfield and Goodison Park. Next door to Epstein's shop, but under different ownership, was a music store called *NEMS*.

It was no secret that Liverpool would be threatened by German bombs during the Second World War, so the Epstein family moved from their south Liverpool, Childwall home to the relative safety of Southport, 15 miles north of the city. Brian attended school there, but found it difficult to settle. His mother removed him and sent him to the fee-paying *Liverpool College*. There he proved troublesome and within a year his head teacher asked his parents to remove Brian.

The family, believing he would better himself outside Merseyside, relocated Brian to a public school in Tunbridge Wells, Kent. Already an itinerant scholar he didn't stay long and continued to move from school to school going next to another Kent establishment and then further south to Dorset. He was now 13 and clearly hating his education. In *A Cellarful of Noise*, he wrote:

> "I had by now developed a conscious hatred of formal education, I was bad at mathematics and all sciences. I had no rapport with the men teaching me.

He moved again, north to *Wrekin College*, a public school in Shropshire. Despite hating it there too, he remained at *Wrekin* until his formal education was complete. Leaving school at 15 without formal qualifications, he told his parents by letter that his ambition was to move to London to become a dress designer. They refused to countenance such an idea and ordered him to return to Liverpool. In his autobiography, Epstein wrote:

> "*On September 10th 1950, aged nearly sixteen, thin, curly haired, pink-cheeked, I reported for duty in the family furniture store Walton, Liverpool.*"

After a short spell in national service in Aldershot, he again returned to Liverpool. In the meantime, Harry Epstein had purchased *NEMS* the music store next to his Walton furniture shop. Brian was made both store manager of *NEMS* and a company director.

Around this time, claims Philip Norman in *Shout! The True Story of the Beatles,* that Epstein acknowledged his homosexuality. In fifties Britain, homosexuality was a criminal offence and those found guilty were liable for imprisonment. To be publicly homosexual was to tread on dangerous ground.

Apart from dress designing, Epstein held ambitions to become an actor. His family were more preferential to acting than dress designing and agreed that training in the profession at the world famous *Royal Academy of Dramatic Art* (*RADA*) in London, may well be a favourable move. At *RADA,* Epstein said he experienced some enjoyable times, but some troublesome times, not getting on with several of his fellow trainees.

At the end of the third term he returned to Liverpool to visit the family. The day before his due return to RADA, Epstein informed his father that he had no further desire to continue his training. In his autobiography, Epstein said he took the decision to stay in Liverpool after spending a fortnight with the *Royal Shakespeare Company* at Stratford. The company, he said, were: "*frightful, phoney, and practised hypocrisy on a grand scale.*

Philip Norman, however offers a different explanation for Epstein's non-return to London. Norman claims that towards the end of his third term, Epstein visited a toilet in Swiss Cottage, London. There he exchanged a few words with another man who informed him that he was an on-duty police officer, basically engaged in entrapment. Arrested, Epstein was charged with importuning. He later appeared at Marylebone Magistrates Court and entered a guilty plea to importuning. He received a fine and a conditional discharge. Norman says that it would have been impossible for Epstein to tell his parents of his experience and most certainly could not publish the information in his autobiography. He was unable to return to London, says Norman, owing to the traumatic effects of the incident.

Following a short spell managing a recently opened Epstein family store in Hoylake, Wirral, in 1958, Epstein's father put him in charge of the record department of the newly opened *NEMS* store on Great Charlotte Street. Working day and night he helped make his department one of the largest musical retail outlets in the north of England.

Impressed by his son's work, Harry Epstein relocated Brian to the family's second city store at 12–14 Whitechapel to run the record department there. Epstein advertised the store as having *"The Finest Record Selection in the North.* He promised customers that any record requested could be obtained. (perhaps that's how the story of Raymond Jones and the *My Bonnie* request originated). In an original move to boost sales, Epstein displayed the top twenty records bought weekly at the store. Though on occasion he was off-hand with some of his staff, he was highly regarded and respected by the majority. Many *NEMS* customers later spoke of him as being polite, well-mannered and smartly-dressed in his sharp suits, although some younger customers did say that they would giggle behind his back on account of his *"posh"* demeanour.
.

In the autumn of 1961, aged 27, and with the store running *"like an eighteen-jewelled watch,* Epstein was *"becoming a little restless and bored."* He was searching for a fresh challenge. Could the Beatles provide it?

Almost certainly Brian Epstein must have been aware of the Beatles when Raymond Jones allegedly walked into *NEMS* to request *My Bonnie*. Aside from selling hundreds of copies of *Mersey Beat*, which included numerous references to the Beatles, Epstein also contributed articles to the newspaper. Regardless of the veracity of the Jones story, Epstein wanted to see for himself a performance by the band of whom many music fans in Liverpool were enthusing. If impressed, he planned to meet the Beatles to discuss the idea of management.

Although the *Cavern*, no more than a couple of hundred yards from *NEMS* Whitechapel, was the obvious venue to see the band, Epstein did not just want to arrive unexpectedly at the club. Bob Wooler, interviewed by Spencer Leigh, explained what happened next.

> "Epstein was intrigued to see what they were like and he phoned Bill Harry at Mersey Beat and asked him to smooth his entrance into the Cavern. Bill arranged this with club owner Ray McFall and doorman Paddy Delaney."

On 9 November, Epstein, accompanied by his Whitechapel store assistant Alistair Taylor, was allowed into the *Cavern* without having to queue and welcomed over the club's PA system by Wooler. He and Taylor stood at the back of the auditorium listening to the session. In *A Cellarful of Noise*, he recalled his thoughts after that first show:

> "I was immediately struck by their music, their beat, and their sense of humour on stage - and, even afterwards, when I met them, I was struck again by their personal charm. And it was there that, really, it all started."

Epstein went backstage to meet the group with George Harrison reportedly asking: "*And what brings Mr Epstein here?*" A bond between those present was immediately established and arrangements were made for a more formal gathering in the near-future.

That same evening, the Beatles performed for the final time at *Litherland Town Hall*, the last in a total of 20 shows at the venue; the first of course was the triumphant appearance on 27 December 1960 following their first trip to Hamburg.

The day following Epstein's meeting with the Beatles, *Operation Big Beat* took place at the *Tower Ballroom* New Brighton, a venue capable of holding 5,000 people. Promoted by Sam Leach, *Operation Big Beat*, was a huge musical event consisting of the best Mersey Beat bands, including Rory Storm and the Hurricanes, Gerry and the Pacemakers, the Remo Four, Kingsize Taylor and the Dominoes and, of course, the Beatles. Tickets for the show cost five shillings. Leach, though nervous at the size of the venue, knew it would not only attract interest on the Wirral, but also on the other side of the Mersey in Liverpool. He arranged for fans to be picked up in buses on St. John's Lane close to the entrance to the Mersey Tunnel. Hundreds made the journey to New Brighton and back when the show ended around 1.30.

The Beatles' first set took place at 8pm, after which they unbelievably drove to *Knotty Ash Village Hall* in east Liverpool, for their second show of the night. Incredibly, after that show, they hopped back in the van and returned to the *Tower*, completing a round journey of about 25 miles, to perform for a second time at 11.30pm. After the show, on the way back to Liverpool city centre, the Beatles and the Hurricanes had a potentially dangerous car chase through the Mersey Tunnel.

Over the next few weeks, Epstein watched the Beatles at the *Cavern* several times. Following one of the performances he suggested they meet again on 3 December at *NEMS*. He wanted to formalise their relationship by proposing himself as group manager. The group brought along Bob Wooler for support, a move which suggests they may have harboured doubts about a potential relationship. Nothing definitive was agreed, as the band needed time to discuss proposals. Pleased enough with deliberations, a few days later John Lennon contacted Epstein to say the band assented to him becoming manager.

In the meantime, promoter Sam Leach had written to A&R representatives of several record companies in the hope they would travel to Merseyside to observe and assess the musical talent on offer. All companies failed to respond. He deduced that if the A&R men would not come to the bands, then the bands would go to them.

The first such were the Beatles, who Leach booked, rather optimistically, for five consecutive Saturday nights at the *Palais Ballroom*, Aldershot, a military town 37 miles from London. The first night, 9 December, was billed on posters and handbills as a "*Liverpool v London Battle of the Bands*" featuring The Beatles and a London group, Ivor Jay and the Jaywalkers.

Leach failed to promote the show sufficiently, for example the local evening paper didn't run an advert because he failed to pay for it in advance. The result was a disaster. Though informed of the event, no record company representatives showed up, perhaps not surprising considering the distance from the capital. Very few people attended too. Photographs taken at the event show an audience of about a dozen people dancing in front of the bored Beatles. Pete Best labelled the night *"a fiasco."* There would be no further speculative trips south.

The Beatles played the *Hambleton Hall*, Huyton on 10 December and travelled afterwards to the *Casbah* to once again meet Epstein. The meeting was not to formalise their relationship but for Epstein to advise changes to their act and appearance.

He recommended the Beatles play songs through to their natural conclusion; the band would on occasion, abandon a song partway through, something that occasionally annoyed some audiences. To further broaden their appeal, Epstein advised they play fixed one-hour sets, containing an extensive range of musical genres which, he believed, would appeal to a wider audience.

Moving on to their stage appearance, Epstein advised uniformity and wanting the Beatles to be rid of their *"dishevelled"* appearance. The band usually wore their own clothes on stage and in consequence, as Billy J Kramer wrote, they often appeared *"unkempt."* Epstein wanted their fans and the music-going public in general to see the change. His recommendations kept coming, including desisting from swearing, smoking, drinking, or eating on stage.

Next on Epstein's agenda was a record contract, informing the grateful Beatles that he was in the process of pursuing one. Epstein was familiar with Tony Barrow, an employee of *Decca Records*. Barrow, a Liverpudlian, was none other than Disker, the music critic of the *Liverpool Echo*. Epstein asked Barrow if he could mention the Beatles to *Decca's* A&R department. Barrow did so and Decca's Mike Smith in turn contacted Epstein. Together they arranged for Smith to attend the *Cavern* on 13 December.

The Beatles played the usual lunchtime session at the club, before Smith's arrival for the evening show. Smith listened attentively, but he wasn't convinced of the band's potential. He was, though, prepared to give the Beatles a second chance and returned to London. Smith later contacted Epstein to inform him that he had scheduled an audition for his fledgling band at *Decca's* London studios on 1 January 1962.

A happy Epstein returned to work transforming the Beatles' image. To demonstrate the group was in visual transition as well as musical, the manager contacted photographer, Albert Marrion, to arrange a photo session for Sunday 17 December. Marrion, the photographer at the wedding of Epstein's brother, Clive, was based over the Mersey in Wallasey. At the shoot, the band teased and annoyed Marrion. The photographer, however managed to finish his assignment and went away to produce an extensive portfolio. The photographs, most of which have survived, show the group dressed in leather jackets, leather trousers, sweatshirts and winkle picker shoes. One of the photos taken that morning was to later adorn the front page of an edition of *Mersey Beat*.

With many of Epstein's recommendations taking shape, on a snowy New Year's Eve 1961, the Beatles, with their equipment in tow, climbed into their van to set off for London. Their driver, roadie Neil Aspinall, faced the difficult task of getting the band and himself safely to the capital in time for their 11.00 am audition. They were almost certain to arrive at the Decca studio cold and tired.

*

Following a long, cold overnight journey, would the Beatles be in decent condition to do themselves justice? Their future may well depend on it.

In the world of Merseyside football, could Everton and Liverpool end the 1961-62 season as respective winners of the First and Second Divisions? Time alone would soon tell.

6. I Feel Fine: January – July 1962

To prove the losing Christmas games were merely a blip and not the start of a prolonged dip in form, Liverpool needed to get back to winning ways as soon as possible. For Everton, continuation of the excellent December 1961 form would suffice. Next fixtures for both clubs were home third round FA Cup ties. First Division strugglers Chelsea, were the visitors to Anfield, while Everton's Goodison Park opponents hailed from the opposite end of the football hierarchy, Southern League minnows King's Lynn.

In the recent past, the FA Cup competition had been a regular source of disappointment for the Merseyside clubs. Everton had won the trophy on two occasions (1906 and 1933), while Liverpool had yet to achieve cup success. They had twice come close to winning the competition, losing the 1914 and 1950 cup finals. Could this be an FA Cup winning year for Merseyside?

Writing on the eve of the third round, Ian St John in the *Post* claimed that some Liverpudlians had suggested to him that Liverpool should not prioritise the cup as a run in the competition might distract from the priority of winning promotion. He was quick to debunk the idea, stressing that players loved the FA Cup and dreamt of the opportunity to play at Wembley. He went further saying he would love to see an all Merseyside final.

> *"Imagine that day with the supporters of both Liverpool and Everton descending on Wembley for a Cup Final,"*

At half time in their tie at a packed Anfield, Liverpool appeared to be cruising into the next round as they remarkably lead Chelsea 4-1. Liverpudlians who enjoyed a dominant first 45 minutes, were shaken by Chelsea's response as the London side reduced the deficit to a single goal with 15 minutes still to play. Despite a very nervous final quarter of an hour and a great deal of Chelsea pressure, Liverpool held on to their lead to record a 4-3 victory.

Although ties against non-league opposition can sometimes be tricky affairs, Everton had little difficulty in despatching a spirited Kings Lynn side 4-0 to move into the fourth round. St John's hope for an all Merseyside final was at least still alive.

A return to league football next and a return to the same old Everton on the road. Sheffield Wednesday inflicted a double whammy on the club's former manager, Harry Catterick, beating his current side 3-1, at Hillsborough. The seemingly regular pattern of results continued as Everton recorded a 3-2 home win over Leicester, a result that kept them in contention for the league title. Lying just three points behind leaders Burnley, it was stating the obvious to Evertonians that their team had to start winning matches away from home if they were to stand any chance of becoming First Division champions.

Liverpool's first post cup tie game was a 5-4 defeat over Norwich City at Anfield. It may have been a thrilling spectacle for neutrals, but it was a worrying one for Liverpudlians and the Shankly in terms of their team's defensive capabilities. Goalkeeper Bert Slater was culpable for at least two of the Norwich goals, the *Echo* claimed, and all were concerned about the quality of the team's last defender. A point was dropped at Scunthorpe United in a 1-1 draw a week later. The gap at the top of the table had worryingly narrowed to a single point over Leyton Orient.

Back to the FA Cup at the end of January and it was Everton's turn to face a struggling First Division side, Manchester City at Goodison. The Mancunians provided little threat and in relative comfort Everton went on to win the game 2-0. Alternatively, one of the lowest ranked teams remaining in the competition, Fourth Division Oldham Athletic were Liverpool's opponents at Anfield. Despite the gulf in league positions, the game was not a straightforward affair. Oldham *"fought gamely"* reported the *Echo,* but Liverpool showed *"just about showed enough quality"* to win the tie 2-1. An all Merseyside cup final?

February was to be a crucial month for both clubs. Against teams around them in the league table, a defining set of fixtures loomed for Everton. Liverpool, needing to re-open a gap at the top of the table, faced, on paper, a winnable set of games in the immediate future.

Liverpool played their fixtures as though defeat was out of the question. In the first, after an *"unconvincing"* goalless first half, the Reds scored three after the break to defeat Brighton 3-1. With Hunt in sparkling form in the club's next two games, Liverpool despatched Bury away 3-0 and Middlesbrough at Anfield 5-1. Hunt scoring a hat trick in each. Orient dropped points over the same period, so come the end of the of the month the gap at the top had indeed re-opened as Liverpool now led Orient by five points. The table made much better reading now.

Ipswich town, an improving team trailing Everton by a single point, were the Blues first opponents in February. Everton struggled from the off and were *"unable to cope with Ipswich's front line,"* said the *Echo*; before the hour they trailed 4-1. A last-minute goal was hardly consolation and another defeat outside Goodison was chalked up.

The season defining set of fixtures continued, up next, league leaders Burnley at Goodison. The Blues battled hard in a thrilling end to end match, but failed to overcome their Lancashire rivals and therefore cut the deficit at the top as the contest ended in 2-2 draw. An away trip to Nottingham Forest was the month's closing fixture and defeat could not be contemplated if a title challenge was to be maintained. Boringly predictable away from home, Everton lost again, on this occasion 2-1.

Now six points off Burnley, the *Daily Post* were confident enough to claim that all hopes of winning the title had finally evaporated. The paper was certain the blame should be apportioned to a particular element of the team set up:

> *"When all allowance has been made, it is the forward line which stands convicted of major responsibility for the Everton decline,"*

Maybe the FA Cup could offer season's salvation for the Blues? Possibly, but the draw could not have been tougher; away to Burnley, the team they shared the points with a week earlier. A spirited first half saw Everton take a goal lead into the break. The second half though was a familiar refrain as *"Everton were totally outplayed."* Burnley scored three second half goals to consign Everton to yet another away defeat and another relatively early cup exit.

In the cup, Liverpool were drawn to play fellow Second Division side, mid-table Preston North End at Anfield, but could not find a way past, what the *Echo* described as, *"a well organised defence.* The game ended 0-0. Liverpool travelled to Preston for the replay three days later; that match was, however, *"almost a carbon copy"* of the first and that too ended in a 0-0 stalemate.

Before the introduction of penalty shoot-outs in the FA Cup, teams were required to play again until a victor emerged. Old Trafford, Manchester, a suitable and convenient neutral venue for both clubs, was chosen for the second replay. Played in freezing temperatures during a snowstorm, after two more hours of goalless football, another replay looked on the cards. Close to the final whistle, the game took an unexpected twist. A young and promising Preston winger called Peter Thompson broke Liverpudlians' hearts as he dramatically snatched victory with a late extra time winner.

Let alone an all Merseyside cup final, the region would not have any representation in this year's final. All efforts, therefore, had now to be concentrated on the league.

With the return of league football on the first Saturday in March, two debutants, one for each team, made the it an historic day for Merseyside football. In Liverpool's game at Walsall and Everton's home match against Wolverhampton Wanderers, goalkeepers made their debuts for both teams, something which had not before happened in the long histories of the respective clubs.

Jim Furnell, an understudy at Burnley, was the busier of the two goalkeepers as Liverpool were held to a 1-1 draw in the Midlands. Gordon West meanwhile, an 18-year-old recruit from Blackpool for £27,500, a record fee for a goalkeeper at the time, had a quieter debut as Everton crushed their Midland opponents 4-0. Both players though received glowing tributes from the *Daily Post* for their debut performances.

> "*Furnell can look back on his debut with complete satisfaction. His most impressive work was the outcoming and timing of his dive at the feet of onrushing forwards.*"

> "*West showed confidence, certainty and promise. Most impressive was the speed, distance and accuracy of his throwing.*"

Furnell's signing was in its own way somewhat controversial. The deal was shrouded in secrecy and forced Shankly to issue a public apology to the displaced Bert Slater; the much-criticised goalkeeper learned of Furnell's arrival in his morning newspaper.

> "*I have had a talk to Bert and I have explained the situation to him. I apologised that it had not been possible to let him know about our new signing before he found out about it second hand.*"

Slater was never to play for the first team again. He returned to his native Scotland in July 1962 to play for Dundee, the club managed by Shankly's brother Bob.

Would the acquisition of two goalkeepers help Liverpool and Everton achieve their respective targets? The Second Division title was looking good for the Reds, but the Blues would have put together a remarkable run of results to win the First Division.

On Thursday 8 March, as Bobby Collins feared it would, his career came to an end at Everton. The *'Little General'* was transferred to Second Division Leeds United for a fee of £30,000. Harry Catterick spoke to the *Echo*:

> "*I felt more than reluctant to part with him as did the board, but because we believed it was in the player's interests and for his future, we decided not to stand in his way. The matter was left entirely to him.*"

Collins, in his autobiography, interpreted events differently. Following a poor run of results which concluded with the 2-1 loss at Nottingham Forest on 24 February, Collins revealed that Catterick and Chairman John Moores called a team meeting to *"clear the air."* He went on:

> *"The Chairman accused me of not giving my all. I was fuming. One thing I could not be criticised for was my work-rate."*

Collins believed the meeting to be the catalyst for his transfer. He felt the board was not at all reluctant to sell him and therefore he had no option but to leave the club. Catterick brought in Dennis Stevens from Bolton Wanderers to replace the Scotsman.

Everton followed up the 4-0 win in Gordon West's debut defeat over Wolves, with an identical score in the next fixture against Chelsea. This was the final victory in March. A 3-1 defeat to fellow title challengers Spurs, in which Roy Vernon missed his only ever penalty for the club, was sandwiched between two draws, the first away to Sheffield United and then at home to Blackpool. If February had not fully ended hopes of winning the First Division, then March almost certainly had. With 16 points left to play for, the team trailed Burnley by seven points and surprise package of the season, rapidly improving second placed Ipswich Town, by six.

Despite recent activity in the transfer market, Catterick remained under pressure for his failure to bring in a goal scoring forward. Cognisant of the criticisms, and reminiscent of many current football managers, he addressed the issue in his *Post* column on 20 March.

> *"No club would just buy for buying's sake. In the history of the game many buys have been panic buys, which invariably don't turn out well. I have tried to bring in top class players to Goodison Park, but I was unable to get their clubs to part, not even for inflated prices."*

Catterick did not reveal who were the top-class players he tried to buy.

Maybe the pressure of expectation got to Everton. In the last eight games of the season, from 4 April to 1 May, with the pressure off, the team embarked upon the season's best run of results. Everton drew four of their last five away games at Bolton, Blackburn, Manchester United and Birmingham prior to defeating Arsenal 3-2 at Highbury in the season's finale. The three remaining home games were all convincing victories starting with a 3-0 defeat of West Ham, followed by a 4-1 win over Birmingham before concluding with their finest result of the campaign against Cardiff City. Evertonians were at least sent home happy that day, witnessing an 8-3 demolition of the Welsh side. Roy Vernon scored a hat-trick and recent signing Dennis Stevens netted his fourth goal in twelve appearances for the club.

The supporters politely applauded the team at the end of the match, though there was a feeling of *"what could have been."* For all their efforts and proximity to the top of the table, most Evertonians regarded finishing the league in fourth place, five points off surprise champions Ipswich Town, as a disappointment. The disappointment may though have not been as profound as it was over at Burnley; the Lancashire club finished league and cup runners-up having lost the FA Cup Final 3-1 to Spurs.

On 10 March Liverpool continued winning ways with a 4-1 victory over Derby County; the *Post* wrote of Roger Hunt, the scorer of two goals:

> *"What a wonderful player he is. He stands out like a beacon light as one of the brightest prospects in the game."*

Following the defeat of Derby, Liverpool placed three players on the transfer list, including Johnny Morrissey, who had made 23 appearances in the 1960-61 season, but failed to be selected for the first team duties during the current season. The *Post* commented:

> *"Everton might do a lot worse than take a chance on John Morrissey, who has proved his ability to play on either wing,"*

A few days later Shankly reported that the club had received *"no offers for any of the players."*

If Liverpool could avoid defeat in their next game, away to rivals Leyton Orient, it would take the most pessimistic supporter to believe the title could not be won. A satisfactory 2-2 draw was the outcome, following an 83rd minute Alan A'Court equaliser. Ian St John believed that as the team held both a five-point lead at the top of the table and two games in hand over Orient, Liverpool *"need only ten points"* from their remaining ten games to ensure the Second Division title.

Four of those points were quickly collected in the next two games which both ended in identical home wins. After failing to score in over 300 minutes of cup football against Preston, Liverpool defeated their Lancashire opponents 4-1, with Hunt again grabbing a brace. A scuffle between St John and Preston defender Tony Singleton resulted in both players being dismissed, which opened the possibility of a suspension for the Scotsman. In determined mood, St John went on to score a hat trick four days later in the next fixture at home to Rotherham.

The team suffered an unexpected 1-0 defeat at mid-table Luton Town on the last day of March, but still maintained a comfortable six-point lead over Orient. *"Some people have inferred"* said St John in his *Post* column on 3 April, *"that players were thinking of international duty and did not put in the required effort against Luton. Nothing could be more untrue."* He went on to add that players *"…always tried, no matter the circumstances."*

Ahead of the home game against Huddersfield on 7 April, Roger Hunt was presented with a gold watch by the club for his double achievement of breaking the club's season goal scoring record and winning his first international cap. He scored in a 3-1 friendly win against Austria three days earlier. The game itself, in which the *Echo* said Huddersfield *"dominated,"* ended 1-1; without surprise, it was Hunt who salvaged a point with a late equaliser.

That point against Huddersfield, and results of their nearest rivals, meant Liverpool need only to draw their next game against Southampton at Anfield on 21 April to win promotion, while victory would yield the league title. Prior to the game, St

John, received the news he didn't want to hear. For his dismissal against Preston he earned a two-week suspension, meaning he would have to sit out the Southampton game.

The attendance of 40,000 was fewer than the club expected for the potential history defining Southampton match, though torrential probably played more than a part in this. Shankly chose Kevin Lewis as St John's replacement and the player did not disappoint as he gave Liverpool a 19th minute lead. Ten minutes later, Lewis netted again to hand Liverpool firm control of the contest. The game there on became a scrappy affair as the heavy rain continued to fall and churned up the playing surface. There were few chances and no further goals, but that mattered little to supporters who were more than happy to see their team eventually win the game 2-0 and with it the Second Division title and finally after eight long years, the promise of First Division football.

Reporting on scenes at the final whistle, the *Echo* commented:

> "*The skies wept, the atmosphere was grey and dismal, but it was still a glorious, unforgettable day for the 40,000 spectators at Anfield on Saturday as thousands of them swarmed on to the pitch.*"

The players headed down the tunnel as the Liverpudlians on the pitch chanted, "*We want the Reds.*" 20 minutes later they returned and all bar St John and Yeats opted to take up positions in the stands alongside Shankly and club directors. The two Scotsmen were hoisted onto shoulders and carried around the pitch, "*bobbing up and down like corks.*"

The triumphant, barely audible manager, addressed the jubilant crowd:

> "*We won the championship in the first month when we were fitter competitively than our rivals. We beat Sunderland and Newcastle twice in that spell and we never looked back. This is the proudest day of my life.*"

After the celebrations, Liverpool played out the last five games of the season, winning three and drawing one, before a final fixture defeat at Swansea. That result didn't matter. All that now mattered was a return to First Division football. The club could now look forward to joining neighbours Everton in the top tier. *'Friendly'* Merseyside derbies could now be consigned to history and replaced by the real thing.

How would the Reds fare against top-class Division One opponents? Were Everton in position to improve upon their fourth-place finish and challenge for the title? Answers to these questions would begin in August

* * * * *

On New Year's Day 1962, cold, tired and nervous the Beatles arrived on time for the 11.00am audition at *Decca*'s recording studios in West Hampstead, London. Brian Epstein, having travelled separately by train, was there to meet them. Decca A&R man Mike Smith annoyed the band and Epstein by arriving late. The Beatles, when told their own amplifiers were substandard, were further annoyed. They would now have to use the studio's own equipment. If they had known beforehand, they could have possibly travelled to the audition by train with Epstein.

The Beatles recorded a total of 15 songs including their own compositions *Like Dreamers Do, Hello Little Girl* and *Love Of The Loved,* as well as *Money (That's What I Want), Till There Was You, To Know Her Is To Love Her* and *The Sheik of Araby.* The entire session took about an hour to complete. A consequence of a long journey, nervous tension and a cold studio did not help the band to perform at their best, though they believed they did well enough to earn a contract. Brain Epstein believed likewise. They returned to Liverpool to await news.

In December 1961 *Mersey Beat* polled its readers asking who they considered Merseyside's top band. Forms were completed and returned to the newspaper's office. On 4 January, results were announced in the paper's new year edition.

The top five bands:

1. The Beatles
2. Gerry and the Pacemakers
3. The Remo Four
4. Rory Storm and the Hurricanes
5. Johnny Sandon and The Searchers

The Remo Four were formed in 1958 by Old Swan born vocalist and guitarist Colin Manley and co-guitarist Philip Rogers. They began as The Remo Quartet, but in 1959 changed their name to The Remo Four. They performed regularly at the *Cavern* and other venues often sharing the bill with the Beatles. Later in the year Johnny Sandon would leave The Searchers to join the Remo Four.

On 10 January Brian Epstein visited the BBC's Manchester headquarters to complete an "*Application for an Audition by Variety Department*". He hoped to obtain an audition in front of radio producers. The application was approved, and in March the band travelled to Manchester play before Peter Pilbeam, a producer for a radio show *Teenager's Turn – Here We Go.*' The recording, the first ever for the group, was aired on the BBC Light Programme (rebranded Radio 2 in 1967) the following day.

Towards the end of the month the Beatles and Epstein finally formalised their relationship. At *NEMS*, with Alistair Taylor as witness, they exchanged contracts. The four Beatles signed the agreement, though Epstein did not. He said he did this with the band's best interests in mind. If they felt they wanted to move on without him, the lack of a formal signature would ease the process. While they wanted him, he would offer the band maximum effort, particularly in the pursuit of a record deal.

Over at the *Cavern*, Ray McFall continued his policy of introducing new bands. One such, a group formed in 1960, were called The Mavericks. Its members included Liverpool born Tony Crane and Billy Kinsley. To capture the mood in the city, *Cavern* DJ Bob Wooler recommended they change their name to The Mersey Beats. The band liked the idea but, under copyright law, had to ask permission of

Bill Harry owner of *Mersey Beat*. He consented. The band adopted the new name though slightly changing it to the singular Merseybeats.

In February, a Manchester band, The Dakotas were also *Cavern* debutants. Having earlier played the *Casbah*, they received a warm reception from the Mathew Street audience and McFall immediately booked them for future performances.

Sometime in March, Epstein was invited to London to discuss the results of the Beatles' audition at *Decca*. Over coffee with representative Dick Rowe, Epstein was bluntly informed of the company's decision. In *A Cellarful of Noise,* he relayed the conversation between the two:

> "Not to mince words Mr Epstein, we don't like your boys' sound. Groups of guitarists are on the way out. I said 'You must be out of your tiny little minds! These boys are going to explode. I am completely confident that one day they will be bigger than Elvis Presley.'"

Epstein stormed off, but not without obtaining a copy of the recordings. He retained confidence in the group and their music. He made it his duty to tour other major record companies, to persuade them of the folly of *Decca's* decision. He first went to *Pye* Records, but was rebuffed there too. Not fazed by the company's rejection, he planned to try elsewhere later.

He returned to Liverpool, and in the early hours of a cold winter morning, at a café in Duke Street in the city centre, he gave the Beatles the bad news; *"No record contract."* He did promise the band he would not be deterred. His persistence angered his father who, he said, *"wanted to know whether I was employed by four leather-jacketed teenagers or by him."*

Back in London, Epstein took the recordings into a *HMV* record store on Oxford Street. The manager suggested that he transfer the songs from reel-to-reel tape to disc, to enable them to be more easily played. Epstein liked the idea and immediately took the tapes to the studio upstairs to have the discs pressed. The studio engineer Jim Foy, impressed by what he heard, especially three original

Lennon-McCartney compositions, contacted Sid Coleman of music publishers *Ardmore & Beechwood*, a subsidiary of *EMI*. Coleman in turn arranged a meeting for early May between the Beatles' manager and George Martin, a record producer at *Parlophone*, another subsidiary of *EMI*.

With more than a couple of months to spare before the engagement, Hamburg was again calling. Thanks to Epstein, the Beatles no longer had to travel overland. Lennon, McCartney and Best flew to Germany on 11 April, without an unwell George Harrison, who followed the next day with Epstein. The trio were given devastating news upon arrival in Hamburg. Waiting to meet them at the airport was Astrid Kirchherr. Showing obvious signs of trauma, she informed them that Stuart Sutcliffe had tragically died two days earlier of a brain haemorrhage.

Kirchherr found Sutcliffe lying on the stairs of their flat, called an ambulance, but the 22-year-old died on the way to hospital. She told the three that her fiancé had been suffering painful headaches for weeks. Several top specialists had examined him, but he always received the same answer: *"We can find nothing wrong."* To overcome the chronic pain, Sutcliffe used ever-increasing amounts of morphine, until his untimely death.

All members of the group were clearly affected by their fellow Beatle and friend's premature passing, but John Lennon seemed to take it worse than the others. As art students, the two studied together; their friendship was the longest of all group members. Though Lennon was regarded as the *"toughest"* of the band, he could not help breaking down.

Sutcliffe's body was flown back to Liverpool for a funeral in his home city. Astrid Kirchherr later wrote to his mother apologising for her non-attendance, saying she was too ill to travel.

The band had to quickly get over the shock of their ex-bass guitarist's shocking, sudden death. At the *Star Club,* they shared the first night bill with legendary US performers Little Richard and Gene Vincent. Excepting Good Friday, it was the first of 48 consecutive nights until their final performance at the club on 31 May.

Audiences who saw the Beatles' performances less than a year earlier may have been surprised and possibly disappointed with the band's appearance. Epstein's influence was clear for all to see. Gone were the leather jackets, the shouting and swearing. In came a smarter dress sense, smarter haircuts and regulated stage-sets. The Beatles were now performing as a professional rock 'n' roll band.

In early May, Gerry and the Pacemakers and Rory Storm and the Hurricanes arrived in the city to share the *Star's* stage with the Beatles. The venue became a veritable brew of international rock 'n' rollers; recording star and wild rocker Jerry Lee Lewis was another to perform at the club that summer.

Brain Epstein didn't stay long in the Germany, he had more pressing business back home. The promised meeting with record producer George Martin went ahead on 9 May. Epstein played him the copied discs and Martin listened attentively. In *A Cellarful of Noise*, Epstein offered his take on events that afternoon. "*I like your discs and I would like to see your artistes,*" Epstein reported. Convinced he had correctly interpreted the producer, Epstein, via telegram, immediately relayed the news to the band in Hamburg.

Appearing on the BBC Radio 4 programme *Desert Island Discs* in 1996, George Martin, however, offered a different take on the meeting:

> "I wasn't too impressed with the discs Brian Epstein played me. There was something there but I couldn't find out whether it was worthwhile or not. What I said to Brian was, 'if you want me to judge them on what you're playing me, I'm sorry, I'll have to turn you down.' He was so disappointed. I felt really sorry for him. So I gave him a lifeline. I said, 'If you want to bring them down from Liverpool, I'll give them an hour in the studio.'"

The Beatles completed their Hamburg residency and returned to their home city. News of Martin's "*lifeline*" arrived shortly afterwards. The band were booked for a recording session at Abbey Road studios on 6 June.

Travelling in relative comfort and arriving in much better condition than they were at *Decca* on New Year's Day, the Beatles set up their instruments for a two-hour session. Much of their own equipment was again deemed unsuitable for recording and therefore dispensed with. Moreover, Martin himself was not present. Responsibility was in the hands of a junior producer, Ron Richards.

The band recorded *Besame Mucho* first, a song with which Richards was very familiar, but not overly impressed. They played their own composition *Love Me Do* next. Richards was more impressed with this original Lennon and McCartney number and sent for Martin. Something in the record captured the producer's attention. He later said. "*I picked up on Love Me Do mainly because of the harmonica sound. I loved raw harmonica.*" Martin remained in the studio and involved himself in the recording process, recommending some changes to the *Love Me Do's* arrangement. On completion, he asked the band to play a couple more of their own compositions. They performed *P.S. I Love You* and *Ask Me Why*.

Martin felt the band had great potential and the individuals a certain charisma. He was not, however, wholly satisfied with all aspects of their recordings, among them Pete Best's drumming. Martin believed the problems, could be resolved and, allowing the band time to deal with them, invited the Beatles to return to the studio in early September.

Returning to Merseyside the following day, the Beatles played another historic show at *Port Sunlight Golf Club*. The band performed for the first time in suits. Prior to the performance, Epstein had taken the four to a tailor in Birkenhead, where they were fitted out in made to measure suits. He paid £40 for each. The venue and its anticipated audience lay behind the change of wear. Expecting the clientele all to be golf club members, attired in lounge suits and evening dress, he had the band smartly dressed. However, many young Beatles fans, uninterested in formal wear, managed to obtain tickets and came along casually dressed. Pete Best later observed: "*It was a great night. Those in formal dress were up dancing before our own fans.*"

Towards the end of June, Epstein established *NEMS Enterprises* (not to be confused with the family's *NEMS* music store). His relationship with the Beatles had been formalised and he was looking to incorporate more beat bands into his fledgling company.

Fully aware of Epstein's work with the Beatles, many bands were desperate for Epstein to take them under his wing. Gerry Marsden, interviewed by the *Liverpool Echo* in December 1963, admitted that he constantly pestered Epstein to manage his group. The singer and guitarist always received the same reply, *"I am too busy with the Beatles."*

Circumstances had now changed. Epstein wrote:

> *"As 1962 progressed, Gerry and the Pacemakers joined me and I decided to form a limited company to cope with tax matters, to ease banking arrangements and generally put my growing band of artists on a proper footing."*

It was a busy July for Merseyside bands such as Gerry and the Pacemakers, recently returned from Hamburg. Many groups played twice a day, having to perform a lunchtime session in the *Cavern* before setting off to play in clubs in other parts of Liverpool or sometimes further afield in St Helens, Southport and North Wales for example.

Also in July, George Martin telephoned Brian Epstein to give him the news he longed to hear. *EMI,* via Parlophone, pleased with the original recordings, had agreed to offer the Beatles a one-year contract with the option of a further four years if the group's musical output proved successful.

All, however, was not well with the Beatles. The *Parlophone* recording session identified a problem with a band member. The other members believed they had a solution to the problem. How were they to deal with it? The three were in a quandary.

On the positive side, the Beatles were guaranteed a recording contract. Progress.

On the football pitch, Liverpool were Second Division champions. Progress.

Everton finished fourth in the First Division. Progress.

Merseyside football and music were on the rise.

7. Ticket to Ride: August – December 1962

In mid-August 1962, Liverpool manager Bill Shankly, knowing his team's supporters were clearly excited to finally be playing First Division football, struck a pre-season note of caution. Throughout the summer, he had written the occasional column for the *Liverpool Echo* and in his final piece on 11 August he wrote:

> "Only the rashest of men would forecast success in the world of football, but any lack of it would not be due to lack of fitness or endeavour by anyone connected with Liverpool Football Club and those thousands of well-wishers are supporting a team which will always give its best. In the seasons ahead we will do our utmost to provide good entertainment and good sport."

Leslie Edwards, chief football correspondent of the *Echo*, balanced positivity with negativity on 15 August, three days before the opening games. Asking himself and the readers the following question: *"Will Liverpool cut a dash in Division One?"* - he answered:

> "In my opinion Liverpool's drive and enthusiasm will prevent them from doing anything other than succeed, but I doubt whether their defence will be able to tie up opponents as it did in the lower division."

As for Everton, ahead of their first game, many optimistic supporters believed their club held more than a decent chance of winning the First Division title, but, with no new recruits, some were more pessimistic. One or two of the pessimists expressed their feelings in letters to the *Echo* and typical of those was Mr P. Harrison of Litherland who gloomily wrote on 15 August:

> *"So, Mr Catterick feels that all is going well? Yet again we are fed the annual promise of jam tomorrow. Alas, unless the urgently required signings are forthcoming I fear that the writing is already on the wall and that we shall make the initial pilgrimage to Burnley resigned to our fate.*

Another correspondent believed that recent Manchester United recruit, Denis Law was a missed opportunity, particularly with the club's poor away scoring record the previous season. Perplexed by Everton's seemingly lack of interest in the player, *"Law"*, the writer claimed, *"is the best forward in the world (including Pele)."*

Everton faced a tough opening set of fixtures starting with the above-mentioned game at Burnley, runners up in both competitions the previous season; dangerous opponents Manchester United and Sheffield Wednesday were scheduled to follow in quick succession. *"These are fixtures,"* said Leslie Edwards writing in the same column as above, *"that Everton should dread. They could ruin their chances of winning the championship within three weeks of the beginning of the season."* The outlook against Burnley, he concluded, was… *"dismal."*

Catterick however believed that unlike the previous season, Everton were fully prepared for the start of this. The team he selected for the game at Burnley read:

West, Meagan, Thomson, Gabriel, Labone, Harris, Bingham, Stevens, Young, Vernon, Veall

Handing a debut to teenage outside left Ray Veall, Everton got off to a poor start at Turf Moor and the fears of both *Echo* journalist Edwards and correspondent Harrison must have immediately heightened. The home side were a goal up within ten minutes.

The Blues, however, did not panic, instead they responded admirably and Vernon equalised before the break. A dominant second half performance led to two second half goals from Bingham and Young as the Blues secured a 3-1 victory. Reporting on the game, Edwards wrote:

> "This was most heartening football for a side which only collected three away victories last season. Everton have really found a way at long last to show their capabilities away from home."

Liverpool faced Blackpool at Anfield for their first game in Division One for eight years. The Shankly team read:

Furnell, Byrne, Moran, Milne, Yeats, Leishman, Lewis, Hunt, St John, Melia, A'Court

Playing for Blackpool was a 17-year-old debutant by the name of Alan Ball. Ball famously went on to win the World Cup with England in 1966, before signing for Everton a few weeks later. The game however did not go to plan. A packed Anfield holding 51,207 spectators, witnessed a shock 2-1 home defeat. The *Echo* reported that Liverpool dominated early proceedings, but *"failed lamentably"* in front of goal. Blackpool *"spied their opportunity after the break"* and midway through the second half scored two goals in quick succession. Many disappointed home supporters had long departed before Lewis reduced the deficit in the 84th minute. As for Alan Ball, his *"performance as a newcomer was exceptionally fine"*, the *Echo* wrote.

Liverpool's poor start continued as they picked up just a single point from two away fixtures. A 2-2 draw at Manchester City was followed by a 1-0 defeat at Blackburn Rovers. The *Echo* claimed that *"Liverpool were not up to First Division standard."* Shankly, it appeared, may well have been correct in restraining the hopes of Liverpool supporters.

In the wake of the Blackburn defeat, Ian St. John in his *Daily Post* column, claimed it was *"the forwards who were to blame"* and they were determined to put it right in the next match. They did so immediately back at Anfield with an excellent 4-1 win in the return with Manchester City. The win was quickly followed by another, a 2-0 home victory over Sheffield United four days later. St John scored one adding to his goal against City.

Everton meanwhile were firmly putting the pessimists in their place. The dreaded start to the season turned out to be nothing of the sort as Manchester United and

Sheffield Wednesday, considered to be serious contenders for the league title, were emphatically put to the sword at Goodison.

On Wednesday 22 August, in front of 70,000 spectators, Everton were three up at half time against a United side fielding Denis Law. The Blues eventually went on to win the game 3-1. Everton secured the double over their Manchester rivals the following week, winning 1-0 at Old Trafford. Sandwiched between these games the Blues trounced title hopefuls Sheffield Wednesday 4-1. Of total goals scored to date, Vernon was responsible for four and Young three.

Everton being Everton, the excellent start to the season was brought to a juddering halt with a 1-0 defeat at Fulham in the next game; the London *'hoodoo'* of last season had struck immediately this.

The day following the United match at Goodison, 23 August, Everton controversially signed a winger for a fee of £10,000. The player, Johnny Morrissey, was recruited from neighbours Liverpool in a deal that angered Bill Shankly. It also bewildered *Echo* reporter Horace Yates.

> *"For the life of me I cannot understand why Liverpool decided to let him go. It could be that they live to regret it before the season is out. If he was a Scotsman and named McMorrissey he would have commanded more than twice the fee."*

Morrissey informed the press that he had no idea he was being sold. He was simply told on the morning of the 23rd to report to Everton's training ground at Bellfield the same afternoon to meet Harry Catterick. The Everton manager clearly had a great deal of confidence in his new signing, putting him straight into the team which defeated Wednesday 4-1.

It took a few weeks to emerge, but it transpired that all was not well at Anfield with the decision to sell Morrissey. It took until mid-September for the story to break and supporters learned that Shankly was extremely unhappy with the Board's action. The *Daily Post* reported on the 15th:

> *"News of a first-class row in the Boardroom of Liverpool Football Club soon after the season started, over the sale of John Morrissey to Everton."*

While Liverpool were in Manchester preparing for their game against City, the Board accepted Everton's bid for the winger. Shankly didn't know of the sale until the following day when the deal was already concluded. Shankly apparently had angrily expressed his absolute disapproval of the Board's action and a rumour circulated that he had threatened to resign in protest.

The situation had resolved itself by the time the dispute made news. The resolution did not prevent the *Daily Post* from trying to get to the bottom of the story, but the manager and the directors, having obviously declared a vow of silence, refused to comment. There was talk of Shankly being linked with the vacant manager's post at Cardiff City, something the *Post* put to him. Shankly admitted that *"Cardiff were interested"* in him, but *"in any event I have a job at Anfield,"* he added abruptly. Shankly was at Liverpool to stay.

Even with the passage of time, questions remain over Shankly's protest. Was he upset that the Board sold his player to Liverpool's closest rival, Everton? After all, Morrissey was a player Shankly seemed prepared to sell just a few months earlier in March 1962. He didn't leave the club then because Liverpool *"received no offers"* for him. Moreover, Morrissey's last first team appearance was at Stoke City way back in May 1961 in a *"nothing to play for"* final game of the 1960-61 season. So, was Morrissey in Shankly's plans? He'd spent all playing time since the Stoke game in the reserves. Or was Shankly, as most historians of Liverpool FC tend to agree, using the sale of Morrissey to gain overall control of transfer policy?

Liverpool continued to struggle away from home losing 1-0 at West Ham and 3-1 to Nottingham Forest. Having managed to pick up just one point on their travels the Reds next away fixture appeared daunting, a trip to Goodison Park. At home Liverpool's form was distinctly better. Two games at Anfield yielded three points with a win over West Ham and a draw against champions Ipswich.

Prior to the Merseyside derby match, Everton were victorious in three of their four games, beginning with home victories over Leyton Orient and Leicester City, 3-0 and 3-2 respectively. A 2-0 win at Bolton Wanderers meant that the Blues had now won three games outside Goodison, equalling the number of away victories achieved the previous season. Naturally for Evertonians, the other of the four matches in the spell was a 3-0 loss to Leyton Orient; and the match was played in which city? ...London.

Scheduled for 22 September, Merseyside was abuzz with excitement and anticipation ahead of the first league derby match in over eleven years. After nine games, the league table showed Everton lying in second place on 14 points, one behind leaders Wolverhampton Wanderers. Liverpool were in 12th place, six points behind their neighbours. Everton were going into the contest as clear favourites. The game was an all-ticket affair for supporters of both teams. Ten days prior to kick off, thousands queued in pouring rain at Goodison and Anfield so as not to miss the chance of watching the long-awaited league clash.

Newspaper columnists and players could not resist joining in the pre-match banter. Roy Vernon found time to offer a bold prediction in his weekly *Daily Post* column: *"I don't mind letting you into a secret,"* he wrote. *"I expect to see Liverpool perish against our defenders. I don't believe there is a better defence than Everton's to be found in any club team."* Ron Yeats, meanwhile, spent the run up to the match ringing up Everton forward Alex Young, a former army colleague, to inform him that he *"would not be getting a kick"* come Saturday. *"Living with him every day for two years, I'd seen all his moves. I know what to expect,"* said Yeats.

There was bad news for Liverpudlians on the morning of the game; Ian St John failed a fitness test and his place was taken by Kevin Lewis. Johnny Morrissey, having made the switch from Anfield to Goodison, would though be in a full-strength Everton side. The teams entered the pitch in pairs, the traditional format for a derby match, to Everton's newly adopted signature tune, *Z Cars*, the theme music of a recent BBC television police drama series.

The game got underway in dramatic fashion; inside the first minute Everton had the ball in the net, but the referee, having judged that scorer Vernon knocked the ball loose from Liverpool keeper Furnell's grasp, disallowed the goal. More disappointment for Evertonians quickly followed as another goal was disallowed; scorer Stevens was judged to be in an offside position.

The controversy did not end there as Everton were awarded a 22nd minute penalty; Liverpool full back Gerry Byrne was adjudged to have handled a goal bound Everton shot. Roy Vernon emphatically dispatched the spot-kick. St John's deputy, Kevin Lewis repaid Shankly's faith in him with an equaliser six minutes later, ensuring the sides went in at half time level. Morrissey's transfer across Stanley Park had caused quite a stir and Shankly's irritation at the deal must have heightened as his former player restored Everton's lead shortly after the hour mark. Liverpool were not done for; in the dying seconds, an Alan A'Court cross was won in the air by Lewis, who headed down for Roger Hunt to grab a second equaliser.

The goal prevented Everton from going top of the table. At the final whistle, the players left the pitch to sustained applause. It had been, according to the *Echo's* Leslie Edwards: *"Hard, exciting, noisy, tense – but no classic"*. Liverpool had *"played above themselves. If they hadn't, they could not have snatched a point."* He found time to praise a player from each side, declaring that Brian Harris of Everton and Jimmy Melia of Liverpool *"had both played like future England internationals."*

Young and Yeats gave their verdicts on the game in their *Echo* columns the following Saturday, paying particular attention to Vernon's early disallowed goal. Predictably, the two viewed it differently. Young said he was standing five yards from the incident and *"Furnell simply dropped the ball,"* he wrote. Yeats was a similar distance away, but claimed that *"Vernon hit Furnell's arm forcing him to drop the ball."* In conclusion, Young said Liverpool were lucky to get a late equaliser, while Yeats argued that *"there's nothing lucky about playing until the final whistle."*

Liverpool were now amid a tough set of away fixtures as up next were league leaders, Wolves. By all accounts Liverpool were much the better team, belying their relatively low league position; nevertheless, they came away from Molineux pointless, losing the game 3-2 to a late Wolves goal. The *Post,* maybe a little over dramatically, called the result *"tragic."*

After beating struggling Bolton 1-0 at Anfield, thanks to a first half Roger Hunt goal, another tough away fixture beckoned at fourth placed Leicester City, but the performance was far from that of the one at Wolves. Leicester dominated from the outset scoring two quick goals before half time and adding another in the second half to win the match by a comfortable 3-0.

The Reds remained in the Midlands for yet another stern test this time at West Brom. Before the game, Shankly was concerned with the form of his goalkeeper Jim Furnell, who, owing to a couple of errors, had been the subject of criticism in the local press. The manager chose to drop Furnell and handed a first team debut to 22-year-old Tommy Lawrence, a player who had joined the club five years earlier. Scottish teenager Gordon Wallace was also handed a debut. Both debutants watched on as Jimmy Melia missed a 19th minute penalty. Soon after, Lawrence conceded the only goal of the game to last season's First Division leading goal scorer and England international, Derek Kevan.

Liverpool had been beaten by some of the best teams in the league so far, but lying 18th in the league and just a point off the relegation places, was a cause of great concern to Shankly. Once again, he turned to the transfer market to help improve the situation. Willie Stevenson, a Scottish League and Cup winner with Glasgow Rangers, had just celebrated his 23rd birthday and was on the verge of emigrating to Australia, after finding himself languishing in the Ibrox reserve side. Shankly got wind of his plan and moved swiftly to persuade his fellow Scot to sign for the Reds. He did so for a fee of £20,000.

Stevenson's debut was on 3 November at Anfield against yet another high-flying side, third placed Burnley. Like Tommy Lawrence, it was an unhappy first outing for the debutant. In front of almost 44,000, Burnley took a first half lead and despite a St John equaliser, the north Lancashire side went on the win match 2-1 with a late goal. Disappointed Liverpool fans left the ground to discover that having played 15 matches, equating to more than a more than a third of the season, their team were now in a dangerous 20th place in the league. Supporters desperately needed their side to pick up points through November.

The Reds travelled to Old Trafford to face a struggling Manchester United in a game, which provided an extraordinary finish. Liverpool were 2-1 down with five minutes remaining, but two minutes later they were 3-2 up thanks to goals from Melia and Moran. Johnny Giles, United's Irish wing half, however unbelievably equalised with the last kick of the match.

Liverpool desperately needed to string some positive results together and two decent fixtures at Anfield against London sides, mid-table Arsenal and bottom placed Leyton Orient, offered an opportunity. A dull first 45 minutes against Arsenal was quickly forgotten seven minutes into the second half with first a goal from Hunt. Replacement penalty taker, Ronnie Moran gave the Reds a 2-0 lead. Despite Arsenal pulling a goal back, Liverpool held on for victory. In what Ron Yeats described as *"the worst conditions I have ever played in,"* through freezing, driving rain and sleet, Liverpool recorded their best win of the season, 5-0 over Leyton Orient. Hunt netted his first hat-trick of the season; Willie Stevenson scored his first Liverpool goal and St. John concluded proceedings with a half hour still to play.

A Roger Hunt double at Birmingham City on 24 November chalked up the third victory in a row. With the December fixtures approaching, Liverpool supporters saw their team move up the table and were now in a much happier place.

League games for Everton could not have gone much better following the derby. Two of the teams which inflicted defeat on Liverpool were comfortably dispatched. Against West Brom, Johnny Morrissey, the *Echo* reported, turned in a *"brilliant performance"* scoring a hat trick in a 4-2 win; Alex Young scored the other.

Next up on 6 October was a top of the table clash with Wolves at Molineux and Everton must have been encouraged by the reports of Liverpool's game at the same venue a week earlier. In a match Everton dominated, *"the only surprise was the period of time in which it took them to score the first goal,"* read the *Echo*.

Everton had to wait until the hour mark for Bingham to head them into the lead. *"From a superb Vernon run and defence splitting pass,"* Young rounded the Wolves keeper to make the final score 2-0. Displacing their opponents, the result moved Everton to the top of the table on goal average.

In front of more than 53,000 at Goodison a disappointing 1-1 draw with Aston Villa followed. The Blues were staring defeat in the face until a 77th minute Vernon penalty rescued a point. Against Ipswich Town a week later at Goodison, Everton produced a much better performance winning 3-1, with Morrissey bagging another double and Vernon, somewhat incredibly, scoring his seventh penalty of the season.

The Ipswich game was sandwiched between Everton's first two matches in European competition. In the Inter City Fairs Cup, Everton were drawn to play Scottish First Division team Dunfermline Athletic in the two-legged tie. The Blues were victorious 1-0 at Goodison, but lost the second leg in Scotland 2-0. Many Everton supporters were obviously disappointed, but the *Echo's* Leslie Edwards was not. *"If this Inter City Fairs Cup is the future then they can keep it,"* he wrote. Everton were kicked from the start and though they gave as good as they got *"they are better off without it and should concentrate their thoughts on winning the league,"* Edwards concluded.

Everton may well have suffered a hangover from their Euro exploits as four days later they struggled to a 1-1 draw at Maine Road against lowly placed Manchester City. Despite his replacement Frank Wignall scoring the Blues' goal, Everton *"missed the skills and artistry of the injured Roy Vernon*, the *Daily Post* reported. Everton, consequently, slipped to second place. Post-match the *Echo* actually believed that Vernon was not injured but had been dropped for his on-field attitude towards officials. Catterick, the paper said, had taken umbrage during the Ipswich game to the player's approach to a linesman, where Vernon, not liking a decision, pointed to his own eyes with two fingers and then gestured similarly to the linesman. Was Catterick using his famed authoritarianism to reprimand Vernon?

Vernon, either recovered from his injury or suitably reprimanded, returned to the first team in Everton's next game on 10 November at home to Blackpool. The player, though not scoring, responded very well creating a couple of goals as Everton produced their best result of the season to date, winning 5-0.

15 minutes into their next game two days later at Nottingham Forest, Everton were two goals down. The opening lines of Michael Charters' report in the *Echo* the following day read: *"This must be one of the finest displays by Everton for seasons, as Vernon and Young took control of the game."* Vernon with two and a Ray Veall goal put Everton 3-2 up before the break. Forest equalised early in the second half, but Jimmy Gabriel had the final say, scoring the winner midway through the second half. The win returned Everton to the top of the table. Their place there did not last long as, with seven minutes remaining, they threw away a 2-1 lead at Blackburn to lose the game 3-2. Everton bounced back in the final game of November beating Sheffield United 3-0.

A defining period awaited in December for both Everton and Liverpool. League leaders Everton faced games against their nearest title challengers Spurs and Burnley; while happier Liverpool supporters were hoping their tenth placed team could maintain the momentum of their recent excellent run of results.

Liverpool did just that in their first December fixture winning 2-1 at home to Fulham thanks to goals from Hunt and A'Court. It was back on the road again to make it five on the spin with a 2-0 victory at Sheffield Wednesday. With just one goal conceded in four games, the *Echo* praised centre half Ron Yeats saying he *"brilliantly held the defence together."*

In Blackpool first and then against Blackburn Rovers, Lancashire provided the opposition for the two fixtures prior to Christmas. The fantastic run was almost ended as Liverpool trailed Blackpool, but a St John equaliser and the bang-in form, Hunt, ensured a 2-1 win at Bloomfield Road. On 22 December, goals from Lewis, St John and Moran gave Liverpool a 3-1 victory over Blackburn.

The *Echo* was full of praise for the huge turnaround in form by Liverpool over recent months. *"With the defence playing well and the forwards scoring more regularly, Liverpool are well placed for a top four finish,"* the paper confidently predicted as the team, though a little way from the top on points, stood in fifth place in the First Division table.

Outside of the derby match, on the first Saturday in December, Everton played their most important game of the season to date against Spurs at White Hart Lane. A crowd of over 60,000 watched two very cautious sides play out the great majority of the game giving little away. There was nothing to separate the teams as the game entered its closing stages. Suddenly a glaring chance arrived at the far post for Alex Young. An Everton shot hit the Spurs post and rebounded to him less than six yards out. Lashing out, he blazed his effort over the bar. Young's miss meant the game ended goalless.

Alex Young's *"sitter"* became the talking point of the match. The Saturday evening *Echo* called it the "miss of the *season,"* By Monday the paper had upgraded it to *"the miss of the century."* In his column the following week, Young explained that he couldn't understand how he missed. The ball, having rebounded from a post, *"came back to me fast. I hit it well. I just don't know how it went over the bar."*

The first of two home games was another disappointing draw, 1-1 with West Ham United. Next up were third placed Burnley. Everton made a *"brilliant start"*; midway through the first half, they had the game virtually won with three goals in seven minutes. Despite a second half Burnley consolation, strikes from Vernon, Stevens and Young ensured a 3-1 victory. In the final pre-Christmas match Everton twice came from behind, to draw 2-2 at Sheffield Wednesday. A mixed bag of results for Everton, therefore in December. Although they were undefeated in four, they had only managed to win one of the games. Regardless, Evertonians were guaranteed a happy Christmas Day as their team stood at the top of the league, with the Boxing Day fixtures to come.

The weather, however, intervened over the holiday and that was it for the Merseyside clubs, and indeed the whole of the football league programme, in 1962. Heavy snow and ice hit all parts of the UK over Christmas.

The lack of football did not, however, stop the clubs from making front page news on Merseyside. On the 27th Everton announced the arrival of a player from Catterick's former club, Sheffield Wednesday; wing half Tony Kay had signed for a huge fee, £60,000. The player arrived at Goodison to tell the press:

> "I joined Everton because they are one of the leading clubs in the land, because they have fine support, a wonderful ground and above all ambition. I know Harry's forthright and he left me in no doubt that I have made the right decision."

Two days later, Everton Chairman, John Moores explained to the *Echo* the reason for the expensive signing.

> "We want 15 or 16 players of high quality challenging for first team places. We are prepared to pay players win bonuses even if they are not selected for the first team. We are near to having the great team we want."

Could Everton's *"great team"* maintain their position at the top of the table in the New Year? Could Liverpool's resurgence continue to challenge their neighbours position? Answers to those questions would have to be put on hold as the extremely poor weather persisted into the New Year. Conditions across all parts of the UK were so bad for so long that the winter of 1962-63 entered metrological history earning the label *'The Big Freeze'*.

Consequently, Everton, Liverpool and most other English football clubs would not play another league match until February 1963. Several matches in the FA Cup competition were though played during the period and with the fine form of Everton and Liverpool, supporters of both clubs were optimistic about their clubs' chances of winning the trophy.

*****

An incredibly transformative month lay ahead for Merseyside's most popular group, the Beatles. They began August 1962 with a regular couple of sessions at the *Cavern* before performing for the first time at the *Grafton Rooms*, a large, famous dance hall on the outskirts of Liverpool city centre. The Beatles topped a bill which also featured Gerry and the Pacemakers and The Big Three.

In mid-August, the band returned to the *Cavern* for an evening session. Pete Best in his autobiography recalled a short conversation he had with a bandmate after the performance. In *The Best Years of the Beatles* he wrote:

> "On the night of Wednesday 15 August, we played at the Cavern and, in the normal way, talked later about the arrangements for the following night, when we were due to appear at the Riverpark Ballroom in Chester. As Lennon was leaving, I called: 'Pick you up tomorrow, John.' 'No,' he said, 'I've got other arrangements.'"

Brian Epstein came to speak to Best after his short conversation with Lennon. Epstein asked if the two could meet at *NEMS* the following day. Slightly puzzled, Best agreed and the next morning arrived on time for the scheduled 10.30 meeting. The drummer picks up the story:

> "Epstein said 'Pete I have some bad news for you. The boys want you out and its already been arranged that Ringo Starr will join the band on Saturday.' I asked the obvious question, 'Why?' Eppy replied: 'George Martin feels you are not a good enough drummer.'"

A distraught Best left the meeting and immediately spoke to his mother Mona. Clearly incensed at developments, she took it upon herself to call George Martin for an explanation. According to Pete Best, Martin informed his mother that he never used the words attributed to him. He explained that he wasn't happy with what he heard on the recording and would prefer to use an experienced, professional drummer at the next session. Martin then told Mona Best that it was never his intention to have her son sacked. *"Why would it be?"* He stressed that it was important, *"not to break up the physical content of the band because it was so integral,"* and had said as much to Epstein.

Pete Best believed that everything was too *"neatly packaged"* and a *"conspiracy had been going on"* behind his back, but none of the Beatles were courageous enough to tell him. It had been left to Epstein to *"do the dirty work."* It later transpired that in a pre-arranged agreement Lennon was to phone Ringo Starr at *Butlin's Holiday Camp* in Phwhelli North Wales the day before Best's dismissal. The phone call took place and Starr was asked if he wanted to replace the Beatles' drummer.

Starr had enough time prior to consider the offer and didn't hesitate to accept. He gave Rory Storm three days' notice to quit the Hurricanes. Not ultimately because of Starr's departure, the Hurricanes were not the same band thereafter. They continued to perform, but the recording successes of Mersey Beat would bypass the once highly popular Mersey Beat band.

Brian Epstein said the idea for Best's dismissal came from his three band mates. In *A Cellarful of Noise* he stated that John, Paul and George came to see him and said: *"We want Pete out and Ringo in."* Epstein listed more than one reason for the decision including, of course, Martin's critique of his drumming ability. He also claimed that though Best was a good friend of John, he did not get on so well with Paul or George; Epstein further added that the three thought Best: *"too conventional to be a Beatle."*

In no time at all, Epstein was made aware of the unpopularity of Best's sacking among fans and other Merseyside musicians. He wrote of being unable to go to the *Cavern* for a few days because of *"placard waving fans chanting 'We want Pete.'"* When he was able to attend the club, he had to do so under a bouncer escort.

The sacking of Best caused a great consternation among Mersey Beat musicians. Gerry Marsden in his autobiography *I'll Never Walk Alone*, wrote:

> *"I really thought it was a tacky sort of thing to do for no apparent reason. I was very annoyed that when I asked Brian Epstein for a reason he couldn't give me a proper answer. It thought it was a sour way to start a recording career, firing a drummer who'd been with them for two years."*

The last word on the incident goes to a chastened John Lennon who told Hunter Davies in *The Beatles: The Authorised Biography*:

> *"We were cowards when we sacked him. But if we told Pete to his face, that probably would have been much nastier than getting Brian to do it. It probably would have ended up in a fight if we'd told him."*

The day following Best's dismissal, the Beatles played their next show at the *Riverpark Ballroom* in Chester. At his meeting with Epstein, Best had been asked to commit himself to playing that evening. He initially said he would, but, unsurprisingly, changed his mind. The group drafted in The Big Three's drummer, Johnny Hutchinson, as a temporary replacement for this show and the following evening's two performances at the *Majestic Ballroom*, Birkenhead and the *Tower Ballroom*, New Brighton.

On Saturday 18 August 1962, the Beatles new permanent drummer united for the first time with his band. Popular music history was made at *Hulme Hall*, Birkenhead when Ringo Starr made his live debut as a Beatle. His preferment as drummer finally established the group which was soon to achieve worldwide fame and success.

Relating the date and episode to Merseyside football, 18 August 1962 was also the day in which Liverpool FC played First Division football for the first time in eight years. Playing Blackpool, an opposition player, one who was to achieve almost legendary status on Merseyside, also made a debut. The player, 17-year-old Alan Ball, would four years later become an England World Cup winner and soon after join Everton to become one of the club's most influential ever acquisitions.

On Wednesday 22 August, the evening that an aggregate of more than 100,000 fans watched two football matches contested between teams from Merseyside and Manchester, a television crew arrived at *The Cavern*. The crew, like many football supporters, travelled from Manchester. Employees of *Granada Television*, they were at the club to film a Beatles' live performance. After receiving dozens of letters from Beatles' fans, *Granada* TV producers investigated the group's growing popularity. They had witnessed a performance at *Cambridge Hall*, Southport on 26 July. Reasonably impressed, on 1 August a producer visited the *Cavern* to check the suitability of the venue before deciding to film on 22nd.

With everything appropriately arranged beforehand, the Beatles performed *Some Other Guy* for Granada's *Know the North* TV programme. During the filming, which took place less than a week after Pete Best's sacking, fans could be heard shouting "*We want Pete!*" at the end of the song. The quality of the recording was, however, deemed unsuitable for broadcast and temporarily shelved. The film was eventually broadcast by Granada on 3 November, with the band's popularity growing.

Looking to expand his stable, next on Brian Epstein's list of potential stars was Billy Kramer who was performing with his backing band the Coasters in Widnes. Epstein had heard that Kramer was considering quitting the music business to take up a full-time post with British Rail in Rugby, Northamptonshire, hence the thirteen-mile trip to the Cheshire town to listen to the young Bootle man. Epstein learned that Kramer had visited Rugby to discuss his potential new job and believed the post offered a good opportunity. His parents were too keen for him to take on the new challenge.

Liking what he heard and saw of Kramer's performance, Epstein immediately contacted the singer's manager Ted Knibbs to discuss a change of management. Knibbs was fully prepared to meet Epstein's offer and contacted Kramer to suggest a meeting in Liverpool the following day. The perplexed teenager arrived as arranged. Writing in his autobiography, Kramer takes up the story:

> "I had no idea what Ted had in mind, but before I knew it, he took me to NEMS and introduced me to Brian Epstein who said he wanted to manage me. I was so knocked out...Shortly afterwards I was called into another meeting with Brian at his office and John Lennon was there. Brian said to me: 'John's come up with an idea. He thinks your name would sound much better if we added the initial 'J' to it. How does Billy J. Kramer sound?'"

Kramer became Billy J. Epstein paid Knibbs £25 for Kramer's contract.

On 4 September, with their new drummer in situ, the Beatles returned to Abbey Road for a second attempt at recording their debut single, *Love Me Do*. The band rehearsed in mid-afternoon, playing a total of six songs, including *Please Please Me*, which George Martin thoroughly disliked. He believed the song too slow and dreary. He told them to go away, rearrange it and bring the revised version along to the next session.

Rather than *Love Me Do*, much to the band's displeasure, Martin had actually chosen a Mitch Murray number, *How Do You Do It* for the group's debut single. Paul McCartney later revealed that although they recorded the song, they didn't consider it a number which suited the Beatles and told Martin so. Though unhappy, Martin nevertheless respected their wishes and abandoned the idea.

The band continued to work on *Love Me Do*, laying down the backing track and overdubbing the vocals. McCartney was unexpectedly given a vocal lead in the chorus, when Martin told the group that Lennon couldn't play harmonica and sing the chorus at the same time. McCartney admitted later that he was terrified at the responsibility. In *Anthology*, he said:

> *"I was suddenly given this massive moment, where everything stopped and the spotlight was on me. When we went back up to Liverpool I remember talking to Johnny Gustafson of the Big Three and he said 'You should have let John sing that line.' John did sing it better than me, he had a lower voice and was a little more bluesy."*

The band recorded the B-side, *PS I Love You*. The session was due to finish at 10.00 pm, but overran until 11.15.

Martin was however, again unhappy with the quality of drumming on *Love Me Do*, and asked the band to return to have another try on 11 September. He again planned to bring in an experienced session drummer, Andy White, to replace Starr.

Martin's removal of Starr begs an obvious question; was Pete Best unfairly sacked? If he was dismissed for his relatively poor drumming skills at the recording session, his replacement fared no better. Fans and many observers at the time therefore believed Best lost his position for non-music reasons. Added to Epstein's list comes John Lennon's alleged jealousy of Best and his popularity with female Beatles' fans.

Returning on the 11th, the band recorded multiple takes of *Love Me Do* with Andy White on drums. They also attempted a revised version of *Please Please Me*, which Martin considered an improvement on the first and a possible future single. The best takes were mixed and *EMI* began pressing *Love Me Do* and *PS I Love You*. The Beatles' debut single was scheduled for release in the UK on 5 October.

On 29 September, a week prior to the song's official release date, Disker, the *Liverpool Echo's*, music critic, gave the single a very favourable review. He wrote:

> "*Love Me Do* is an infectious medium paced ballad with a haunting harmonica accompaniment which smacks home the simple tune and gives the whole deck that extra slab of impact and atmosphere essential for the construction of a Top Twenty smasher. The Beatles come out with flying colours."

Disker was of course Tony Barrow, the *Decca* employee who helped arrange the Beatles audition for the company earlier in the year. He was now, however, also an employee of *NEMS Enterprises*. Epstein, fully aware of the importance of publicity, didn't hesitate to employ Barrow as press officer. Born in Crosby, north Merseyside in 1936, as a 17-year-old sixth form schoolboy, Barrow was employed as freelance record reviewer for the *Echo*. In 1960 he moved from Crosby to London to work for *Decca*.

Barrow, writing as Disker wrote some fantastic reviews for many Mersey Beat records. The *Love Me Do* feature was given special prominence too. Laid out in its own box, the article was accompanied by a photograph of the Beatles at the recording session. The following Saturday, and something unusual for the column, Disker again reviewed *Love Me Do* following the song's official release. He also advertised the Beatles forthcoming shows, including a performance at the *Tower Ballroom, New Brighton*.

Again, a simultaneous football related link. In mid-September, following a defeat at Leyton Orient, Everton were displaced at the top of the First Division by Wolverhampton Wanderers. On Saturday 6 October, the day after the release of *Love Me Do*, Everton defeated the league leaders 2-0 at Molineux to return to the top of the table.

Ringo Starr's presence in the band brought all parties together to sign re-written contracts. On 1 October, the four band members and Epstein signed anew. Starr signed using his real name, Richard Starkey, and the fathers of George Harrison and Paul McCartney also signed, as the pair were under 21 and required parental consent.

Epstein busied himself trying to generate as much radio and TV airplay for the band and their single. In early October, the Beatles made their first appearance on Radio Luxembourg, one of the earliest commercial radio stations broadcasting to the UK. The station was an important source of rock 'n' roll music for many teenagers in the early 1960s. The band made their TV debuts on 17 October with an appearance in Manchester on a Granada Television local programme, *People and Places*. The show was broadcast live at 6.35. The group performed two numbers, *Some Other Guy* and *Love Me Do*. Twelve days later they returned to Manchester to film a second performance.

In the meantime, in Hamburg, there was a voracious demand for Merseyside bands. Some, however, were more successful than others. Gerry and the Pacemakers were appreciated by German audiences. Kingsize Taylor and the Dominoes likewise. Beginning in July, The Searchers, now minus Johnny Sandon who quit the band to join The Remo Four, played an incredible 128 one-hour nightly performances at the *Star Club*. Bands such as The Big Three, never really enjoyed their German experience. One member, lead guitarist Adrian Barber, quit to become stage manager at Hamburg's *Star Club*. The Bluegenes, probably because of their penchant for jazz, were on occasion booed off the stage. When the band returned in 1963 as the Swinging Blue Jeans, playing sets dominated by rock 'n' roll, they were much more successful.

The Beatles played another fortnight in Hamburg in November and soon after their return to the UK were back in the studio to record their second single, *Please Please Me*, and its B-side *Ask Me Why*. The recording took three hours to complete. Having initially *"thoroughly disliked"* the song, George Martin addressed the band over the studio's talkback system and announced: "*Congratulations, gentlemen, you've just made your first number one.*" To discover the reality of the bold prediction, the band would have to wait until the new year. The single was scheduled for release on 11 January 1963.

Having succeeded in obtaining a recording contract for the Beatles, Epstein could now concentrate on his next project, Gerry and the Pacemakers. He urged George Martin to come to Liverpool to see the band in performance, preferably at the *Cavern*. Martin eventually agreed, but also had his own reasons for coming to the city; he had plans for a live recording of the Beatles at the *Cavern*. He needed to reconnoitre the club to discover if his plan was feasible.

On the evening of Martin's choosing, 9 December, the Pacemakers were not on the bill at the *Cavern* or indeed any other venue in the area. In haste, Epstein organised for the band to play to an under fifteen audience at the *Majestic Ballroom,* Birkenhead. Happy with the evening, in *A Cellarful of Noise* Epstein wrote:

> *"Gerry was splendid with the kids and George was very impressed – particularly singing How Do You Do It… Gerry was not signed on the spot. George simply said: 'Come to London and we'll give you a test.'"*

Having seen and heard the Pacemakers, Epstein and Martin, accompanied by his assistant Judy Lockhart-Smith later to become his wife, travelled to the *Cavern*. Martin was not impressed with the acoustics in the claustrophobic cellar. He informed Epstein that it didn't appear a suitable location for a live recording, though he would not totally abandon the idea. He was, however, impressed by a Beatles' support act, The Fourmost.

Epstein admitted that he hadn't spotted the potential of the band, but Martin convinced him that *"they were ripe for development,"* saying *"I would like to meet them sometime and see if we can make a hit or two."*

The four young men, Brian O'Hara, Billy Hatton, Mike Millward and Dave Lovelady, began performing in 1959 as The Four Jays before changing the band's name to The Fourmost. When approached by Epstein, they took some persuading to turn full-time professional. All of them were either working as apprentices or were full-time college students. It took until summer 1963 for Epstein to convince them otherwise.

In late December, the Beatles returned to Hamburg to see out 1962 in performance at the *Star Club*. Kingsize Taylor and the Dominoes were also in residency at the club. Group leader Teddy Taylor asked the Beatles if they would assent to a recording of their show. It has since been suggested that John Lennon agreed to the proposal if Taylor bought the band's beer for the night.

Whatever the reason, the recordings, eventually over three nights, went ahead. They were produced by the club's stage manager, ex-Big Three guitarist Adrian Barber. Using a microphone placed at the front of the stage, he recorded the sessions on a Grundig home tape machine. The complete recording contained 26 songs of which only two, *I Saw Her Standing There* and *Ask Me Why,* were Beatles' compositions. All others, including *Roll Over Beethoven* and *Hippy Hippy Shake*, were covers.

The tapes, deemed to be of poor quality, remained in the possession of Taylor. In 1977 he put together an album titled, *The Beatles Live! At the Star-Club in Hamburg, Germany: 1962*. The band attempted to block its release and in April of that year the group's lawyers served a writ demanding the album be shelved. Taylor counter argued that at least one of the Beatles had granted permission for the recording to be made.

The High Court rejected the Beatles' attempts to block the album's release, with the judge accepting Taylor's arguments. *The Beatles Live!* was released later that month in Germany and in the UK the following month.

*

All that was in the future. At the close of 1962, the Beatles were a group very much on the up. They had a record at number 22 in the UK charts and another due for release in early January, which their producer predicted would reach number one. Group manager Brian Epstein was building his empire and had high hopes for his other artists such Gerry and the Pacemakers and Billy J Kramer.

The Merseyside football clubs were very much on the up too. Everton held a healthy three-point lead at the top of the First Division. Liverpool, though eight points off the neighbours, were on a fantastic run, having won their previous seven matches. The FA Cup was next on the fixture list, but heavy snow and freezing conditions all over the UK threatened to wipe out all football games in January. The bad weather, moreover, made road travel extremely hazardous, something that could affect the more itinerant Beatles.

8. I Like It: January – July 1963

On 2 January 1963, the freezing weather wiped out the whole of the third round FA Cup competition. Unlike most clubs, Liverpool had only to wait seven days for their tie to go ahead against Third Division side Wrexham. 9,000 Liverpudlians expectantly travelled the relatively short distance from their home city to North Wales. Reports gave Wrexham a fair amount of credit for their efforts against the First Division side, but Liverpool's quality in front of goal showed in the end as strikes from Hunt, Lewis and Melia gave the Reds a 3-0 victory and a ticket into the fourth round.

Everton also faced mid-table Third Division opposition away in the cup; their game against Barnsley took place three days after the Liverpool tie. Barnsley proved stubborn opponents and it took until the 72nd minute for Everton to take the lead through Brian Harris. Stevens and Vernon scored the second and third goals for Everton to record a 3-0 win and match Liverpool's victory.

The freezing conditions had firmly taken a grip on the country by mid-January and subsequently, virtually no league football was played before the next round of the cup came around. On 26 January Liverpool played their fourth round tie, and they couldn't have chosen a much tougher draw, away to fellow First Division side, third placed Burnley.

A sell-out crowd of almost 50,000 witnessed a thrilling, evenly fought contest. Liverpool took a first half lead with Kevin Lewis once again on the scoresheet. Burnley responded well in the second half and a John Connelly equaliser ensured a 1-1 draw and a replay at Anfield.

Everton were drawn once more against Third Division opposition, though on paper it appeared a harder tie than their first; their opponents, Swindon, were top of the division when the game took place on 29 January. Nevertheless, it proved to be a much easier affair than the game with Barnsley. Thanks to goals from Vernon and Gabriel, the Blues raced into a two-goal lead inside 15 minutes. Strikes from Bingham and Morrissey, and another from Vernon, led to a convincing 5-1 victory. Everton already knew of their next round opponents, West Ham, at Upton Park, London.

Come February the first league game for either side may well have been the derby match scheduled for the 9th, but this too fell afoul of the weather. The poor weather did not though prevent Everton from once again entering the transfer market. On 7 February, the club made a bid for Glasgow Rangers' winger Alex Scott, but were in fierce competition with Tottenham for the highly-rated Scotsman's signature.

On the morning of negotiations, at Glasgow Rangers' stadium Ibrox, Tottenham appeared to be in pole position to sign Scott, but proceedings, as outlined in the *Echo* below, were to take a dramatic twist.

8.30 – Scott in talks with Spurs' manager Bill Nicholson
10.30 - Scott leaves Ibrox and returns home. Nicholson leaves Ibrox
12.10 – Nicholson returns to Ibrox
12.20 – Scott returns to Ibrox. A reporter asks, *"Is it Spurs?"* Scott doesn't speak, but nods his head in the affirmative
1.45 – An angry looking Nicholson emerges from Ibrox and simply says to journalists, *"I'm leaving Scotland now, goodbye,"* before stepping into a taxi.
1.55 – Harry Catterick steps out of a taxi and enters Ibrox
2.30 – Catterick and Scott emerge from Ibrox smiling. The Everton manager informs the waiting journalists that he has signed the Rangers' player for £39,000.

Scott, and Everton's other acquisition Tony Kay, did not have to wait too long to make their league debuts. The Division One programme finally resumed a few days later and it was to be a tough introduction for the two on 12 February, away at title rivals Leicester City. *"Everton were totally outplayed,"* reported the *Echo*, as Leicester took a two-goal lead into half time. 15 minutes into the second half Leicester scored a third; a Vernon reply ended the game 3-1. The league table at the end of the day's games showed Everton trailing Spurs by a point with Leicester a point off the Blues.

Everton did themselves no favours in their next game recording a disappointing 0-0 draw at home to Wolves. Worse news followed; Spurs won to open a two-point gap at the top of the table. A 2-0 defeat of Nottingham Forest the following week kept the Blues in touch as the fifth round cup ties approached.

Liverpool's 1963 league programme eventually got underway on the evening of 13 February at home to Aston Villa with the team turning in a very impressive performance in front of 53,000 people. Two goals apiece from St John and Hunt gave the Reds a comfortable 4-0 win. The *'Big Freeze'* had certainly not halted Liverpool's momentum, continuing where they left off in 1962.

The following Saturday, Wolves arrived at Anfield and they were despatched in similar fashion. Unlike Villa, Wolves did manage to score, but another double from St John, equalled this time by Kevin Lewis, led to a 4-1 victory. Liverpool had incredibly recorded their ninth successive league victory. Everton's game scheduled for the same afternoon was postponed so Liverpool's victory moved them to within four points of their neighbours.

A potentially serious incident provided the biggest talking point of the Wolves game, however. A crowd of over 53,000 were in attendance. In the Kop, crammed to capacity, a crush barrier collapsed, injuring several spectators. Treatment was administered on the side of the pitch and though a few spectators had to attend hospital, thankfully no-one was seriously hurt.

The incident provided the club with a clear warning that parts of the ground were susceptible to overcrowding. Writing to the *Echo* a few days later, several correspondents, who were on the Kop for the Wolves game, urged the club to cut the number of people allowed in that section of the ground.

All focus now turned to Liverpool's concluding match in February, the FA Cup replay with Burnley. The club believed the ground was safe and on the evening of the game it was again full, a couple of hundred below 58,000. The Liverpudlians in the ground were left stunned as Burnley took a surprise 25th minute lead, but fans were relieved to see St John equalise on the stroke of half time. There were no further goals in the second half and two desperately tired teams battled on into extra time.

As the match entered added time in extra time, a second replay appeared inevitable. In the concluding piece of action, the ball was played back to the Burnley 'keeper, Adam Blacklaw. St John chased down the pass, forcing Blacklaw to kick out at the ball which hit the Liverpool man. As the two players scrambled for the loose ball, St John was brought down for a penalty. Up stepped Ronnie Moran to slam the ball home with the last kick of the game. *"I haven't heard or seen such jubilation at the final whistle for years,"* wrote the *Echo's* Leslie Edwards.

The fifth round draw handed Liverpool yet another difficult tie, this time away to Arsenal. Before that game, Liverpool were scheduled to play three league matches in seven days with the last of those also away to their cup opponents.

In the first of those games, Liverpool suffered a 2-0 home defeat to title chasing Leicester City. Shankly spent much of his post-match interview complaining about Leicester's tactics, accusing the Midland's club of being a very negative team which relied on playing on the break and using the long ball. Liverpool's two further league matches were away from home and yielded the same results, 2-2; the first at Ipswich followed by the FA Cup rehearsal with Arsenal at Highbury.

Having got close to the leaders during the excellent run of victories, the two points accumulated in the two latter matches all but ended hopes of a Liverpool title challenge; Spurs had been on a fantastic run recently and now led the Reds by nine points. Most hopes were now fixed on winning the cup for the first time in the club's history.

"Cup Fans Invade London," read the front page of the early edition of the *Echo* on Saturday 13 March.

> *"Travelling on trains, in dozens of coaches and with some supporters of either team sharing cars and vans, thousands of Liverpudlians and*

Evertonians are arriving in the capital to cheer on their teams in the FA Cup this afternoon."

Playing with confidence, Liverpool were very impressive from the outset at Highbury; latching onto an accurate Roger Hunt through ball, Jimmy Melia gave the Reds a 1-0 half time lead. Since taking over penalty duties, Ronnie Moran was proving to be a reliable exponent of the art, as he repeated his last minute fourth round heroics to double Liverpool's lead in the second half. They remained very much in control of the game and, despite Arsenal scoring in the 85th minute, deservedly progressed to the sixth round.

At Upton Park, Everton's cup tie was a bad-tempered affair; in the first half, players fought and scrapped for possession and there was little in the way of chances. On the hour, a West Ham corner found its way to the far post and, as the ball reached him, Everton's wing half Denis Stevens finished up on the turf, having appeared to be pushed over by Hammers' centre half, Bobby Moore. Players on both sides, as well as thousands of Evertonians, were though shocked to see the referee point to the penalty spot.

The spot kick was delayed as missiles thrown by some Evertonians rained down onto the pitch, One Evertonian, for some unknown reason, ran to the centre circle to confront Roy Vernon and had to be removed by five policemen. With the situation calmed, the West Ham penalty was duly despatched and though Everton exerted intense late pressure they failed to find an equaliser and the single goal ensured yet another relatively early cup exit.

On the Monday following the game, the *Echo* reported that Harry Catterick had confronted the referee in the tunnel to explain his reasons for the award of the penalty. The official told the Everton manager that Stevens had handled the ball before he was pushed to the ground. If Everton could have gone on to win the tie they would have been rewarded with an away sixth round fixture against Liverpool, as it was, the Reds would now play West Ham at Anfield.

For their next league game at home to West Brom, Liverpool handed a debut to a young local right back, Chris Lawler. Albion took the lead twice before, yet again, another late Moran penalty made the score 2-2. In their next game, Liverpool did Everton another massive favour winning 3-1 at Turf Moor, Burnley to all but end the Lancashire club's hopes of winning the league.

The poor weather had left a huge backlog of fixtures and by mid-March, Everton faced the prospect of 16 games before the end of the season. Four of those games, three of them away from home, had to played before the end of the month. First up were champions Ipswich Town at Portman Road. *"Everton played first class football with poise and rhythm as they crushed Ipswich 3-0"*, the *Echo* reported. Alex Young scored two and *"it would not have been an injustice had Everton doubled the* score."

Despite going behind early on, Manchester City were beaten 2-1 four days later at Goodison Park with Young again on the scoresheet and Morrissey netting the decisive winner. Supporters left the ground to good news; playing each other, Leicester and Spurs drew their game 2-2. Everton were now three points off Spurs and one off Leicester having played two fewer games.

It was a return to London and Arsenal for one of the games in hand. *"It was a wonderful game; a thrill a minute,"* Harry Catterick's verdict on the match; but it was not a wonderful result. Everton failed to take advantage, losing the game, 4-3, making it five trips to the capital without victory, so far this season. To end March on a miserable note, on their travels the Blues were beaten again, 2-1 at Sheffield United. As the league title appeared to be slipping away, the only consolation, was Alex Scott's first goal of his Everton career.

As Everton were losing in Sheffield, Liverpool were playing their biggest game of the season to date, their FA Cup sixth round home tie with West Ham. The Londoners were not easy opponents as West Ham played aggressively from the start. *"They looked the team most likely to score in the first half,"* the *Echo* reported. However, having failed to score when they held the upper hand, *"West Ham appeared to settle for a draw and the chance of a replay,"* the report added. The following week in his column, Ron Yeats agreed with this assessment; *"I got the impression that about halfway through the second half they decided that a draw will do,"* he wrote.

West Ham ultimately paid the penalty for their over-cautious approach as Roger Hunt struck the only goal of the game in the 81st minute. *"The crowd went wild and dozens of young boys ran onto the pitch to celebrate."* The cup win kept Liverpool's season alive; they were through to their first semi-final since 1950. Two days later they learned of their opponents, Leicester City.

Liverpool's next scheduled game was the re-arranged derby match with Everton at Anfield on Monday 8 April. Everton though had to play two games before meeting their neighbours. First up, Aston Villa at Goodison on 1 April and nothing short of victory would suffice. Would Everton have the mental and physical capacity to maintain their title challenge?

* * *

On New Year's Day 1963, the Beatles flew from Hamburg to a freezing London. The group spent the night in the capital before taking to the air again, flying to Scotland the following day for a five-night tour of the country. On the 8th the band were back on TV, recording an appearance on a Scottish Television children's show *Roundup* where they mimed *Please Please Me*. Brian Epstein had cleverly arranged for the recording, to be aired on the 11th, to coincide with release of the single. Throughout 1963, TV audiences were to see more and more of the in-demand Beatles.

In the meantime, Epstein had lost patience with Billy J Kramer's backing group, The Coasters. He didn't think the band were taking the music business seriously enough. Kramer felt the same, writing in his autobiography: *"Some of them were reluctant to give up their day jobs to become full-time professional musicians."* Epstein moved to replace The Coasters with a band now performing regularly at the *Cavern*, Manchester based The Dakotas. Everyone concerned signed a formal contract on 6 January.

The main reason for Epstein's swift change of Kramer's backing group was an upcoming first trip to Hamburg's *Star Club* for the teenager. Kramer had something of a mixed introduction to the nefarious delights of the German port city. Though enjoying performing in the city, the long nights, daytime periods of boredom and occasional arguments with his new backing group, Kramer endured a few personal problems. He said he *"drank heavily,"* often with Gene Vincent who was also in residency at the club. To stay awake he *"became addicted to amphetamines."* On more than one occasion, because of his mounting problems, Kramer doubted that he would make it in the music business.

In spring, the band's time in Hamburg came to an end and they returned to Liverpool. The return was Kramer's saviour as his drinking very much diminished, as did his dependency amphetamines. His reversion to a *"more normal"* was essential as Brian Epstein had arranged for the ensemble to record their first single with George Martin at Abbey Road on 8 May.

Booked for a performance on the popular show *Thank Your Lucky Stars* on Sunday 13 January, the Beatles made their most important television appearance to date. The show, recorded at ATV Studios in Birmingham, was made for the ITV network. The show was aired the following Saturday evening.

First aired in April 1961, *Thank Your Lucky Stars* was ITV's answer to the BBC's *Juke Box Jury*, the leading TV pop and rock 'n' roll programme. Usually miming in front of a live studio audience, *Lucky Stars* featured many top performers of the day. Although the Beatles were at the bottom of a seven-act bill playing *Please Please Me*, it was a major coup for them to appear on the much-watched Saturday evening programme. The Beatles made a second appearance on the show on 26 February on a bill featuring Billy Fury as the headline act.

More television appearances followed, this time for the Granada TV's *People and Places* and *Here We Go*. The band were busy in the radio studio too. On 22 January, the Beatles made three recordings in London for BBC Radio's Light Programme.

The following day in the atrocious freezing weather, the band began the long drive back to Liverpool. They were determined to fulfil a booking at the *Cavern*. Few would have been surprised if they cancelled the show. To make matters worse, they made the journey with a damaged windscreen; Paul McCartney in *Anthology* remembered the perilous trip; Neil Aspinall was ill, so assistant road manager, Mal Evans was driving:

> "I do remember one incident: going up the motorway when the windscreen got knocked out by a pebble. Our great road manager Mal Evans was driving and he just put his hat backwards on his hand, punched the windscreen out completely, and drove on. This was winter in Britain and there was freezing fog and Mal was having to look out for the kerb all the way up to Liverpool."

Somehow, they managed to arrive on time. They shared the evening bill with The Fourmost and Freddie Starr and the Midnighters. Later to become famous as a comedian, Starr had recently joined the group taking over from Gus Travers as lead singer. The Midnighters did go on to record a couple of singles, but they failed to make an impact on the UK charts.

The *Cavern* was now at its height with almost every session a sell-out, particularly if the Beatles were on the bill. On Sunday 3 February, the club put on an eight-hour music show titled "*Rhythm and Blues Marathon*". The Beatles topped a bill which also included a Manchester based band called The Hollies; other acts completing the line-up were The Fourmost, The Merseybeats, The Roadrunners, Earl Preston and the TTs, the Swinging Blue Jeans and Kingsize Taylor and the Dominoes featuring Swinging Cilla.

Hailing from Liverpool's famous Scotland Road, Swinging Cilla was 19-year-old Priscilla White who, after leaving school, went to college to train as an office administrator. At 16, she began working as a typist at British Insulated Callender's Cables (BICC) in Stanley Street, just a couple of hundred yards from the *Cavern*. White became a regular at the club and was offered the job as a part-time cloakroom attendant.

Encouraged by a workmate, she began to give impromptu stage performances, backed by Mersey Beat bands such as Rory Storm and Kingsize Taylor. She impressed promoter, Sam Leach, who booked her first solo show at the *Casanova Club*, on London Road, where she appeared as Swinging Cilla.

In what was effectively an audition, at a show in Birkenhead and backed by the Beatles, Brian Epstein was there to see her perform. The manager was less than enthralled. In December 1963, Cilla told the Liverpool Echo: "*I sang Summertime without rehearsal. The music was in the wrong key. I knew I had blown it.*"

She had another opportunity to impress a few months later at *The Blue Angel* club where she was backed by a modern jazz band and sang in jazz style covering numbers such as *You Made Me Love You*. "*I was more relaxed and Epstein liked my performance,*" she told the *Echo*. "*Why didn't you sing like that before? he asked.*" Epstein signed up the young singer and changed her surname to Black.

The evening prior to the *Cavern* marathon show, the Beatles began a nationwide tour supporting a 16-year-old singing sensation named Helen Shapiro. As a 14-year-old, in 1961, Shapiro achieved a UK number three hit single with her first song, *Don't Treat Me Like A Child*. This was followed by two UK number one singles *You Don't Know* and *Walkin' Back To Happiness*.

The tour began in Bradford and most musicians had to set off from London to make the long, hazardous trip in freezing temperatures. The Beatles, having played the previous evening in Sutton Coldfield, Warwickshire, had a shorter, but no less hazardous journey, making the trip in Neil Aspinall's Commer van.

Supporting Shapiro may have been viewed as something of a come-down, as the Beatles found themselves bottom of the bill. Ringo Starr didn't think so. He believed Shapiro's chart success made her the star. As the newest member of the Beatles he was still getting used to performing with and accompanying his new band mates. In *Anthology*, Starr said the tour helped him bond with the band.

> "*The togetherness of this tour helped a lot. At first I was worried about who I was going to share with at the hotels, but mostly it was me in with Paul, and John and George sharing another room.*"

The first half of the Shapiro tour ended in Sunderland on the 9 February. On the 11th, the Beatles returned to Abbey Road to record ten songs for their debut album *Please Please Me*. The session began at 10.00 a.m. and recording stopped for lunch at 1.00 pm. George Martin and the engineers went off to the pub, but were surprised to see on their return an hour later that the Beatles hadn't taken a break at all. Drinking only milk, they continued to rehearse through the lunch hour.

Recording continued into the afternoon and, after a short break, on into the evening. Working their way through their live set song by song, the number of takes varying on each, recording finished at 10:45 pm. A whole album of 14 songs completed in less than 13 hours. Side one included *I Saw Her Standing There, Ask Me Why* and *Please Please Me*, with side two containing titles including *Love Me Do, There's a Place* and *Twist and Shout*.

After the recording, the group were required to be photographed for the album cover. In the wake of a couple of suggestions, George Martin settled on the use of *EMI's* headquarters at Manchester Square, London for the backdrop. The result was the iconic colour image of the group looking down from an upper floor of the building's stairwell.

For Merseyside's other leading band, Martin was as good as his word. He auditioned Gerry and the Pacemakers and they returned to Abbey Road in late February to record their first single, *How Do You Do It*. The song, written by Mitch Murray, apart from the Beatles, had been offered to Adam Faith and Brian Poole and the Tremeloes, but both had turned it down. Martin, having heard the band performing the song when he came to Merseyside in December 1962, believed it perfect for the Pacemakers.
The song was released on Monday 4 March and on 20 March, it charted at number 39; a week later it made the top twenty.

The Beatles were busy composing during the Helen Shapiro tour, now in its second phase. Lennon and McCartney composed a song they believed good enough for a single release. Epstein and George Martin agreed and on 5 March the band recorded *From Me To You* at Abbey Road.

In late March, *EMI* released *Please Please Me* the album and on 24th the Beatles made a triumphant return to Liverpool with a sell-out performance at the city's *Empire Theatre*. It was their first performance in Liverpool in over a month. *Please Please Me* the single was at number two in the charts at the time, being kept from top spot by a Cliff Richard and the Shadows song, *Summer Holiday*. The Pacemakers, *How Do You Do It*, had climbed to number ten, in the same week.

*

Into spring, weather prospects were much brighter, as were the prospects for Mersey Beat. What about the prospects for Mersey football? Liverpool were some way off challenging for the title, but had a great deal to look forward to at the end of April, an FA Cup semi-final tie against Leicester city. It was Everton who were challenging for the First Division championship. If they were to achieve their ambition, they had to win their 1 April match away to Aston Villa.

Decades later, the game remained permanently fixed in the memory of Alex Young: *"I think that was my best ever 90 minutes"*, he wrote in his autobiography. *"It was one of those rare glory days when everything I tried came off."* Young scored one of the goals and Jimmy Gabriel the other in a 2-0 victory. The win kept Everton in the title hunt.

On Saturday 6 April, many First Division games were postponed, among them matches involving Liverpool, Spurs and Leicester, as the annual England v Scotland Home International contest at Wembley took place. Three Liverpool players were in action, St John for Scotland and Byrne and Melia for England. Spurs had six representatives in total, three for each country and Leicester's Gordon Banks was keeping goal for England. Scotland went on to win the game 2-1.

The Wembley international offered Everton an excellent chance to close the gap on Spurs and Leicester as they faced Blackburn at Goodison. Everton, they had done previously when they had the chance to play games in hand, failed to take advantage. Evertonians departed the ground disappointed and frustrated as their team played out an unsatisfactory 0-0 draw. Two days later, the derby match at Anfield.

Coming quickly after the international game and Everton's weekend fixture, the build-up and press coverage to the second derby match of the season could not compare with that of the first. As for the game itself, Leslie Edwards wrote in the *Echo* the following evening:

> "I never saw a derby which reflected more credit on the teams for sustained effort, for tremendous skill and tremendous speed. The 56,000 crowd must have gone away enthralled by a contest which showed our city sides as among the finest in Britain. I wouldn't criticise any players, as the majority played with great poise and great sense."

The teams *"cancelled each other out"* and neither could find the back of the net. A 0-0 draw the result. Edwards though was very displeased with the reaction of supporters of both sides. He stated:

> "Some engaged in barracking players throughout the match for doing nothing wrong other than performing for the opposition."

Having observed the players congratulating each other at the final whistle, Edwards believed they thought the result fair. Ron Yeats and Alex Young agreed; they both concluded in their newspaper columns that neither side deserved to lose the game.

Leicester played and won their match the same evening to stretch their advantage over Everton and move to the top of the table, which now read:

> Leicester played 34 points 48
> Spurs played 33 points 47
> Everton played 33 points 45

The season now entered a tense period. The crucial Easter weekend in which, incredibly, most teams would play three games in either four or five days. In the first of those games on Good Friday, Liverpool could do Everton yet another favour by defeating Spurs at Anfield. At half time, Everton players and supporters, and of course Liverpudlians, would have been in despair as Spurs led 2-0. At the final whistle, despair would have been replaced by total surprise; Liverpool had, barely unbelievably, rattled in five second half goals to win the game 5-2.

Ron Yeats, unsurprisingly, believed that Liverpool's first half performance *"was as bad as any first half"* in which he had played for the Reds. Conversely, the second half *"was probably the finest."* For the record, the scorers were Melia (2), Stevenson, St John, and Lewis. Perhaps the biggest winners on the day though were Everton, with Spurs losing and Leicester not playing.

With the excellent news from Anfield, Everton travelled to Blackpool the following day. For the game, Harry Catterick handed the captaincy to his ex-Blackpool goalkeeper Gordon West, in recognition of his service to both clubs. Everton did what they needed to, winning the game, played in heavy rain, 2-1.

Scheduled first for Easter Monday and the Tuesday following were two games against Birmingham City. In the first of those at Goodison, Everton, *"never looked like champions"* the *Echo* reported. They had to twice come from behind to draw the match 2-2.

On the same afternoon, Liverpool were engaged in yet another remarkable match with Spurs at White Hart Lane. Spurs once more held a two-goal lead at the break, this time 3-1. The second half, however, was not to be a replica of the Good Friday contest, but it was to be memorable for one player in particular, Jimmy Greaves. He scored an amazing four goals in twenty minutes as Spurs went on to win yet another incredible match, 7-2.

With the news of that result and their poor performance the same day meant an Everton win in the return match with Birmingham at St. Andrews was vital. Everton responded in fine fashion, though only winning by a goal to nil, they totally dominated the contest to pick up two valuable points. Without doubt, with six to play, Everton's biggest match of the season was on the horizon on 20 April, a home fixture against Spurs.

After a mixed bag of holiday results, the league table could not have been closer on the morning of the Spurs game, reading:

> Leicester played 37 points 51
> Spurs played 36 points 50
> Everton played 36 points 50

Spurs were ahead of Everton on goal average as the game at Goodison kicked off in front of 68,000 spectators. The post-match *Echo* headline read: *"Tottenham Not-So-Hotspur."*

> *"The margin of victory, 1-0, gave no hint of the hammering Tottenham had to take. They might have been beaten four or five-nil. It wasn't their fault that they weren't, but Everton's for missing some glorious chances."*

Alex Young scored the only goal of the game and though Spurs exerted some late pressure, Everton held on for a much-deserved victory. Leicester drew their game 0-0 on the same afternoon, handing top position to Everton on goal average. The Blues also held a game in hand over their rivals. That game, against Arsenal at Goodison, was next up on Wednesday 24 April.

It was a rough contest against the north London club. Goalkeeper Gordon West picked up an early leg injury, seriously affecting his mobility. In today's game, he would certainly be replaced, but in the days before substitutes, West was forced to play on.

Everton took the lead in the first half through Roy Vernon, but played the second half consciously trying to protect their goalkeeper. It almost paid off; Arsenal though managed to grab an equaliser. Alex Young was convinced later that a fit West would have prevented the goal. Still the draw moved them a point clear of Leicester and three of Spurs. All three teams had now played 38 games with four remaining.

Saturday 27 April: *"D Day for Liverpool and Everton: The Biggest Day in Merseyside Football in Over a Decade,"* read the headline in the early edition of the *Liverpool*

Echo. It was FA Cup semi-final day for Liverpool at Hillsborough and a vital league game at West Ham for Everton. Harry Catterick in the same *Echo* edition stated, *"We cannot afford to lose the game. If we do so, I fear we will lose the championship."*

Recalling the recent game at Anfield in which Liverpool were beaten 2-0 by Leicester, Bill Shankly was asked about the tactics their opponents were known to employ. He replied: *"The match is about how my team play. If we play to our abilities it won't matter how they play, we will win the game."*

Out of a total of 65,000, almost 30,000 were Liverpudlians. They saw Leicester start the game quite predictably, not committing too many players forward. Leicester had not produced a meaningful attack when in the 18th minute, they won a free kick out wide on the right. The ball was crossed in, winger Mike Stringfellow lost his marker and headed home to put Leicester one up.

Liverpool spent virtually the whole of the next 70 plus minutes hammering away at the Leicester defence, but owing to a succession of missed opportunities and an irrepressible performance from the outstanding Gordon Banks in goal, they failed to find the breakthrough and lost the game 1-0.

Even with the passage of time, St John had not forgotten the game, especially the performance of the Leicester goalkeeper. Writing in his autobiography, he said:

> *"Banks was in the form that served England so well in winning the World Cup in 1966. He dived everywhere, caught, flicked and punched everything... Our dressing room was like a morgue after the game."*

Thousands of Liverpudlians left the ground in despair, firmly believing that a wonderful opportunity to win the cup for the first time in the club's history had been missed. The knowledge that the other cup finalists were fourth to bottom placed Manchester United, a team they had beaten a couple of weeks earlier, only added to the despair.

Two days later, an angry Leslie Edwards in the *Echo* asked:

> *"Were there ever less worthy winners of a semi-final than Leicester? Has there been a team that played worse tactically and got away with it? Leicester's deep defence didn't deserve to win the game, they simply hit the ball as hard as they could anywhere up the field."*

The enormously disappointing result impacted on Liverpool's remaining league games. The players and supporters had seemingly little appetite for the final six fixtures. The team won just one game, 5-1 against Birmingham City in front of 23,456, the lowest attendance of the season; they drew another and were defeated in the other four. After putting together a magnificent run of results in mid-season, Liverpool finished the league in eighth position.

For Merseyside football, hopes now rested on Everton, beginning with their game at West Ham. The team lost the services of injured goalkeeper Gordon West, who had been ruled out for the remainder of the season. Winger Morrissey was also absent through injury. They were replaced by Albert Dunlop and Derek Temple, respectively. Temple repaid his manager's faith, scoring an early goal. Roy Vernon doubled Everton's lead before half time. Though West Ham scored late, the 2-1 victory kept Everton at the top of the table.

With three games to play in the space of a week, the league title was firmly in their hands and theirs to lose; only three victories though would guarantee success. First up, a home game with Bolton Wanderers on the first Saturday in May.

> *"Everton were unrecognisable from the team that hammered Spurs in their last home match. They fumbled and floundered their way through the game. The only explanation for this was tension amongst the players and the crowd of 52,000 nail-biting, anxious, worried spectators.*

The words of the *Echo's* Michael Charters, who described the anxiety as it persisted for over an hour of the match, until finally a Roy Vernon strike in the 71st minute put Everton in front.

> *"It was as though a pin had burst a giant balloon and the pent-up frustration exploded into a massive roar."*

Bolton piled on the pressure as Everton desperately guarded their goal until the relief of the final whistle. Still top with two games remaining. West Brom next on the 7th.

The *Echo* didn't call it such, but the gist of its report suggested that against West Brom, Everton were *"unrecognisable"* from the side that played Bolton three days earlier.

> *"They took charge of the game and moulded it to their will in a manner befitting prospective champions and victory was achieved without a weak link in the chain anywhere."*

Everton did receive a stroke of fortune early in the game, as a West Brom defender picked up an early injury, left the field of play and was unable to return to the action. Everton dominated there on and a Young goal sent the Blues into the break one up. Another strike from the Scotsman plus a Vernon goal and an own goal ultimately gave Everton a convincing 4-0 victory.

One game remaining against Fulham at Goodison and victory would bring Everton the First Division title for the first time since 1939.

The anticipation was great and the tension palpable as the game got underway. Unlike the previous home game against Bolton, the tension was eased early on. Vernon scored after just five minutes and the crowd of 63,000 had barely finished celebrating when three minutes later he struck again. Anxiety briefly returned when Fulham pulled a goal back in the 20th minute. The negative feeling was however short-lived; eight minutes later Alex Scott re-opened Everton's two-goal.

The second half was reasonably comfortable before Vernon rounded off a perfect day for himself, and for everyone connected with Everton, as he bagged his hat-trick to record a fantastic 4-1 win. The final whistle signalled celebrations all around Goodison.

Supporters, who were asked before the game not to come onto the pitch, cheered and sang the players' names as they performed a lap of honour. Unfortunately, there was no trophy presentation, but it did not prevent thousands of ecstatic fans staying to absorb the atmosphere and to wallow in the moment. They chanted for John Moores who appeared in the stand to take the applause.

Interviewed by the press minutes later, a visibly delighted chairman believed the club policy of spending big had clearly and justifiably brought reward. He said:

> "We received much criticism for the signings of Kay and Scott for a total of £100,000 during the winter freeze, but those decisions have been fully justified,"

Two of Everton's key players, scorers of 42 league goals between them, wrote of their emotions following the team's fantastic achievement. Alex Young stated:

> "This is the greatest thing that has ever happened to me in football. Never shall I forget those final five minutes of the Fulham game as the crowd were stomping and shouting so much that my head was reeling so much with the noise."

Hat-trick hero Roy Vernon probably deserves the final word on the club's triumph.

> "I tingle every time I think about Saturday's match including the tremendous tumultuous reception, the fun in the dressing room after the game and the demands from the press for photographs and interviews. It all adds up to a wonderful picture that will live with me long after my playing days are over."

Thanks to substantial financial investment, skilled management and enthusiastic support, Everton had risen from relegation candidates in 1960 to First Division champions in 1963; without doubt, a remarkable achievement.

* *

On 5 April, the Beatles were awarded a silver disc, for sales of more than 250,000 copies of their single *Please Please Me*. In the presence of George Martin, they accepted the award at *EMI* studios. The band's latest single, *From Me To You*, went on general release the following week

A performance on the BBC's *625 Show* was another first for the Beatles. Although they had made eleven appearances on regional and independent television programmes in Britain, this 13 April show was their TV debut for the corporation and therefore their first exposure to a nationwide audience.

The updated weekly music singles' chart was published the following day and it made historic reading for Merseyside musicians and fans. A Mersey Beat group were at number one; it was not, however, the Beatles who achieved the momentous milestone, but Gerry and the Pacemakers with their song, *How Do You Do It*. The band went on to hold the top spot for a total of three weeks.

The simultaneous achievements of the bands and football teams were in evidence again. Everton's victory over Tottenham Hotspur on 20 April moved the club back to the top of Division One for the first time in 1963, three days after the Pacemakers made number one.

The relative success of *Love Me Do,* the even better chart performance of *Please Please Me* and the increasing number of TV appearances made the Beatles a band in ever more demand. Some shows outside of Liverpool were selling out and they were performing on occasion in front of audiences numbering in the thousands. Epstein had promised the band a holiday at the end of April, but the week prior he had booked a heavy schedule containing daily treks back and forth, from north to south.

In an afternoon show, on Sunday 21 April the Beatles were second on the bill for the *New Musical Express* 1962-63 *Annual Poll-Winners' All-Star Concert*, held at the *Empire Pool*, Wembley, London. Topping the 14-act bill were Cliff Richard and The Shadows. The venue was filled with 10,000 music fans.

It was back north for a performance on the 23rd at Southport's *Floral Hall* and the following day a return to London to play the *Majestic Ballroom* in Finsbury Park, London. Organised by Epstein for his acts only, this show was one of the first of a special series called *Mersey Beat Showcase*. The Beatles shared the bill, in front of two thousand fans, with Gerry and the Pacemakers, The Big Three, and Billy J Kramer and the Dakotas. The following day, the whole Showcase moved on to play the *Fairfield Hall Ballroom* in Croydon, Surrey, once again playing to a full house.

Epstein was well on his way to creating a musical phenomenon. The Beatles played two more shows in the north of England in Shrewsbury, Shropshire and Nantwich Cheshire, before flying out of the country on the 28th for holidays in Europe.

McCartney, Harrison and Starr began a two-week break in Tenerife. John Lennon and Brian Epstein meanwhile went off on their own holiday together in Barcelona. The pair's trip, however, was to be the source of much discussion and cause no shortage of trouble as rumours of a gay relationship between the two spread. In *Lennon Remembers*, by Jann S Wenner, the Beatle remarked:

> "It was enjoyable, but there were big rumours in Liverpool, it was terrible. Very embarrassing. It started off all the rumours that he and I were having a love affair, but not quite – it was never consummated. I was pretty close to him because if somebody's going to manage me, I want to know them inside out."

Paul McCartney in *Anthology* suggested that Lennon agreed to the holiday to assert his authority within the group:

> "Brian invited John along. John was a smart cookie. Brian was gay, and John saw his opportunity to impress upon Mr Epstein who was the boss of the group. I think that's why he went on holiday with Brian. And good luck to him, too - he was that kind of guy; he wanted Brian to know whom he should listen to."

Ramifications awaited in Liverpool as the persistent rumours continued. In the non-too distant future, the ramifications would involve Lennon and a special friend of the Beatles.

While the Beatles were holidaying, they received fantastic news. On 2 May, the latest music chart was issued and it made great reading for Mersey Beat. The Beatles' *From Me To You* had reached number one, pushing Gerry and the Pacemakers into second position. The one-two remained the same the following week, 9 May.

On 11 May, Everton defeated Fulham 4-1 at Goodison Park to win the First Division title. The club's achievement along with those of the Beatles and the Pacemakers provides yet another remarkable example of the synchronised success of Merseyside football and Merseyside music.

It was now time for one of Epstein's other budding stars to attempt a shot at chart success. On 8 May, Billy J Kramer recorded and released *Do You Wanna Know A Secret,* a Lennon and McCartney composition which also featured on the Beatles' album *Please Please Me*. The song went on to spend a total of eleven weeks in the top twenty, peaking at number two in early June. *Do You Wanna Know A Secret*, made Kramer a household name.

After their much-deserved holiday, the Beatles returned to the UK to join a nationwide tour headed by American recording star Roy Orbison. The touring party also included Gerry and the Pacemakers. Although Orbison topped the bill, he was soon demoted to second due to audiences' reactions to the Beatles. The American, fully aware of the band's popularity, graciously accepted the promoter's decision.

Partway through the tour The Beatles were given their own BBC Radio series called *Pop Go The Beatles*. The four shows, the first of which was recorded on 24 May and broadcast on 4 June, featured a mix of music and conversation. A different guest act chosen by the BBC featured each week.

The tour reached Liverpool on 26 May. It was a fantastic homecoming at the *Empire Theatre* for the Beatles, now headlining, and Gerry and the Pacemakers. The Pacemakers had played Liverpool recently, but this was the Beatles first show in their home city for over six weeks, demonstrating the increasing national popularity of the band.

In early June, Brian Epstein and George Martin, using the tour as a perfect vehicle for publicity, released the new Gerry and the Pacemakers single, *I Like It,* another Mitch Murray composition. The song, which first charted on the 6th, did not take long to become a smash hit for the band, reaching number one on the 26th. This, only the band's second single, remarkably became their second consecutive number one hit.

On 18 June, Paul McCartney reached the milestone age of 21 and to celebrate the occasion, held a party at his Aunt Gin's house in, Huyton, Liverpool. The Fourmost performed at McCartney's request, while guests included Gerry and the Pacemakers, Billy J Kramer and Cliff Richard's backing group, The Shadows, who had been performing in Blackpool.

As a consequence of John Lennon's holiday with Brian Epstein, the party turned into something of a disaster and embarrassment. Lennon's friend, *Cavern* DJ and promoter, Bob Wooler allegedly mocked the Beatle saying his trip to Barcelona with Epstein was not a holiday but a *"honeymoon."* Lennon, fuelled by alcohol, shocked those present by launching a physical attack on Wooler, resulting in a black eye for the DJ.

Lennon was taken home and Brian Epstein drove Wooler to hospital. A sober Lennon two days later sent Wooler a telegram of apology reading: *'Really sorry Bob - terribly worried to realise what I had done - what more can I say."* Unfortunately, the local press and the *Daily Mirror* got hold of the story. The *Mirror* ran the story on the 21st.

> *"Guitarist John Lennon, 22-year-old leader of The Beatles 'pop' group, said last night: 'Why did I have to go and punch my best friend? 'I was so high I didn't realise what I was doing.'*

> *Yesterday Wooler said: 'I don't know why he did it. I was booted in the face. I begged him to stop. I have been a friend of the Beatles for a long time. I have often compered shows where they have appeared. I am terribly upset about this - physically as well as mentally.'*
>
> *John Lennon, in London with the Beatles said: 'I had a great deal to drink at the party and very little to eat. By the time this happened I didn't know what I was doing. Bob is the last person in the world I would want to have a fight with. I can only hope he realises that I was too far gone to know what I was doing.'"*

Somewhat sarcastically, the *Mirror* ended the article: "*Lennon helped to write The Beatles' latest hit tune, From Me To You.*"

The Beatles returned to touring and to the studio to record their next single *She Loves You*, at Abbey Road on 1 July. They also recorded their debut EP containing four songs from the *Please Please Me* album. Side one contained *Twist and Shout* and *A Taste of Honey*. The B-side featured *Do You Wanna Know A Secret* and *There's A Place*. Although all the songs were available on a Beatles album, the EP went on to sell an incredible 800,000 copies.

Another Liverpool band, overlooked by Brian Epstein, were too in the recording studio. The Searchers returned from Hamburg to take up their usual residency at the *Iron Door* club. There, on tape, they recorded some of their sessions and sent them off to *Pye Records*. With the sound of Mersey Beat a growing phenomenon and liking the sound of the band, Pye signed The Searchers and placed them in the hands of producer Tony Hatch. In early July, they released their first single, *Sweets for My Sweet*, which, after a slow start, gradually crept up the charts and by 31 July had reached number three in the UK charts.

In Liverpool, the local press had finally recognised the musical phenomena on its doorstep. On 27 July, the *Echo* produced a *Big Beat Special* featuring on the front-page Billy J Kramer and The Big Three, a band Brian Epstein had lost patience with and dropped earlier in the year. Without Epstein, The Big Three had signed to *Decca* and at the time of the *Echo* special had released their second single, *By The Way*. It went on to reach a peak of 22 in the charts, a better position than their first record, *Some Other Guy* which only scraped into the top forty making number 37 in April.

The Big Three also recorded a number called *The Cavern Stomp,* which had to date failed to make the charts (it would not do so). The title came from a dance of the same name performed at the *Cavern*. The *Echo* invited its readers *"to experience the dance"* and, in a series of photographs, detailed the moves required to do so.

In a feature called *Rock Around the Clock,* pages two and three were dedicated to a day in the life of the Beatles. One of the closing articles featured an interview with TVs *Thank Your Lucky Stars* producer, Philip Jones. He commented:

> *"The Liverpool Beat not only appeals to Scousers but to all Britain's teenagers and their elders. The aim of the show is to bring you the latest and the best from the world of pop music and that quite definitely includes anything new from Merseyside."*

Merseyside was dominating the charts. On the last day of July, it contained hit records by The Beatles, Gerry and the Pacemakers and Billy J Kramer and the Dakotas, as well as containing singles by other Liverpool artists, Billy Fury and Frankie Vaughan. The Swinging Blue Jeans had also produced a minor hit, *It's Too Late Now*, which had just slipped out of the top forty after peaking at number 30 a week earlier.

*

The first half of 1963 had produced three Mersey Beat number one records, two for Gerry and the Pacemakers, *How Do You Do It* and *I Like It*, and one for the Beatles, *From Me To You*, as well as hit records for other Merseyside bands. On the football front Everton were league champions and set to compete in the European Cup for the first time in the club's history. Liverpool had made more than a decent return to the First Division and agonisingly just missed out on FA Cup success.

Could the current crop of musicians, and perhaps other Mersey Beat hopefuls, continue the incredible run of success in the remainder of the year? Could Everton and Liverpool again challenge for honours come the return of the football season in August?

9. You'll Never Walk Alone: August - December 1963

Reflecting developments and investment on the pitch, in the summer of 1963, Goodison and Anfield were both undergoing redevelopment in preparation for the forthcoming season. Everton were adding a lower tier to their Bullens Road stand and Liverpool were redeveloping the stand on Kemlyn Road.

There were barely redevelopments of club squads through the summer though. Everton had sold Billy Bingham to Port Vale and Frank Wignall to Nottingham Forest because, said manager Harry Catterick, *"both players wanted to leave as they could not be guaranteed first team football."* Catterick had brought in just one player, Jimmy Hill aged 27, from Norwich as cover for Roy Vernon or Dennis Stevens.

There were no summer changes to the first team squad at Anfield, though manager Bill Shankly had spent the end of July and the beginning of August desperately trying to sign an outside left. An attempt to entice Michael O'Grady from his old club Huddersfield Town had fallen through when the player renewed his contract with the Yorkshire club. O'Grady's decision made Shankly more determined not to let his alternative target slip through the net.

"I'm delighted to be joining a club like Liverpool. I knew nothing about it until I read it in the newspaper this morning," said 20-year-old Peter Thompson as he was introduced to the press at Anfield on the afternoon of 12 August. For a fee of £44,000. paid to Preston North End, Shankly informed the press that he had the winger he desired.

> *"I have known Peter since he was a boy of 15 at Carlisle. He's a great player and I think he will do exceptionally well for us,"*

Expectations for the coming campaign were high on Merseyside. Everton, as reigning champions, were obvious candidates for trophies; the bookmakers had them as favourites to retain the league title. Liverpool, apart from the final few fixtures when there was little to play for, had clearly proven the previous season that they were one of the division's leading sides.

The annual Charity Shield match, the curtain raiser to the English football season between the First Division champions, Everton and FA Cup winners, Manchester United was played at Goodison Park on 17 August. The game was not a great spectacle. *"I rate this as one of the least worthy games we have seen in this city for seasons,"* commented Michael Charters in his *Echo* match report. He accused the players of *"deliberate fouling"* and *"strolling around in possession."*

Though Evertonians were, in the opinion of Charters, unhappy with the entertainment on offer, they were at least happy with the result. Everton won the game by a convincing 4-0, with goals from Gabriel, Stevens, Temple and a Vernon penalty. A downside to the match, Vernon picked up an injury, ruling him out of the opening league game a week later.

The fixture list had remarkably arranged for Fulham, the team Everton defeated in the final game of the previous season to win the title, to visit Goodison for the season's opener. The Everton team:

West, Parker, Meagan, Gabriel, Labone, Kay, Scott, Stevens, Young, Temple, Morrissey.

Following the match, Harry Catterick said in assessment that recent recruits Kay and Scott, *"had their best games since joining the club. Kay controlled the game from the middle and Scott played with speed and craft."* Scott scored, Vernon's deputy, Temple added a second and a Fulham own goal completed the scoring, as Everton got off to the perfect start, running out comfortable 3-0 winners.

Thousands of Liverpudlians, eagerly anticipated the season's opening game, descended on the city's *Exchange Railway Station* on the morning of their match at Blackburn Rovers. British Rail had put on four special trains to take supporters to the match.

Just after midday a station announcement informed hundreds that the last special train due to depart was full. Dozens of fans, determined not to miss the match, clambered over barriers and climbed through train windows. Police had to prevent hundreds more following and those supporters, some of whom had the foresight to purchase train tickets in the days preceding, were left disappointed and had to miss the game.

Despite hundreds missing out, *"Liverpudlians made up about half of the crowd,"* the *Echo* reported. The Liverpool team for the match:

Lawrence, Byrne, Moran, Milne, Yeats, Stevenson, Callaghan, Hunt, St John, Melia, Thompson.

The massed ranks of Liverpudlians saw their team go into the break a goal down. A period of Liverpool pressure led to a 65th minute penalty kick. Taker Ronnie Moran's shot was saved by Blackburn 'keeper, Else, but Moran followed up to tap in. With 15 minutes remaining, Ian Callaghan, *"who always looked likely to score,"* said Horace Yates in the *Daily Post*, netted the winner. A great start too for Liverpool who now faced two home games in succession.

At Blackburn, Peter Thompson's debut was, said Yates, *"sensationally successful."* 50,000 fans were hopeful of a repeat performance in the winger's first home start against Nottingham Forest. Again, the Reds were a goal down at half time and again equalised, this time through an own goal, early in the second half. The equaliser was followed by the match winner. To the surprise of the majority in the stadium, it came not from a Liverpool player, but from the Forest centre forward and recent recruit from Everton, Frank Wignall.

Three days later, Liverpool had the opportunity to atone for their defeat at home to Blackpool in the concluding game of August. The local press concluded that Liverpool were outplayed by their opponents, who were two up at half time. Liverpool were *"pedestrian"* in the second half and supporters on the Kop slow handclapped. Many of them had given up and gone home before Melia pulled a goal back, but Liverpool *"never looked likely to equalise."*

Everton's second fixture, and their only other game in August, was against Manchester United at Old Trafford. Thousands of Evertonians saw their team get off to a flying start with a fit again Roy Vernon scoring after just eight minutes. The game from there quickly went downhill. United were 2-1 ahead by half time and in the second half scored another three to complete a 5-1 hiding.

August on Merseyside was not meant to be like this. Everton hammered in their first away game; Liverpool unacceptably losing their two opening home games. Both teams had mustered just two points leaving Everton in 15th and Liverpool 17th in the league table. Could September bring a change of fortune?

Not immediately for Liverpool. The return fixture with Forest resulted in a 0-0 draw and before the next fixture an under pressure Shankly told the press:

> "Don't think it is only the fans who are disappointed, nobody feels it more than the players. I hope the game against Chelsea will be the beginning of a scoring burst by our attack."

The attacking players responded with St John scoring two and Hunt one in a 3-1 victory.

Two days later, Liverpool repeated their early season habit of replicating results. Playing Wolverhampton Wanderers, the team recorded another 3-1 away win. The England manager, Walter Winterbottom, was present to see, *"Wolves smashed by a side without a weak link,* according to the *Echo:*

> *"Liverpool's English players, especially the goal scorers* (Hunt, two and Melia) *impressed the watching Winterbottom as the side showed sureness of touch, speed and strength on the ball."*

"Saturday will see the home bogy laid," wrote St John prior to the game with West Ham United; but what was it with Liverpool and replication. Not only was the result, a 2-1 defeat, an exact replica of previous home games, the sequence of goals was virtually identical. Goals from Martin Peters and Geoff Hurst gave West

Ham a two-goal half time lead before Roger Hunt pulled one back in the second period.

Surely disgruntled home supporters would not witness the same outcome in the return home fixture with Wolves two days later? Playing West Ham, St John picked up an injury and his place in the team was taken by reserve centre forward Alf Arrowsmith. In the first minute, with his first touch of the season, Arrowsmith scored the opening goal. His strike opened the floodgates. The *Echo* headline read, *"A Six-Goal Salvo Shattered the Anfield Hoodoo."* Hunt with another two, Callaghan and the first of the season for both Thompson and Milne completed the rout.

Liverpool's penultimate September fixture was an away game at Sheffield United. From the outset, United successfully deployed the offside trap constantly frustrating Liverpool's forwards. The Yorkshire club gradually took control of the game, before going on to record victory. An opportunity, not to be missed, the *Echo* could not resist a pun on United's win and nickname: *"Liverpool Find the Blades Much Sharper in Front of Goal,"* the sub-editor penned, referring to the fact that the Blades of Sheffield scored three goals without reply.

A 3-1 away win at Bolton got Everton's September off to a great start. The *Post* claimed that *"Everton outplayed, out-thought and outshone their opponents."* Young was *"lethal in front of goal, scoring two and setting up Temple for the other."* There was however a downside to the victory as Vernon, Jimmy Gabriel and left back Mick Meagan picked up injuries.

Catterick did not hesitate to find a replacement defender. He set off for Scotland the following day. By Monday, he had signed the Partick Thistle left back, Sandy Brown, for a fee of £30,000. Brown was immediately handed his debut for the home game against Burnley on Saturday 7th.

It was a chastening start for the Scotsman. Burnley were 4-1 in front by half time as *"Labone had his worst ever game,"* according to the *Post*. A much-improved start to the second half heralded an unlikely comeback; Hill, replacing the injured Vernon, scored his first goal for the club and a Scott strike made the score 4-3 with

25 minutes remaining. A storming finish however failed to produce an equaliser and Everton recorded their first home defeat in almost two years.

Everton's went on a decent run of results in their three remaining September fixtures. A 2-0 home win over Bolton and a 0-0 draw at Ipswich was followed by a 3-2 win against Sheffield Wednesday at Goodison. The latter match was sandwiched in between the most anticipated game for years by all those associated with Everton football club, the European Cup Preliminary Round tie with Italian champions Inter Milan.

Evertonians bemoaned the fact that they had been drawn against one of the best European teams and bookmakers' favourites. Manager Harry Catterick preferred to remain pragmatic about his team's chances. He told the *Echo*:

> "We are hopeful and quietly confident of progress despite the quality of the opposition. We've got to meet the best teams sooner or later if we are going to do well. We know they play a different type of football, more defensively minded, but we think we can overcome this."

The Italian side set up pretty much as Catterick expected, giving little away while carrying a substantial threat going forward. A Roy Vernon goal was controversially disallowed for offside, but thereafter the Blues rarely threatened the Inter goal. The Italian side were content on not conceding and the game finished 0-0. The *Echo's* Leslie Edwards wrote:

> "Everton showed nothing to encourage a belief that they could accomplish in Italy what they failed to achieve at Goodison. The Italians were happy with a draw they regarded as a victory."

45 years later Alex Young was still in awe of the Inter performance at Goodison. Writing in his autobiography, he stated:

> "We had never experienced anything remotely resembling Inter Milan's tactical approach and had been unsettled by their ability to counter-attack with such tremendous pace and skill."

Catterick's conclusion immediately after the game: *"Our forwards have a lot to learn from this type of football."* They didn't have long to learn, the second leg scheduled was set for the following week. The manager faced the huge problem of overcoming the formidable Italian defence, and had to attempt to do so with a weakened team. Out of the team were Gabriel and left back Meagan, whose replacement, the recently signed Sandy Brown, was ineligible to play.

On the day of the game, at the famous *San Siro* stadium in Milan, Catterick chose wing half Brian Harris to play out of position at left back and surprised all by selecting 18-year-old Liverpool born Colin Harvey for his debut.

The game was a rough, tough affair with heavy challenges by both sides and although on the back foot for much of the first half, Everton defended with discipline. The sides went in goalless at half time. However, one of Inter's overseas' stars, a member of Brazil's 1962 World Cup winning squad, Jair, broke the deadlock in the 48th minute to put the Italians one up. Facing a team fully adept at defending leads, Everton seldom looked like scoring and were beaten 1-0 on the night, the aggregate score too.

Catterick, though upset, was proud of his debutant Harvey and his team:

> *"Considering we played a makeshift eleven, to hold Inter Milan to a single goal in three hours of football is something Merseyside can be proud of. Everything I asked of the lads we did and the tactics we employed almost came off."*

Maybe Evertonians were right to curse the luck of the draw. Inter Milan went on to defeat Real Madrid 3-1 in the final in Vienna.

Everton had to lick their wounds and try to overcome the defeat as soon as possible. In four days' time, they faced another stern test, and one of the sternest of the season, Liverpool at Anfield. To add to the misery of their European Cup exit, Alex Young picked up an injury and would miss the derby match.

The surprise for supporters, before the start of the game, was the relatively poor league positions of both teams. Only separated by goal average, Liverpool were 10th and Everton 11th. It was not supposed to be like this!

Compared to the *"full-blooded game in Milan, this was like a Sunday School picnic,"* wrote Horace Yates in the *Post*. It was *"not a vicious game. Both teams were expert and willing to make the match a test of football rather than brute strength."* A local player grabbed the post-match headlines. Ian Callaghan scored twice within five minutes either side of half time to open up a two-goal Liverpool lead.

Everton exerted tremendous pressure on the Liverpool goal following Callaghan's second. Vernon pegged one back in the 75th minute, but, hard as they tried, Everton failed to find an equaliser. The win moved Liverpool up to eighth in the league; the Blues slipped to twelfth. As a consequence of European Cup participation, Everton had played just eight games to date, at least two fewer than all other teams.

The games in hand were to be played in October. Along with the pre-scheduled four league games, this provided a heavy schedule for Everton. Liverpool too were to play four scheduled games in October.

What a month, though! Everton beat Arsenal, Birmingham, Aston Villa, Sheffield United and Spurs in five of their six fixtures. Their only defeat coming, where else, London, 4-2 to West Ham. Derek Temple was the star player, scoring four of the twelve goals. Everton's defence, apart from the West Ham game, played exceptionally well too, conceding just two goals in the five victories.

Though playing only four games during the month, it couldn't have gone any better for Liverpool either. All four, against Aston Villa, Sheffield Wednesday, West Brom and Ipswich Town, ended in victory, with eleven scored and four conceded. Hunt and St John between them shared six of the goals.

At the end of October Liverpool headed Everton on goal average; both teams had played 14 and accumulated 19 points. Remarkably three other teams, Manchester

United, Spurs and Arsenal had played the same number of games and totalled the same number of points. All five clubs were two points behind leaders Sheffield United, with a game in hand. The Merseysiders, lying in fourth and fifth, were clearly much better positioned than at the end of September. It was supposed to be like this!

Next up on the first weekend of November, for Everton – Blackpool away; for Liverpool, the scourge of Anfield, Leicester City.

No surprise. Leicester, with the only goal of the game in the 29th minute, ended Liverpool's excellent run with a 1-0 victory. St John must have been reaching the point of boredom in his seemingly never ending praise of goalkeeper Banks. *"I have never seen a finer series of* saves," he wrote in his *Daily Post* column.

Everton *"failed to get a grip of their opponents, Blackpool,"* the *Echo* reported, relying on a Vernon goal to earn a point. The best player on the pitch, the report added, was Blackpool's Alan Ball who *"played with skill and refused to shirk a challenge."*

Everton and Liverpool supporters had, for a few weeks prior, received a lot of criticism in the press for their behaviour travelling to away matches. On several occasions, they had caused a lot of damage to train carriages, ripping seats and smashing lights. Concerns over behaviour were not only restricted to public transport. During October, criticism was levelled at home supporters, especially at Goodison. Missiles had been thrown at opposing goalkeepers. In Everton's game with Spurs a dart was found in the goalmouth at the Gwladys Street end of the ground.

Against Leicester, the Kop threw objects, such as apple cores and toilet rolls, at Gordon Banks. Not feeling threatened, the goalkeeper laughed off the incidents. However, a piece of wood, over a foot long, was aimed at Banks, making the situation much more serious. The football authorities and the press pressurised the clubs to act, especially Everton.

Back to the football and Liverpool recorded another away victory, 2-1 at Bolton. Callaghan scoring a second half winner. The victory did not prevent the *Echo* from criticising the performance.

> "The attack was not very impressive. They moved the ball slowly. They will need to be better in front of goal against better opposition."

The criticism continued after the next fixture.

> "Liverpool hardly looked like potential champions. They played stop-go football and their eventual victory was due to the gifts of their opponents."

The *Echo's* summary of the 2-0 win over Fulham the following week at Anfield. More importantly, the two St John goals moved the Reds into second place in the league.

Liverpool visited Old Trafford to face Manchester United in the penultimate game of November. A close encounter was expected with Liverpool holding a slender one point advantage over their opponents. Thanks to a Ron Yeats headed goal, Liverpool recorded a fantastic 1-0 victory.

The post-match headlines were all about the Liverpool captain and goal scorer, Yeats. A few minutes before his winning goal, Yeats went up field to contest a Liverpool corner. In doing so, he clashed with United goalkeeper Harry Gregg. The United player was eventually stretchered from the pitch with a broken collar bone. He was replaced in goal by centre forward, David Herd. The incident incensed United supporters and their feelings were further inflamed when the Liverpool centre half scored shortly afterwards.

Bill Shankly speaking to the press at the end of the drama announced: *"Ron Yeats is the greatest centre half in the world."* Clearly protecting his player, Shankly said Yeats had dealt excellently with the threat of quality players such as Denis Law and Bobby Charlton. The Liverpool manager noticeably didn't want the story to be about the centre half's unfortunate episode with Gregg.

In the final game of November, the *Post* claimed that Liverpool, playing Burnley in their next game: *"were shredding the home supporters' nerves."* Fans had to wait until the 70th minute for St John to open the scoring; a Roger Hunt penalty gave the Reds a 2-0 victory. Hunt had taken on penalty duty because of Ronnie Moran's two recent misses from the spot. The question; would he retain responsibility for the rest of the season? Even better news for Liverpudlians leaving the ground, their team were top of the league.

At the beginning of November. Everton struggled to maintain their excellent October form. The draw at Blackpool was followed by a 4-2 home defeat to Blackburn Rovers. Centre half Brian Labone was given a torrid time by Rovers' centre forward Fred Pickering, scorer of a hat-trick. The defeat was compounded by Tony Kay's second half dismissal, for which he would likely receive a suspension.

Away to Nottingham Forest, and with goalkeeper Andy Rankin making his debut, Everton appeared to be returning to form as they led 2-0 with a quarter of the game remaining. Labone however picked up a hamstring injury in the 70th minute and was switched to play centre forward. Full back Parker fell victim to the same injury ten minutes later. He was taken off, but did not return. Effectively trying to see out the game with nine men, Everton could not hold on. Forest scored two goals in the final five minutes to draw the game 2-2.

Everton's next fixture made news for football and non-football reasons when Stoke City arrived at Goodison on 23 November. In response to the hooliganism, the club erected four feet high, 20 feet deep barriers behind both goals. A minute's silence was held before the game in memory of US President John F. Kennedy, assassinated the previous day. During the silence, a spectator in the crowd, referring to the President of the Soviet Union, called out, *"Long Live Khrushchev,"* and was removed from the stadium.

For the opposition, the highly-respected veteran England international, 48-year-old Stanley Mathews, returned to the Stoke City team after a ten-week absence. He performed well enough to earn sustained applause from all sections of the ground at half time. Thanks to goals from Kay and Temple, Everton went on to win the game 2-0, and in so doing recorded their first victory of the month. The final fixture of November was 0-0 stalemate away to Wolves. The point left Everton in seventh place in the league.

Liverpool's excellent run of results had taken them to the top of table on goal average over Blackburn Rovers, though league remained very tight at the top. Although several positions separated the Merseyside clubs, in terms of points, only three divided them. Also in November, unable to force his way back into the side having been replaced by Tommy Lawrence, Liverpool reserve goalkeeper Jim Furnell submitted a transfer request, which the club accepted. He left for Arsenal a few days later.

It was London opposition for both clubs on the first Saturday of December, Everton at home to Chelsea and Liverpool away to Arsenal. Both teams led 1-0 (Vernon for Everton and Callaghan for Liverpool). Both teams were pegged back by late equalisers and had to settle for 1-1 draws. As you were in the league table.

Three days later, and devoid of goalkeeper West, Labone, Parker, Gabriel and Kay, it was Everton's turn to face Arsenal at Highbury. Catterick's makeshift side failed to cope with the rampant London club who raced into a four-goal half-time lead. Two further second half goals completed a 6-0 humiliation.

Everton remained in the capital for their next fixture at Fulham. The London hoodoo appeared to be broken as goals from Brian Harris and Alex Young gave Everton a two-goal lead on the hour. Fulham pulled a goal back, but in injury time the Londoners struck again to level the scores at 2-2. The hoodoo remained after all.

In their final pre-Christmas match, Everton hoped to gain revenge for the embarrassing 5-1 defeat earlier in the season at Manchester United. They showed few signs of doing so in the first half, failing to score, thankfully their opponents did likewise. However, in the second half *"It was inspired inspiring stuff from Everton,"* said the *Echo,* as the Blues ran in four goals without reply to win the match very convincingly. Harris, Stevens, Temple and Vernon all on target.

Everton supporters could celebrate Christmas in a happier frame of mind; could they celebrate the New Year similarly after their next two games, a double header against Leicester beginning at Filbert Street on Boxing Day. As Liverpool often found against this opponent, Everton too discovered Leicester 'keeper Banks in superlative form. They couldn't find a way past him and gave away two *"soft"* goals to lose the game 2-0.

A chance to atone the defeat came two days later at Goodison, the final match of 1963. Atone they did not. The *Echo* reported that: *"Everton's play was ponderous and predictable… Leicester got the ball forward quickly and were rewarded for their play."* They moved into a two-goal half time lead. They added another ten minutes into the second half and, *"when the gates opened with twenty minutes still to play, the Everton support poured out of the ground."* A guaranteed unhappy start to the New Year for Evertonians.

A top of the table clash with Blackburn Rovers followed Liverpool's draw at Arsenal. Captain Ron Yeats, playing his 100th game for the club, received a rapturous welcome from supporters. However, the *Post* reported, Liverpool showed *"a lack of bite up front as Blackburn's direct methods paid off."* Blackburn were two up before Roger Hunt pulled a goal back in the 85th minute. The Lancashire side's 2-1 win put them top of the league.

St John's 100th game came next at Blackpool. Liverpool effectively played most of the game with ten men, following an early injury to Jimmy Melia. He played the game out on the left wing for nuisance value only. Despite the numerical disadvantage, Liverpool proved to be the better team throughout. St John scored the only goal in a 1-0 victory. Unlike his team mate Ron Yeats, St John could celebrate his milestone match with victory.

A few dozen under 50,000 turned out for the Boxing Day game with Stoke. A St John goal was cancelled out by a Stoke equaliser leaving the teams level at half time. Cue the Roger Hunt show in the second half. In a 30-minute spell, the striker ran in an incredible four goals, as rampant Liverpool blew away their opponents. Sandwiched between Hunt's goals was one by Alf Arrowsmith to leave the final score 6-1. The Kop, in celebratory Christmas mood, belted out a rendition of the Beatles' *She Loves You* towards the end of the game.

The return fixture with Stoke two days later was postponed due to fog, leaving the First Division league table at the end of 1963 to read:

Blackburn played 26 points 34
Spurs played 24 points 33
Liverpool played 23 points 32

Having played 24, Everton were in tenth on 28 points, still in touch with the leaders, but Liverpool were in a much stronger position going into 1964.

Next up, as ever, on the first Saturday of the New Year, the FA Cup third round with Liverpool at home to Derby County and Everton away to Hull City.

* * * * *

On Saturday 3 August, just four days short of six years since the Quarry Men first played the venue, the Beatles assembled for their final show at the *Cavern*. It was perfectly reasonable to believe that the band had outgrown the club, said Bob Wooler interviewed by Spencer Leigh for his book *The Cavern*:

> "I can't blame Brian Epstein as he had seen how crowded the Cavern got and he had to think of The Beatles' safety."

Wooler said that Epstein promised owner Ray McFall that the Beatles would return to play the club. They never did. Tony Crane of support act, The Merseybeats, told Leigh:

> "We were on just before the Beatles and we were delighted with our reception as everybody was cheering and going mad. The Beatles all had

> *long faces and John Lennon was saying, 'We never should have come back.'"*

The Beatles had become too big for the *Cavern* and *NEMS Enterprises* had become too big for its offices in Whitechapel. Epstein chose to move the business to new premises situated nearby at 24 Moorfields. In *A Cellarful of Noise,* he described the change:

> "Moorfields is a charming little street near Exchange Station in Liverpool. We bought new furnishings, new people and a seething sense of urgency. A brand-new switchboard was installed with two telephonists. We took on office boys, a general manager, an accountant, and a press officer."

Six months later he transferred the whole enterprise to London. It had become too big for Moorfields.

Gradually, The Searchers first single *Sweets For My Sweet*, crept up the charts. On 8 August, it finally reached number one in the UK, were it remained for two weeks. The song was to herald a period of unprecedented chart success for Merseyside musicians. *Sweets For My Sweet* was shunted from the top of the charts by Billy J Kramer and the Dakotas next single, *Bad To Me*, yet another Lennon and McCartney composition.

The smash hit single left Kramer and his backing band on a high as the next *Mersey Beat Showcase* got underway on 12 August, the first of six consecutive dates in Llandudno, a north Wales seaside resort town. Only three Merseyside acts were on the bill, Kramer, the Beatles and another recent Epstein discovery named Tommy Quickly.

Born in the Liverpool district of Norris Green, 18-year-old Quickly, real surname Quigley, came to Epstein's attention during an audition in Widnes. He fronted a band called the Challengers, who Epstein didn't rate. He rated Quigley though and took him on as a solo artist. Holding high hopes for his latest find, Epstein changed the singer's name and handed him a Lennon and McCartney composition, *Tip Of My Tongue*, for his debut single. The song failed to chart.

Epstein was undeterred, writing in his autobiography a year or so later *"He is going to be a star."* Quickly went on several tours with his Mersey Beat co-performers including three with the Beatles and one each supporting Gerry and the Pacemakers and Billy J Kramer. He eventually released five singles, but all went the same way as the first, ending in disappointment. Despite the lack of success, he remained part of *NEMS Enterprises*, but must go down as a rare Epstein failure. He stayed on the books until finally leaving *NEMS* in 1966.

Disker, *Liverpool Echo's* music critic and Brian Epstein's press officer, Tony Barrow, travelled to Llandudno to interview the Mersey Beat performers, placing the emphasis on fame, its rewards and drawbacks. Interviewing Quickly first, the teenager told Disker he had no problems going about his daily life as very few people recognised him. Billy J Kramer told a different story. He said:

> *"When our first single was high in the charts I could walk into a shop and nobody would recognise me. But now with my picture in the paper and my TV appearances, I do get recognised more often, but I don't want to start dodging off without doing photos. I do wish I could just pop into the Cavern though."*

John Lennon also mentioned the downside of newly found fame and the response of the audiences at their shows, which he clearly found annoying.

> *"At theatre shows we can't even hear ourselves singing when half the audience screams through every number. It ruins it for the other half. We've pleaded with the screamers, but it hasn't made a scrap of difference."*

The Beatles, like it or not, were going to have to get accustomed to audience reactions at live performances. The present was the future.

If proof were needed that the Beatles were becoming anything other than a national phenomenon, then it arrived in the weeks after 1 August 1963, the date their next single *She Loves You* was released. The song went on to become the band's first to sell a million in the UK.

She Loves You entered the charts on 31 August, where it remained for 31 consecutive weeks. It reached number one on 14 September replacing *Bad To Me*, making it three unbroken number ones for Mersey Beat. *She Loves You* stayed at the top for a month, and though it lost the position for a short period to another Mersey Beat hit, it returned for a second spell at the top on 3 December.

The day after the release of *She Loves You*, yet another Lennon and McCartney number, *Hello Little Girl*, was released by the Fourmost. Although the song is credited to the duo, it is widely believed to be John Lennon's first ever composition. Though not achieving the heights of other Mersey Beat singles, *Hello Little Girl* managed to reach number nine in the charts at the end of October.

At the end of August, the Beatles entered yet another phase of TV work. In July, a Manchester-based BBC producer Don Haworth approached Brian Epstein with an idea for a documentary to be titled *The Mersey Sound*. Epstein agreed and granted Haworth exclusive access to the band for a specified time.

Shooting began of 27 August in Southport where the band were in performance and continued until the 30th. On the first day's shoot, the Beatles were filmed performing on stage without an audience. Haworth later edited in film of fans from concerts; songs were later dubbed onto the footage. The final day of shooting took place at Ringo Starr's Dingle home. The oft seen footage shows the drummer and George Harrison, chased by hundreds of teenagers, running to a car, jumping in and driving off. *The Mersey Sound* was broadcast on the BBC on 10 September.

Following a round of concerts and TV appearances, the Beatles went on separate holidays in Greece, France and the USA at the end of the September.

With the Beatles out of the country, Brian Epstein took the opportunity to fully launch the career of one of his new artists. Cilla Black, unsurprisingly singing a Lennon and McCartney composition, released *Love Of The Loved*, which the *Liverpool Echo's* Disker gave an excellent review. He labelled Black: *"The Red Headed Raven with the Jet-Black Voice."* After signing full time with Epstein, Black quit her job the same week and immediately began a nationwide tour with Gerry and the Pacemakers.

Epstein was ultimately disappointed with the song's reception. The highest chart position it reached was an unsatisfactory 30.

Another Mersey Beat non-Epstein band The Merseybeats, performers at the Beatles' final ever *Cavern* show, released a September single. It too was a disappointment. Recorded on the *Fontana* label, *It's Love That Really Counts*, failed to break the top twenty, achieving only a chart position of 24.

Sometime in October, the term *'Beatlemania'* became part of the national vocabulary. In *A Cellarful of Noise*, Brian Epstein wrote that he thought the phrase came about *"because of the group appearing at the Royal Command Performance."* This show, however, did not take place until 4 November and there is plenty of evidence to suggest that the term was already in use.

The Beatles' press officer Tony Barrow said its usage began after the band's appearance on the ITV show *Sunday Night at the London Palladium* on 13 October. The show pulled in an amazing 15 million viewers. The Beatles performed an unprecedented four songs, *From Me To You, She Loves You, I'll Get You* and *Twist And Shout*. Barrow said the TV performance garnered so much publicity it actually made his job easier. He said he rarely had to contact members of the press afterwards, as they began contacting him.

The first known printed reference of the term Beatlemania is credited to the *Daily Mail* a week later. On 21 October, the newspaper headlined an article: "*This Beatlemania.*" The *Daily Mirror* published the largest feature yet in a national newspaper dedicated to the rapidly growing sensation. On 2 November, a headline in the newspaper screamed *"BEATLEMANIA! It's happening everywhere... even in sedate Cheltenham."* The article went on: *"Everyone, everywhere is catching it."* On the same day, the *Daily Telegraph* ran a piece on *'Beatlemania'*, comparing Beatles' concerts to Hitler's Nuremberg rallies.

Discounting the Hamburg trips, the Beatles began their first European tour in Sweden on Friday 25 October playing the first of a week-long set of concerts. None sold out, although hundreds of fans did wait at venues to greet them. It was however, their return to England which made headline news.

The band flew into London Airport where a crowd of 10,000 waited in heavy rain to greet them. The Beatles initially thought the fans were there to see the Queen, but soon realised the extent of their popularity back home. The media were out in force too; newspaper journalists, dozens of photographers and a BBC camera crew were present to document their first major airport reception.

As Beatlemania swept the country in October, Gerry and the Pacemakers third single was making its way up the UK charts. The song, *You'll Never Walk Alone,* went on general release at the beginning of the month and charted at 22 for the first time on 10 October. A show tune, composed by the American pair Richard Rogers and Oscar Hammerstein, the song may have seemed somewhat unusual for a popular music band to record. Gerry Marsden in a *Liverpool Echo* interview in December, explained how it became part of the band's repertoire.

> *"I went to see the film Carousel one afternoon. We'd played the Cavern and it was raining, a horrible day, this would have been about 1959. I was particularly impressed by one song in the show and went to seek out the sheet music."*

Having done so, he persuaded his fellow band members to perform the song live. The Pacemakers played it to the packed audience at the 1960 *Liverpool Stadium* show headlined by Gene Vincent, and from there on performed it at almost every one of their subsequent concerts.

At the recording, Marsden reported that although:

> "George Martin liked the song, he felt it slow-paced... to compensate, he brilliantly added a string section. It was the most worrying period of our lives waiting for it to make the grade. Most of us at the time thought it was a horrible mistake."

A horrible mistake it was not. Three weeks after release on 6 November, *You'll Never Walk Alone* made number one overtaking the Beatles' *She Loves You* in the process. There it remained before the same Beatles song leapfrogged it on 3 December.

At Anfield, the tradition at the time was to play the top ten chart songs in reverse order, so playing over the PA system as the teams ran out, was the song standing at number one. On Saturday 30 November Liverpool defeated Burnley 2-0 at Anfield to move to the top of the First Division league table for the first time in over a decade. Amazingly, this was the final weekend that *You'll Never Walk Alone* spent at number one in the UK charts.

In taking *You'll Never Walk Alone* to number one, Gerry and the Pacemakers became history makers. They were the first artists to have their first three singles all reach the top. *You'll Never Walk Alone* was the third of the singles after *How Do You Do It* and *I Like It*.

On 29 October 1963, Merseyside lost one of its original successful stars. Michael Holliday died of a suspected drug overdose in Croydon General Hospital, Surrey. He is buried in Priory Road Cemetery, Anfield.

The Beatles were not the headline act at the *Royal Command Performance* on 4 November. Appearing in front of the Queen, they were only seventh on the 19-act bill, but they were to become headline stealers. They began playing their opening song, *From Me To You,* before the curtains opened and when they came into view some younger audience members began screaming. They then performed *She Loves You,* followed by *Till There Was You.*

When the applause died down after the third song, John Lennon delivered his now famous announcement, which guaranteed the headlines in all the next morning's newspapers. He cheekily told the audience:

> "For our last number, I'd like to ask your help. The people in the cheaper seats clap your hands. And the rest of you, if you'd just rattle your jewellery. We'd like to sing a song called Twist And Shout."

Although their appearance on the *Command Performance* was a triumph, the Beatles declined all subsequent invitations to return to the show. Lennon in *Anthology* stated:

> "We were asked discreetly to do it every year after that, but we always said, 'Stuff it.' So, every year there was a story in the newspapers: 'Why no Beatles for the Queen?'"

A delighted Epstein said of the band's performance and the reaction to it:

> "London was brought to a standstill by the screaming youth of the south of England. The Royal Family, the wealthy and the great were captivated by the naturalness of the four young men and we were proud of it."

Epstein later recalled that demand for Beatles' concert tickets was overwhelming. He wrote:

> "The Beatle Queue became a feature of British life. With transistors and blankets, hot water bottles and with or without their parents blessing, the young people of provincial England braved every weather hazard for a small slip of paper which would permit them to hear their idols."

In Liverpool, the *Daily Post* chose to examine the snowballing phenomenon. Analysing young women's reactions to the Beatles, its Women's Editor, Diana Poulson, first interviewed an unnamed psychologist about the seemingly "*hysterical*" reaction to the group. He said:

> "There is a sexual element to it. Young people today are bored to death. They consider their lives boring and unexciting. This crazy, wild excitement is a way of rebelling against it. They like to go wild. It's similar to a football crowd I suppose."

Poulson then took a trip to the *Cavern* to interview teenagers attending a lunchtime session. She put the psychologist's analysis to a few of them. 16-year-old Edna Lewis of Speke responded:

> "There is nothing sexual. It's just that the noise and the movement picks you up and you go with it. We're not in 'love' with the Beatles."

Anne Lotus, 15, of Huyton said:

> "When they play, we cheer. It's just audience participation. People have been interested in listening to music for hundreds of years. Even in Elizabethan England people liked listening to the lute, I suppose."

Poulson's conclusion; it was all a temporary phenomenon and that *"it will all soon pass."*

It would not pass soon anywhere in the UK. Queues began to form the night before a Beatles' concert at the *Liverpool Empire*. Supported by Billy J Kramer, The Fourmost and Cilla Black, in a show compered by Rolf Harris, when the box-office opened there was an estimated 10,000 waiting to buy the 5,000 tickets on sale for the two-scheduled 22 December shows.

Two days earlier, and precisely eight months on from the release of their debut album, the Beatles released their follow-up, *With The Beatles*. There were advanced orders of 300,000, and it quickly sold more than half a million copies, taking it straight to the top of the album charts.

A week later the Beatles released their next single, *I Want To Hold Your Hand*. It too was a phenomenal smash hit, with pre-orders of more than a million. A week after release it was number one displacing *She Loves You*. The Beatles now stood at one and two in both the UK album and singles' charts.

More significantly, *I Want To Hold Your Hand* was released in the USA and proved an instant hit there too. The song paved the way for their subsequent visit to the States. The Beatles had come to the attention of influential US TV host Ed Sullivan. By a remarkable coincidence, he was at London Airport when the group returned from their Swedish tour and was taken aback by the reception they received.

Sullivan contacted Brian Epstein with a view to having the band appear on his show. The two men met in New York in December and agreed to the Beatles performing in Sullivan's New York TV studio on Sunday 9 February 1964 and again one week later in a Miami hotel.

In December. all Brian Epstein's artists were engaged in UK tours. Playing to packed theatres and cinemas. One show, titled *The Billy J Kramer Pop Parade*, featuring The Fourmost and chief support act Johnnie Kid and the Pirates, performed in venues from Bolton to Brighton. Prior to Christmas, Gerry and the Pacemakers, supported by Cilla Black and The Searchers, completed a tour of Scotland.

Beginning on 27 December and running on until the 11 January 1964, the Beatles ended 1963 and began the new year, playing a series of Christmas shows. A mixture of music and short comic sketches, the show took place at the *Astoria Cinema* in Finsbury Park, London. Tickets went on sale on 21 October 1963, and by 16 November all 100,000 had sold out.

In the final music chart of 1963, the Beatles held the first and second positions, with other Mersey Beat bands also very prominent. Singles by Billy J Kramer and the Dakotas (*I'll Keep You Satisfied*), The Searchers (*Sugar And Spice*) and The Swinging Blue Jeans (*Hippy Hippy Shake*) had all achieved respectable chart positions. The latter two songs were in fact still climbing.

* *

The second half of 1963 had then been a remarkable period for Merseyside music. The Beatles had conquered the UK creating *Beatlemania* and were preparing for a trip to the USA. Other Merseyside artists had achieved stunning chart success too.

On the football front, Liverpool were third in the First Division with Everton not far off their neighbours.

Could the musicians and the football teams of 1963, maintain the high standards they set themselves in 1964?

10. Needles and Pins: January - July 1964

Liverpool and Everton (though a few points in arrears) were serious contenders for the First Division title. Looking ahead to the closing fixtures of the season, Liverpool centre half Ron Yeats writing in the *Echo*, and Everton forward Roy Vernon in his *Daily Post* column agreed that the Easter weekend of three games in four days would be crucial to hopes of winning the league title.

Before the resumption of the league programme it was, as ever, the FA Cup to kick off the new year. Liverpudlians and Evertonians were more than hopeful of good runs in this season's competition, so much so that there was a great deal of talk about the possibility of an all Merseyside cup final, should the competition's draw prove sympathetic. The third round draw offered decent chances to progress as both clubs faced lower league opposition; Second Division Derby County for Liverpool at Anfield and Third Division Hull City away from home for Everton.

From Anfield, the *Echo* used a chant from the Kop for its post-match headline. Supporters sang the recent Beatles number one, *She Loves You*, which the *Echo* turned into "*Arrowsmith: They Love Him Yea! Yea! Yea!*" (without the final H on yea). This was in recognition of centre forward's Alf Arrowsmith scoring an incredible four goals in a very comfortable 5-0 win.

Alternatively, Everton's tie proved problematical. The team were a goal down inside ten minutes and struggled to break down opponents Hull. Alex Scott, however, managed to equalise early in the second half, which earned his side *"a hardly deserved"* replay, the *Echo* reported. The Blues also struggled in the replay. They went a goal behind early on again and were still so with 20 minutes remaining. Finally showing some form, they managed to get on top and went on to win the game 2-1.

Hopes for a Merseyside FA Cup success were elevated with the news that Liverpool's bogy team and last season's losing finalists, Leicester City, had been defeated 3-2 at home to Leyton Orient (when heard over the PA system at Anfield, a loud cheer erupted) and following a replay, pre-tournament favourites Tottenham Hotspur were knocked out by London rivals Chelsea.

In fourth round games at the end of January, Liverpool were again drawn at home, on this occasion to Third Division Port Vale, but were surprisingly held to a 0-0 draw. Everton faced a tough tie away to Second Division league leaders, Leeds United, a team containing one of their ex-players and supporters' favourite, Bobby Collins. They too were held to a draw,
1-1.

Liverpool scored an early goal in their replay to lead at Port Vale. Goalkeeper Tommy Lawrence *"was unemployed for more than an hour,"* stated the *Echo*. Vale however rallied and equalised to take the contest into extra time. Liverpool's superior fitness eventually told and a Peter Thompson goal earned the Reds a hard fought 2-1 victory.

Everton's replay was also hard fought, but for different reasons. The referee was very much in the action having to book several players as tough tackling and arguing dominated much of the game. On the football side, Everton were the better team. Jimmy Gabriel gave the Blues a goal lead early on and Vernon scored the second and final goal with 20 minutes remaining. No easy matter, but the Merseyside clubs had, after much struggle, progressed to the fifth round.

In their first league match in January 1964, Liverpool found themselves a goal down at half time *"to a far superior Chelsea team."* The Kop were very subdued, offering little encouragement until a Roger Hunt equaliser in the 69th minute brought them to life. The team, and Alf Arrowsmith in particular, responded to the crowd's urgings. The centre forward snatched an 84th minute winner.

Another London team the following week, West Ham away and Liverpool were again a goal down at half time. Despite *"hammering away at the West Ham goal"* the Reds failed to pull back the deficit. West Ham 'keeper Standen was *"outstanding"* and on the two occasions they did manage to beat him, the goal post came to his rescue.

For Everton's January league games, manager Harry Catterick, by dropping star players Roy Vernon and Alex Young, shocked supporters before the first at Burnley. He told the press:

> *"I am sure that players of their ability will appreciate that they are out of form at the present and a couple of games in the reserves will help them recover their form."*

As half time approached, it was looking like poor judgement on the manager's behalf; Everton trailed Burnley 2-0. Alex Scott pulled a goal back from the penalty spot before the break and goals from Gabriel and Morrissey in *"a superb second half,"* gave Everton a 3-2 victory. Was Catterick's dramatic action justified?

Back at Goodison for the game against Ipswich, supporters didn't think so. *"We want Young,"* they chanted as their team toiled and trailed by a goal to nil. Young however was playing elsewhere in the reserves. It took yet another Scott penalty to rescue a point and save Catterick from the total wrath of Evertonians.

The second derby match was due on the second Saturday of February, but before the fixture both teams faced Sheffield opposition. Against Sheffield United, the *Echo* selected Liverpool wing half Willie Stevenson as its man of the match:

> *"He varies his production of the ball admirably. He can knock a short telling pass or punch a long one down the centre with the artistry of a top-class player."*

Liverpool, totally dominated their opponents. St John netted a hat trick, Hunt scored two and Peter Thompson another, as the Reds battered United 6-1. A supporter leaving the ground was heard to grumble that the goals had *"come a week early; they should have saved some for next week's game at Goodison."*

Everton faced United's neighbours Wednesday at Hillsborough on the same afternoon. The team, *"showed a toughness missing in recent games."* Jimmy Gabriel, playing centre forward in place of Young, scored the opening goal in the first half of *"a game they totally controlled."* The second half continued in the same fashion as Scott and a recalled Vernon each bagged a goal to give the Blues a convincing 3-0 victory.

On the eve of the derby match the league table read:

>Spurs played 28 points 39
>Liverpool 26 – 36
>Blackburn 29 – 35
>Everton 28 – 33 (8th position)

In such a position, a derby day defeat could prove fatal to Everton's championship hopes. In his pre-match report, *Echo* football correspondent Leslie Edwards wrote:

>*"Rarely in the long history of derby matches have the two teams had greater incentive to win; never before has the rivalry been so intense. It is likely to be a close fought match and a hard one. The Gabriel versus Yeats duel is likely to be the key to the game."*

An all ticket sell-out crowd of 66,000 packed into Goodison. Everton had the better of the opening exchanges and took an early lead through a deflected Vernon effort which deceived 'keeper Lawrence. Liverpool failed to respond and shortly before the half hour, Gabriel doubled the lead. The pressure was now on Liverpool to respond, but they carried little threat until the 80th minute when St John scored to give supporters some hope of a comeback. Those hopes were quickly dashed when Vernon scored his second on 88 minutes to restore Everton's two goal advantage and an eventual 3-1 Everton victory.

Leslie Edwards, the following Monday, reported:

"No argument about this derby; it was palpably Everton from start to finish. They surprised their own fans and shocked Liverpool's by the ease with which they sailed through 90 minutes of tough, thrilling football."

The win put Everton firmly back in the title race. The league, however, was on hold in mid-February with the return of the FA Cup and tough ties awaited both. Having recently replaced Leeds in that position, Everton were away to Second Division leaders Sunderland. Liverpool faced a very difficult away trip to Arsenal.

At Highbury, Arsenal were on top early on. Tommy Lawrence was forced into making some excellent early saves. Then in the 15th minute the Reds took the lead with their first meaningful attack of the game. A Milne cross was headed in at the far post by St John. Seven minutes before half time. Arsenal centre forward Joe Baker and Ron Yeats tussled for the ball and went down together. Both rose and exchanged punches. The referee intervened, broke them up and promptly dismissed both.

Arsenal put Liverpool under intense second half pressure, but the defence held out well. In injury time, a Liverpool break led to a penalty when ex-Reds' keeper Furnell brought down Arrowsmith. The 'keeper however redeemed himself by saving Hunt's spot kick. It mattered little though as the final whistle blew moments later to give Liverpool a 1-0 victory putting the side through to the sixth round.

Over at Roker Park, Everton's goalkeeper Gordon West endured a nightmare start. He was beaten by a weak shot for Sunderland's opening goal and shortly after he deigned to drop a corner kick to a grateful Sunderland player and Everton were two down. Sunderland scored a third shortly after half time all but ending the tie. Vernon scored a late goal, but it was little consolation and Everton yet again exited the cup far too early.

Liverpool were rewarded with a decent sixth round draw at home to Second Division Swansea City and talk of winning the *'double'* emanated from some supporters

Liverpool's next league encounter was away to lowly placed Aston Villa. In front of just 13,748 spectators, Liverpool only managed a relatively disappointing 2-2 draw. Villa's neighbours, Birmingham City, were up next at Anfield. The Reds took a first half lead through Moran, but City equalised early in the second half. A draw was looking likely until St John struck a 75th minute winner.

Everton meanwhile played three league games before Liverpool's sixth round cup tie, starting at home to Birmingham. The Blues showed improved form winning the game 3-0. The win was though followed by a disappointing 0-0 draw against a team recently thrashed 6-1 by Liverpool, Sheffield United.

Everton's next fixture clashed with Liverpool's cup tie, so the game against Aston Villa at Goodison was switched to the final Friday evening of February. The Blues were a goal down inside seven minutes, but went on to play *"some exceptional football"* and midway through the second half led by four goals to one. A late Villa goal resulted in a 4-2 Everton victory. The win leapfrogged Everton to the top of the table leading their neighbours by a point. Liverpool did though have the significant consolation of having played three games fewer.

1964 was a leap year, so the scheduled date for Liverpool's much anticipated FA Cup sixth round tie at Anfield was 29 February. Underway, most inside the ground, were shocked to see Swansea take a surprise 35th minute lead against the run of play. The Welsh club's 15,000 travelling fans celebrated wildly. Unbelievably they were celebrating even more just four minutes later when their team doubled the lead.

A shocked Liverpool upped their game in the second half; a 63rd minute Peter Thompson goal restored hope. Liverpool strove desperately for the equaliser. With ten minutes to play they were handed a fantastic opportunity to do so when Ian Callaghan was upended in the area. The referee pointed to the penalty spot. Who would take the kick?

Hunt, having missed in the last round at Arsenal, clearly spurned the opportunity. The Kop, aware of the on-field indecision, chanted *"Moran! Moran! Moran!* A short discussion between the Liverpool full back and captain Yeats followed and

Moran stepped forward. He ran up, gave the ball an almighty thump, but it flew wide of the goalkeeper's right hand post. Liverpool failed to pull back the deficit and, for the second consecutive season had, unbelievably, missed another wonderful opportunity to win the cup for the first ever time.

Asked afterwards, first on the penalty indecision, Shankly told reporters that Moran was designated penalty taker and the players knew he had responsibility. On the match overall, he commented:

> *"Unbelievable. Unbelievable. I have never seen the boys play better. Their goalkeeper was magnificent. We could have scored 14 and yet we are out of the cup."*

Swansea went on to play and lose the semi-final to another Second Division side, Preston North End, who in turn went on to play and lose the final 3-2 to a last-minute West Ham United goal.

Liverpool had now to concentrate all thoughts and efforts on winning the league. They had played fewer games than all challengers so, with a total of seven games to play, faced a busy month of March. Everton too were in the hunt. They were a point clear of their Merseyside rivals, but had played three games more. They faced a great challenge to retain the title.

* *

When it came to broadcasting popular music, the BBC chose to up the ante, adding a new programme to its output. On 1 January 1964, *Top of the Pops*, presented by DJ Jimmy Saville, was opened by the Rolling Stones, singing yet another Lennon and McCartney composition, *I Wanna Be Your Man*. Dusty Springfield, The Dave Clark Five and The Hollies appeared before the first Mersey Beat band The Swinging Blue Jeans performed their hit single, *Hippy Hippy Shake*. Although not making a personal appearance, the Beatles closed the show with the UK's number one song, *I Want To Hold Your Hand*.

The Beatles didn't make a personal appearance on *Top of the Pops* as they were still performing their London *Christmas Show*. When the run eventually ended, the band were ready to go international. The USA awaited in February, but before that it was France. On 14 January, they flew to Paris to perform 18 days of concerts at the capital's *Olympia Theatre*. Performing on a nine-act bill, and playing two or sometimes three sets a day, they were booked to close the show.

Following the Beatles first performance on the 16th, the *Liverpool Echo* gave its readers an insight into the thoughts of the French press on the young Liverpudlians now taking their capital by storm. *Le Parisienne Libre* commented:

> *"Their most revolutionary aspect is their hairstyle. What headgear! But on the musical or stage style, it is granddaddy rock."*

France Soir was more complimentary, stating:

> *"These 20-year-olds win over by their extraordinary rhythm. The four young men are gay, relaxed, sometimes funny and are good musicians and good singers."*

While performing in Paris, after spending five weeks at number one, *I Want To Hold Your Hand* was knocked off the top of the UK charts. The news was, however, more than compensated by reports coming from the USA, the single had reached number one in the Billboard Hot 100 chart. Hearing the news when they returned to their hotel, Paul McCartney couldn't contain his excitement. In *Anthology*, he said:

> *"A telegram came through to Brian from Capitol Records of America. He came running in to the room saying, 'Hey, look. You are number one in America!' Well, I can't describe our response. We all tried to climb onto Big Mal Evans' back to go around the hotel suite: 'Wey-hey!' And that was it, we didn't come down for a week."*

Back in the UK, the hits kept coming for Merseyside artists. At the end of January, The Searchers reached number one for the first time with their rendition of

Needles And Pins, a song part-composed in the USA by Sonny Bono. John McNally of the group said that the band heard a British singer, Cliff Bennett, perform the song while they were both resident in Hamburg the previous year. The Searchers took the song to *Pye Records* who agreed to record and release it.

In February, there were so many Merseyside acts in the singles' charts they kept each other from reaching the top. In one week alone in the middle of the month, The Searchers were at number one while the top ten included numbers by the Beatles, Gerry and the Pacemakers, The Merseybeats, The Swinging Blue Jeans and Cilla Black, an incredible accomplishment. While the battle of the Merseyside acts was taking place in the UK charts, the Beatles departed for the USA. The only British based journalist accompanying the band was the *Liverpool Echo's* George Harrison (another one).

Touching down at New York's John F Kennedy Airport on 7 February, the band received a tumultuous welcome. More than 5,000 fans, mostly young girls, were crowded onto the upper balcony of the airport's arrivals' building, waving placards and banners. A couple of hundred reporters, photographers and personnel from radio and television clamoured for the band's attention.

The Beatles faced the press in their hotel, the *Plaza,* the following morning. They then left for their now famous walk and photo session in Central Park, where their every move was shadowed by around 400 female fans. In the afternoon, they were escorted to *CBS* studios on Broadway for the first of several rehearsals for their debut appearance on *The Ed Sullivan Show*. During the journey, their cars were charged by fans and mounted police were forced to intervene to keep order.

On 9 February, shortly after 8.00 pm Eastern Standard Time, Ed Sullivan announced *"Ladies and gentlemen...the Beatles!"* After a few seconds of rapturous cheering, the band belted out *All My Lovin'*. This was followed by the mid-tempo *Till There Was You*. The songs received enthusiastic responses, but nothing which could be described as uninhibited.

The next number though was met with a much more excited vocal response. The Beatles struck up *She Loves You* and the studio went wild. After a break, they returned to play *I Saw Her Standing There* and *I Want To Hold Your Hand*. The audience reacted in much the same way as they did to *She Loves You*.

When the viewing data came in, the figures revealed that the Beatles' live performance had broken American TV audience figures. The show itself was witnessed by just 728 people in the studio, but on TV by an estimated 73 million in more than 23 million US homes. This figure comfortably smashed the record for television viewing figures in the States.

The following day the Beatles were booked to perform at the *Washington Coliseum*. They were due to fly to the American capital, but were forced to travel by rail, as an East Coast snowstorm caused all flights to be cancelled. Arriving at Washington's Union Station the band were greeted by 2,000 fans who braved the eight inches of snow.

The *Coliseum* was a boxing arena, so the band performed 'in the round' before a surrounding audience numbering over 8,000. Also booked to perform were The Chiffons and Tommy Roe. The Chiffons, however, were unable to make it due to the snowstorm and they were substituted by two acts, Jay & The Americans and The Righteous Brothers. During their twelve-number set, many fans pelted the band with jelly beans after a New York newspaper had reported the Beatles discussing their liking for them. An act that seriously annoyed all four.

After the show, the entourage attended a reception at the British Embassy where the four band members issued raffle prizes to benefit the *National Association for the Prevention of Cruelty to Children*. They then mingled with the invited guests. However, they left in disgust after one of the guests cut off a lock of Ringo Starr's hair. The four walked out telling Brian Epstein never to subject them to such an occasion again.

The following day, the Beatles returned to New York City for two concerts at Carnegie Hall. Tickets went on sale on 27 January and were sold out in less than 24 hours. 2,900 people saw each of the two shows.

The Beatles then travelled to Miami for the second Ed Sullivan Show, due to be broadcast from the *Deauville Hotel* on Miami Beach. The warm Florida weather was in total contrast to New York and Washington. Recalling their time at the hotel, Paul McCartney commented in *Anthology*:

> "We had never been anywhere where there were palm trees. We had a great time down there. We'd look down on the beach where the fans would write 'I love John' in the sand, so big we could read it from our rooms."

Sunday the 16th, Sullivan introduced them again and began by recognising the importance of the previous week's show:

> "And now, this has happened again. Last Sunday, on our show in New York, the Beatles played to the greatest TV audience that's ever been assembled in the history of American TV...Ladies and gentlemen, here are four of the nicest youngsters we've ever had on our stage ... the Beatles! Bring 'em on!"

They followed pretty much the same format as the first show, three songs at the start and, after a short break, another three at the end. At the conclusion, Sullivan brought them over and told them that Richard Rodgers, the co-composer of *You'll Never Walk Alone*, had contacted Sullivan to say that he was *"one of their most rabid fans."*

Liverpool Echo journalist George Harrison interviewed Sullivan at the end of the Miami show. He began by asking: *Why did you take on the Beatles?*

> "They are the best harmony combination I have ever heard. They are not rock 'n' roll. Their style is essentially their own and they seem to be improving all the time. They will stay at the top long after Beatlemania has run its course. The Beatles are real professionals. That's about the highest compliment that anyone in show business can pay another."

Though some newspapers and magazines did, much of the US press did not agree with Sullivan. In major newspapers and magazines, the Beatles performances on the Sullivan show and in concert earned mixed responses. On the negative side:

The Washington Post:

> "Just thinking about the Beatles seems to induce mental disturbance. They have a commonplace, rather dull act that hardly seems to merit mentioning, yet people hereabouts have mentioned scarcely anything else for a couple of days."

The Boston Globe

> "They sound like a group of disorganized amateurs whose voices seem to be fighting each other rather than blending."

The Chicago Tribune

> "We think the three B's of music — Bach, Beethoven and Brahms — have nothing really to fear from the Beatles."

...and on the positive side:

The New York Times

> "In nine days, the Beatles made a deep impression on the American subculture. They can look back with gratification on the dominance of the Liverpool sound on those American radio stations. They can also look back at the staggering sky-rocketing sales of their records."

Newsweek

> "They shout, they stomp, they jump for joy and the audience responds in a way that makes the old-time revival meeting look like a wake.

Two days after their Ed Sullivan appearance, the Beatles visited the training camp of boxer Cassius Clay - later known as Muhammad Ali - who was preparing for his 25 February fight against heavyweight world champion, Sonny Liston. At the gathering, which took place at Miami's Fifth Street gym, the five got into the boxing ring where they mockingly sparred and joked.

The Beatles, preparing to depart Miami, via New York, for England on 21 February, where, for the final time on the tour, they were interviewed by the *Echo's* George Harrison. He first asked Ringo Starr what he made of it all.

> *"It is like coming to the end of a holiday, but when you have to go, you have to go. This American tour has been the greatest thing in my life."*

Answered by McCartney, he put his final question to the band: *"When will you break up?"*

> *"As soon as we find out that this game of being the Beatles isn't fun anymore, we shall pack up and quit"*

Eric Heffer, a Labour Party, Liverpool City Councillor, wrote in February to the Lord Mayor asking if he would consider the city holding a civic reception for the Beatles. Heffer wrote, saying: *"the band are in their own way, wonderful ambassadors for the city."* The Mayor liked the idea and put the suggestion to Brian Epstein, who replied saying he too thought the idea excellent and would forward a proposed date in the near future.

* *

Into the closing months of the football season, Liverpool had to quickly re-assemble and get over their shock cup defeat at the hands of Swansea. Playing their next league game at Hillsborough, Liverpool appeared to be nursing a hangover from the tie. 2-0 down early in the second half, they finally managed to rouse themselves and clawed their way back into the game, thanks to a 70th minute St John goal. Defeat, though appearing inevitable, was avoided, thanks to a last-minute Willie Stevenson equaliser.

The first half performance at home to Ipswich in the succeeding fixture was as laboured as the previous one at Wednesday, but supporters were relieved to see another St John goal give the Reds a half time lead. What a contrast in the second half. Liverpool ran riot, running in goal after goal to record a thumping 6-0 victory. Liverpool were back!

Not likely. A very disappointing display at Fulham followed. The *Daily Post* believed that Liverpool were *"too defensively minded"* on a muddy Craven Cottage pitch. They fell behind midway through the second half and did not show the wherewithal to find an equaliser and went on to lose the game 1-0.

On the day Liverpool faced Ipswich, Everton played league leaders Spurs at White Hart Lane with Alex Young restored to the side. In his post-match *Echo* report on the possible season defining match for the Blues, Horace Yates wrote:

> *"The Catterick conquerors played the game with an artistry that commanded the utmost admiration. Vernon is storming back to peak splendour, while Young is livelier and more diligent."*

The reason for the flattering assessment, a very impressive 4-2 victory. Everton were a goal down early but, thanks to goals from Young and Stevens, went in at half time 2-1 up. Spurs equalised on the hour, but the Blues did not panic and from there on played the last third of the game impressively. Two Vernon goals gave them a much-deserved win.

A few days later Harry Catterick shocked English football by placing a bid for Blackburn Rovers' centre forward Fred Pickering, scorer of a hat trick at Goodison earlier in the season. Rovers accepted the whopping British transfer record offer of £85,000. Pickering was *"an old-fashioned bustling centre forward."* But, whose place would he take?

Evertonians reacted to Pickering's arrival with bemusement and anger. They viewed him as a direct threat to terrace hero Alex Young. Some supporters told the local press they would show their dissent and not attend the next home match. Catterick fully understood this reaction but, despite the four goals at Spurs, felt he needed to add firepower to his side.

Selected ahead of Young, Pickering went straight into the team for the next game against Nottingham Forest at Goodison Park. How would he fare? The centre forward totally dominated the Forest defence and incredibly scored a hat trick in his team's 6-1 rout of the opposition. Pickering was applauded from the pitch by supporters and, somewhat unusually, by his new team mates. Catterick's new signing had, for now, silenced the dissenters.

The table following's Everton victory and Liverpool's loss at Fulham on the same day read:

> Spurs played 33 points 44
> Everton 34 – 44
> Blackburn 35 – 43
> Liverpool 32 – 42

Extremely tight, but crucially for Liverpool, they still held games in hand. Before those games, Liverpool and Everton both received news they didn't want to hear. Ron Yeats, for his dismissal at Arsenal, and Roy Vernon, for accumulation of bookings, had both received 14 day suspensions. The two players had, ironically, written at the start of the year how important the upcoming Easter fixtures would be and they were now both suspended for a portion of those games.

Before Easter, Liverpool's next game at Anfield, switched to a Friday evening owing to the Grand National, was a seemingly decent fixture against relegation threatened Bolton Wanderers. With Chris Lawler deputising for Yeats, a comfortable evening it turned out to be. First half goals from Arrowsmith and St John resulted in a 2-0 victory. Liverpool, for at least 18 hours or so, were top of the table.

The next day, Everton had to be at their strongest to overcome a determined third placed Blackburn Rovers, perhaps smarting from the recent loss of their centre forward. Blackburn took a deserved lead in the first half, but Everton showed great resilience to fight back. Scott and Vernon netted a second half goal each to give Everton a 2-1 victory. The *Echo* praised Tony Kay stating that he *"stood head and shoulders above all others on the field."*

Everton supporters left the ground to the surprising news that Spurs had been beaten 3-2 at home by Manchester United, so combined with the win over Blackburn they were now, unlikely as it may have appeared prior to kick-off, back on top of the First Division, having demoted Liverpool to second place in the process.

The packed Easter period of fixtures were on the horizon and what a set for Liverpool; two games with Spurs, the first away on Good Friday 28 March with the return at Anfield on Easter Monday. Sandwiched between was another away match against non-other than bogy team Leicester City, victors of the past five meetings between the clubs.

Everton's games by comparison appeared more straightforward. Two games with West Bromwich Albion, the first at Goodison on Good Friday, the second not until the Tuesday evening, after the Spurs v Liverpool game. In between, Everton's Saturday fixture was at home to Blackpool.

Yeats and Vernon agreed at the beginning of the year that the Easter programme would be crucial in determining the destination of the title. Would they be proved right?

Good Friday arrived and 57,000 supporters crammed into Anfield for the Liverpool v Spurs encounter. Liverpool, much the better side, began positively. The defence comfortably kept Spurs at bay while the attack always looked threatening. It was no surprise therefore when Roger Hunt netted in the 28th minute to send the Reds into a half time lead.

The second half continued in the same vein. St John and Thompson *"tormented the Spurs defence,"* Hunt scored two further goals in three minutes to complete his hat trick. His third triggered of a burst of Beatles' songs among the travelling support. A late Spurs strike only changed the score line not the result; Liverpool winning by a fully deserved 3-1.

Liverpudlians were further cheered with the news from Goodison that Everton had dropped a point in a 1-1 draw with West Brom. *"Everton laboured throughout"* the *Echo* reported, *"...looking a shadow of the team which beat Spurs."* Colin Harvey replaced the suspended Vernon but he failed to inspire. His side fell behind in the first half and did not look like scoring. The Blues were thankful to a late own goal, the source of their point.

Catterick had to respond in the home game with Blackpool. He did so, recalling Young to replace Harvey. His team responded too and had the game all but won inside 18 minutes. Pickering, who had a poor game the day prior, atoned for his display by scoring two goals in the space of ten minutes. Scoring a late goal Blackpool briefly threatened, but Young finished the game with Everton's third in the 88th minute.

Could Liverpool overcome Leicester City at Filbert Street? Liverpool, the *Daily Post* reported:

> *"...tackled the fixture with all the precision of a skilled surgeon. When Hunt's strike beat Gordon Banks for the first time in five games, Liverpool's players celebrated as if it was the goal that secured the title."*

A late Alf Arrowsmith goal gave the Reds a 2-0 win. *"The bogy team tag was deflated to a shrunken memory,"* the *Post* concluded. The gap between the Merseysiders remained the same, but Spurs dropped more points, effectively reducing the title chase to a Merseyside two-horse race. The *Post* boldly stated: *"It must be Everton or Liverpool now!"*

Playing their next game against Spurs a day earlier than their neighbours, Liverpool could put the pressure on Everton with an Easter Monday win. There was tremendous demand for the match, queues forming as early as eight o' clock on the morning of the game. One hour before kick off the turnstiles were closed and 15,000 disappointed fans found themselves locked out.

Ron Yeats returned to captain the side. Liverpool began the game nervously as though aware of the consequences of failure. Spurs, without the injured Greaves, failed to take advantage, appearing to be playing to avoid defeat. in the 36th minute the game burst into life, an opening goal was quickly followed by two others.

The first was came via a stroke of fortune. A misdirected St John cross floated over the goalkeeper's head and landed in the far corner of the net. The same player scored a more conventional goal two minutes later to double the lead. Liverpool supporters did not celebrate for long; within a couple of minutes Spurs pulled a goal back.

Arrowsmith restored the two-goal lead in the 53rd minute. Not in the least performing like the side that dominated English football at the beginning of the decade, Spurs laboured and rarely threatened. Liverpool went on to record a 3-1 victory to intensify the pressure on Everton.

After a slow start at West Bromwich Albion the following evening, Everton found themselves a goal down inside seven minutes. They reacted well, however. Vernon equalised four minutes later, but right on the stroke of half time Albion restored their lead. Everton *"failed to turn up in the second half,"* the *Echo* claimed, as their opponents scored another two. Vernon's late strike was no consolation and the Blues slumped to a 4-2 defeat.

Advantage Liverpool. A point clear with two games in hand, the league was now theirs to lose. Everton were at Stoke City on the first Saturday in April, while on the same afternoon, Liverpool faced another difficult fixture, improving, now in third place, Manchester United at Anfield.

The *Echo* extolled:

> *"Never for one moment was victory in any doubt. Liverpool's win was achieved with an air of easy superiority. Bill Shankly's boys stand head and shoulders above all."*

In front of another sell-out crowd, with thousands again locked out, two goals from Arrowsmith and another from Callaghan gave Liverpool a conclusive 3-0 victory. The Anfield stadium announcer gleefully informed supporters that Everton lost 3-2 at Stoke City. The league title was within touching distance.

On the following Monday evening, Manchester United won their game in hand over Everton to move ahead of them on goal average. The top of the table now read:

Liverpool played 37 points 52
Manchester United 39 – 49
Everton 39 – 49

Liverpool's next fixture was away to Burnley, but it wouldn't be played on the upcoming Saturday, 11 April, as the annual Scotland v England international match was scheduled for the same day. Milne and Hunt were representing England so the Burnley match was re-scheduled for the 14th. Scotland won the game 3-1.

Everton and United did play on the afternoon of the international. The Blues were held to a 3-3 home draw by Wolves, United won their game. United's victory meant Liverpool could not win the title against Burnley. The club would have to sweat a little longer.

Before the next set of fixtures, a shocking Sunday newspaper report was to rock English football, but more so Everton and Sheffield Wednesday Football Clubs. On 12 April, the *Sunday People*, in a front page exclusive, alleged that in December 1962, three Sheffield Wednesday players had taken a bribe to lose a match at Ipswich. One of the accused players was Everton's Tony Kay, who signed for the club a couple of weeks after the alleged offence.

Prior to the Ipswich game, the three players were handed £50 each by an ex-professional footballer, Jimmy Gauld, to ensure an Ipswich win. Ipswich did win the game 2-0. Kay, ironically, was awarded man of the match for his performance and given a rating of 9 out of 10 in the same newspaper.

The three were eventually convicted of conspiracy to defraud, with Kay receiving a £150 fine and a four-month prison sentence, which many people deemed harsh. He served ten weeks and on his release, he learned that the FA had inflicted a further career ending sentence, banning him from football for life. Although this was later rescinded to seven years, it was too late for Kay, by then he was 35 years old. Despite investing a substantial sum in the player, Everton never appealed the punishment and Kay never returned to the professional game

Everton's title challenge had unravelled before the Kay story broke, but the news added to the despondency around Goodison. They had lost one of their star players and they would soon lose their hold on the league title.

Conversely, on 14 April, Liverpool arrived at Turf Moor Burnley on a high. They played with great verve and were *"a sheer joy to watch"* reported the *Echo*, as Burnley were blown away. The margin of victory, 3-0, *"did not do justice to the overwhelming superiority of the team."*

Though four games remained, Liverpool's far superior goal average, meant a point at home to Arsenal on the forthcoming Saturday, would all but guarantee the title. The great majority of Liverpudlians were desperate to be at Anfield to see history in the making. Queues formed early and an hour before kick-off all gates were closed. Some supporters complained to the press that they had attended all home games and were now to miss the most important of all.

It didn't take long for those inside to celebrate as Liverpool went ahead on six minutes, St. John sliding in an Arrowsmith cross. On the half hour, there were further celebrations when Tommy Lawrence saved an Arsenal penalty. Arrowsmith went from provider to scorer in the 40th minute to put Liverpool two in front.

The celebrations were well and truly underway during the half time interval and continued into the second half as Liverpool ran Arsenal ragged. Two goals in quick succession by Peter Thompson and another from Roger Hunt put the Reds five up on the hour. Although Callaghan missed a 64th minute penalty, it mattered little.

The players took it easy until the final whistle sounded. This was the cue for an explosion of joy from all corners of the ground.

The *Echo* takes up the story:

> "Everybody obeyed the instructions to stay behind the terraces except a few boys. The Liverpool players went down the tunnel to accompaniment of the chant "We won the League" and calls for Yeats and manager Shankly.
>
> Then the eleven returned to the field almost immediately to a rapturous reception from the terraces, and a standing ovation from everyone in the stands. The roar when they ran in front of the Kop increased by 50 per cent. I don't think I have ever seen such an Anfield scene. It almost baffled description by its warmth and intensity."

Shankly was the focus of much of the acclaim for the team's success, but he was quick to share praise with everyone involved at the club. He conveyed his thoughts in the *Daily Post* the following Monday. He wrote:

> "Liverpool's triumph is no one man affair. It has been due to a united effort from the boardroom to the groundsman. Every cog in the machine has functioned perfectly. I can honestly say that I have never asked anything from anyone without getting a 100% effort. My training and coaching staff have done a wonderful job.

In his autobiography, Ian St John wrote of how he and Ron Yeats celebrated the title win that night. They went to a pub, the *Maid* of Erin, off Scotland Road (soon after demolished to make way for the second Mersey Tunnel) where they drank beer and sang with supporters. The players' wives knew roughly of their vicinity, but when eventually found their husbands were showing the effects of over-celebration. *"A different world to today's modern football,"* St John noted.

* * * * *

In the first week of March, Cilla Black's recording of the Burt Bacharach and Hal David number *Anyone Who Had A Heart*, displaced The Searchers at number one in the UK charts. Black's ballad remained at the top for a total of three weeks. The first recording of the song by US singing star Dionne Warwick reached the top of the US charts in December 1963. Warwick's original was released in the UK in 1964, but by that time Black's version was already in the top twenty.

When the Liverpudlian eventually reached number one, Warwick expressed her anger. She claimed that Black's version was merely *"a replica of her own"* stating, for example, that if she had *"coughed then Black would have done the same."* Clearly aware of Warwick's displeasure, Cilla Black interviewed on TV in 1996 said: *"It was a UK number one for me. Dionne was dead choked and she's never forgiven me to this day."*

On the same day as *Anyone Who Had A Heart* reached number one, Billy J Kramer and the Dakotas latest record, *Little Children*, entered the charts. The group at the time were on a nationwide UK tour sharing top billing with US star Gene Pitney and supported by The Fourmost and Swinging Blue Jeans.

On Monday 2 March, the Beatles began their next project. Having joined the actors' union, Equity, the band began shooting their as-yet untitled first movie, *A Hard Day's Night*. The filming would take up almost two months of their lives. On the occasional days away from shooting, they could be found at Abbey Road recording tracks for the accompanying album.

The band had a break from movie making and recording in mid-March to make their debut appearance on *Top of The Pops*. Recorded in London, the Beatles filmed their latest single *Can't Buy Me Love*, which was aired on the BBC on Wednesday 25 March.

While the Beatles were away filming, Brian Epstein was busy arranging no less than a World Tour for the band. Set to begin in the Danish capital, Copenhagen on 4 June, from there the band were to take a short hop to the Netherlands and then fly off to the other side of the world to perform in Hong Kong, Australia and New

Zealand. To conclude the tour, the Beatles were programmed to return to Australia to perform in Brisbane on 30 June.

With the heavy touring schedule ahead of them and the filming behind them, the band had the month of May to themselves. They took the opportunity to holiday abroad.

While the Beatles were away sunning themselves, it was the turn of Gerry and the Pacemakers to hit North America. In late April, accompanied by manager Brian Epstein, the band toured Canada and the USA. In between concerts, they made an appearance on the *Ed Sullivan Show*. On 22 May, having returned to Liverpool, Gerry Marsden spoke to *Mersey Beat* newspaper about the Pacemakers' experiences in North America. He began by saying that he had been a little worried before the group's first live appearance in Toronto. "*I needn't have bothered, the audience were great and set the mood for our whole stay over there,*" he said.

The band performed three more live shows, in Montreal and Toronto, before their first US concert in Massachusetts. They then flew into New York's JFK Airport to rehearse for their first appearance on the *Ed Sullivan Show*, scheduled for Sunday 3 May. More than 1,000 fans were there to greet them.

Before a TV audience of over 17 million, the band performed their first two UK number one hit singles and closed the show with their latest, *Don't Let The Sun Catch You Crying*. The song went on to reach number four in the US charts, two places higher than its final UK chart position. In the studio audience were members of Liverpool's football team, who were playing a series of close-season friendly matches in the US at the time. Marsden said:

> "*We invited the team to see the Ed Sullivan show, and it was nice to have a chat with them about our home town - though most of the players seem to hail from Scotland.*

Marsden added that Sullivan *"was so pleased with the way we went down that he asked us to record another show before we left, which we did.*" That performance was aired the following Sunday. During their stay in New York, the group had plenty of spare time, which they spent sightseeing. Marsden was amazed at the reception they received from fans.

> "They were fantastic. We had a chauffeur driven Cadillac to take us round New York, complete with telephone, and the kids found out the number and kept ringing up whilst we were in the car! We had a bodyguard of 12 hefty men, but we still got mobbed. We had police guarding the hotel, the lift and our room, and there were fans crawling up drainpipes and in through the cellars to get to see us."

Epstein next arranged for Billy J Kramer and the Dakotas to tour the States and appear on Ed Sullivan's show. *Little Children,* which they performed on TV along with their other recent chart hits, was at number five in the US charts when they arrived in New York on 5 June.

Kramer and his band then went on to perform in cities which were not part of the Beatles or Pacemakers' itinerary. They travelled to San Antonio, Texas where they played a total of four shows. From Texas on the 13th, Dakotas' guitarist Robin MacDonald spoke to the *Liverpool Echo*:

> "San Antonio is fabulous. We didn't expect the terrific reception we received based on the strength of a couple of hits. The whole group is surprised and chuffed."

Epstein was not with Kramer and his backing band in the States; he was on the other side of the world accompanying the Beatles on their tour of Hong Kong and Australasia. Once more, the *Echo's* George Harrison was the only officially invited journalist.

On 10 June, the Beatles played two shows to *"screaming fans"* in Hong Kong. John Lennon constantly urged them to *"shut up."* Speaking to journalist Harrison, Paul McCartney commented on Lennon's pleas: *"Nothing he said mattered. It was like trying to push the gushing water back up Niagara Falls."*

The following day, in torrential rain, they arrived in Sydney to begin the tour of Australia. On the 15th Harrison sent a report to the *Echo*. He informed readers that the band travelled from Sydney to Adelaide where *"four thousand screaming fans"* were waiting outside their hotel to greet them. George Harrison (the Beatle) said that the reception was: *"...louder and longer than anything heard in the* USA.*"*

In the next city, Melbourne, *"a quarter of a million-people lined the streets from the airport to the city centre.*" At the band's accommodation, Harrison added:

> *"Fire hoses were turned on the crowds of teenagers besieging the hotel, climbing fire escapes and attempting to get into the band's rooms."*

Inside their hotel, Harrison asked the Beatles whether they were now prisoners of their own success. John Lennon responded:

> *"No I don't think so. We never go out much in England, so we don't feel like prisoners, though everybody else seems to think we are."*

Tonsillitis had laid Ringo Starr low forcing him to miss the beginning of the tour. His place had been taken by stand in drummer, Jimmy Nichol, who had performed with Billy Fury in the recent past. Starr was well enough to begin duties in Melbourne. When Nichol checked out of the hotel and went outside, Harrison wrote, *"nobody recognised him."*

Although the Beatles were *"totally amazed"* at attendances and the reactions of fans, by the 19th, they were complaining about aspects of the tour. *"There's nothing to do,"* said Ringo Starr. *"This morning I got up and had breakfast and at eleven o'clock I went back to bed."* George Harrison commented, *"time drags."* Lennon complained of feeling *"restless."* On his 22nd birthday, the 18th, Paul McCartney telephoned his father back in Liverpool. He said he felt very emotional at the fact that he was 13,000 miles away and could not celebrate with the family. *"The price of fame."*

On the day of McCartney's birthday and the day following, the Beatles played two Sydney concerts to an aggregate 20,000 fans. The band were bombarded with jelly beans and koala bears. At one time McCartney stopped playing his guitar and pleaded with those responsible to desist. They did not.

The Beatles then flew to New Zealand to play the first of six days of concerts in Wellington. On arrival, they received a Maori welcome at the airport, After Wellington they moved on to Auckland, Dunedin and Christchurch. In Auckland, dozens of university students demonstrated against the band. they waved placards reading, for example, *"We Hate the Beatles"* and *"Beatles Go Home."* Some minor skirmishes occurred between students and Beatles' fans.

As in Australia, New Zealand hotels were permanently besieged. In Auckland, the Beatles encountered unwillingness from local police to provide adequate protection. Auckland's Inspector of Police told the group's management: *"We didn't want them here and I don't know why you brought them."*

The Beatles returned to Australia to play their final two concerts in front of a combined audience of 11,000, at the *Festival Hall* in Brisbane. The following day, 1 July, they began their long return journey back to England. The world première of their movie *A Hard Day's Night,* awaited the band in London on 6 July.

Brian Epstein had responded to the Liverpool Lord Mayor's request to hold a civic reception in honour of the Beatles. He organised the event, scheduled for 10 July, to coincide with the city premiere of *A Hard Day's Night.*

While Gerry and the Pacemakers, Billy J Kramer and the Beatles were performing in venues across the globe, they and other Mersey Beat artists continued to dominate the UK music charts and, increasingly, the US charts. *Little Children* replaced *Anyone Who Had A Heart* as UK number one on 19 March, where it stayed for two weeks. On 2 April, the Beatles, with *Can't Buy Me Love,* replaced Billy J Kramer at the top.

The practically implausible simultaneous football and music achievements continued in 1964. A year earlier, on the weekend in which Everton won the First Division title, the Beatles reached number one for the first time with *From Me To You.* On 18 April 1964, the date Liverpool won the First Division title, *Can't Buy Me*

Love was on its 16th day as UK number one. The Beatles, Liverpool and Everton in unison.

A week later, the Beatles were replaced at the top by The Searchers hit, *Don't Throw You Love Away*. The Beatles' apart, The Searchers number one proved to be the last produced by the generation of Mersey Beat bands, though several would make the top ten. The musical phenomena had reached the peak of success. Cilla Black overtook The Searchers in May singing *You're My World*. Black's single remained at number one until the end of June.

Over in the US, from early February, the Beatles dominated the Billboard Hot 100. The run of number ones, totalling fourteen consecutive weeks, began with *I Want To Hold Your Hand* and concluded with *Can't Buy Me Love*. At one point in March, the band held the top four chart places with *She Loves You* holding top spot, followed by *I Want To Hold Your Hand, Twist And Shout* and *Please Please Me*. Gerry and the Pacemakers, Billy J Kramer and the Dakotas, The Searchers, The Swinging Blue Jeans and Cilla Black, all made the top thirty at least, though none of them reached number one.

The world premiere of *A Hard Day's Night* went ahead at London's *Pavilion Theatre* on 6 July. On the 10th, the Beatles flew from London to Liverpool's Speke Airport where 3,000 fans were gathered to greet their arrival. Paul McCartney in *Anthology* fondly recalled the welcome as they drove toward the city centre:

> *"There were crowds everywhere, like a royal do. It was incredible, because people were lining the streets that we'd known as children... And here we were now with thousands of people - for us. It was strange because they were our own people, but it was brilliant."*

On the police escorted five-mile drive from the airport to Liverpool Town Hall, the location of the civic reception, an estimated 200,000 people lined the route. Hundreds of police officers were on duty and were much needed as thousands of fans on several occasions breached the cordons and stopped the cavalcade.

The band eventually arrived just before 7.00 pm, almost a half hour behind schedule. They were welcomed by the Labour MP for Liverpool Exchange, Bessie Braddock. Invited guests included friends and family of the group, the Bishop of Liverpool, Everton Chairman John Moores and various invited local musicians. Uninvited, for example, were Pete Best, Allan Williams or any member of Stuart Sutcliffe's family.

Following a meal, The Beatles appeared on the balcony where they waved to the thousands of gathered fans. Brian Epstein should have been standing alongside, but he later said he was unable to extricate himself from the attentions of Beatles' admirers. Such was the crush in the surrounding streets, it later emerged that St John's Ambulance personnel treated 381 people, the majority having suffered fainting fits. Another 35 were transported to hospital, though examinations revealed no serious injuries.

John Lennon told the assembled invited press:

> "It beats our previous best reception in Adelaide by a mile. We were wondering what kind of reception we would get. We never expected so many people to turn out for us."

An eight-year-old boy was lifted on to an office window ledge on Dale Street, about fifty yards from the Town Hall balcony. Corinthian columns on the 18th century building slightly obstructed his view. He was though able to see Paul McCartney and John Lennon waving and smiling to the screaming, excited crowd below. He saw some people faint and receive treatment. It reminded him slightly of one of the city's overcrowded football grounds where people were sometimes pulled from the terrace and treated on the running track. The whole spectacle he found unbelievably amazing.

The Beatles disappeared inside a few minutes later. The boy clambered down from the ledge. His intention was to make his way to the *Odeon Cinema* on nearby London Road, where the Beatles were due to arrive to view their new movie. The boy had, however, lost his companions in the crowds outside the Town Hall. Nervous and frightened he chose instead to walk home, which at first seemed to him miles away. He was in fact only a few hundred yards from home. He needed to walk along Dale Street, past the entrance to the Mersey Tunnel and across the road to reach his tenement flat. His home was actually closer to the *Odeon* than it was to the Town Hall, but that mattered little. Still a little fearful, he returned home. Without the presence of the young boy, at 9.00 pm, the Beatles arrived at the cinema to be greeted by more screaming hordes of fans.

The memory of an eight-year-old child is not always reliable, but a memorable event, such as the Beatles appearance on the balcony of Liverpool Town Hall, holds a greater chance of recollection. I was that boy and the event remains ingrained in my memory. I saw the Beatles!

At the end of July, both the single and album of *A Hard Day's Night* reached number one in their respective charts. The single remained at the top for three weeks and the album for a remarkable 21 weeks. An incredible conclusion to this period in the history of Mersey Beat.

* *

On 1 January 1960, if someone would have suggested that Everton and Liverpool would both have won the English First Division within four and a half years... Yet, this is precisely what happened.

On 1 January 1960, if someone would have suggested that a group of teenage musicians then calling themselves The Quarry Men (later the Beatles) would have "*conquered the world...*"

Yet, this is precisely what happened.

From the beginning of the decade to the mid-sixties, the simultaneous rise of the Merseyside football clubs and the Mersey Beat musicians from despair and obscurity to national and international fame and success was nothing more than extraordinary.

11. ...and in the end: 1964-2016

Some of those who have passed away since 1964:

Brian Epstein – 1967
Alan Caldwell (Rory Storm) - 1972
John Lennon – 1980
Bill Shankly - 1981
Billy Fury - 1983
Harry Catterick - 1985
John Moores – 1993
Roy Vernon – 1993
Johnny Carey - 1995
Bob Paisley – 1996
Frankie Vaughan - 1999
George Harrison -2001
Billy Liddell - 2001
Alex Scott - 2001
Bob Wooler – 2002
Brian Labone - 2006
Gordon West – 2012
Bobby Collins - 2013
Dave Hickson - 2013
Cilla Black – 2015
Ray McFall - 2015
Tony Barrow – 2016
Allan Williams - 2016

As of January 2017:

Pete Best is still performing, Gerry Marsden leads the Pacemakers, John McNally performs with The Searchers; original member, Ray Ennis, remains active with the Swinging Blue Jeans as do Tony Crane and Billy Kinsley of the Merseybeats.

Billy J Kramer recorded an album in 2012, while his backing band the Dakotas continue to perform live. Ringo Starr has recently recorded an album. Finally, still recording *and* performing - Paul McCartney.

Printed in Great Britain
by Amazon